DATE DUE			

RESEARCH PERSPECTIVES ON THE GRADUATE PREPARATION OF TEACHERS

RESEARCH PERSPECTIVES ON THE GRADUATE PREPARATION OF TEACHERS

Anita E. Woolfolk, *Editor*

Rutgers University

Prentice Hall, *Englewood Cliffs, New Jersey 07632*

LIBRARY OF CONGRESS
Library of Congress Cataloging-in-Publication Data

Research perspectives on the graduate preparation of teachers / Anita
E. Woolfolk, editor.
        p.   cm. -- (Rutgers symposia on education)
    Bibliography: p.
    Includes index.
    ISBN 0-13-774357-2
    1. Education--United States--Graduate work--Congresses.
I. Woolfolk, Anita. II. Series.
LB2372.E3R47 1989
378'.1553'0973--dc19   88-20962
                                                           CIP

Editorial/production supervision and
 interior design: Mary A. Araneo
Cover design: Ben Santora
Manufacturing buyer: Peter Havens

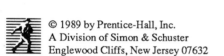

Printed in the United States of America

10 9 8 7 6 5 4 3 2 1

ISBN   0-13-774357-2

Prentice-Hall International (UK) Limited, *London*
Prentice-Hall of Australia Pty. Limited, *Sydney*
Prentice-Hall Canada Inc., *Toronto*
Prentice-Hall Hispanoamericana, S.A., *Mexico*
Prentice-Hall of India Private Limited, *New Delhi*
Prentice-Hall of Japan, Inc., *Tokyo*
Simon & Schuster Asia Pte. Ltd., *Singapore*
Editora Prentice-Hall do Brasil, Ltda., *Rio de Janeiro*

To Liz

RUTGERS SYMPOSIUM ON EDUCATION

Louise Cherry Wilkinson, Series Editor

CONTENTS

PART V: CONCLUSIONS

SERIES FOREWORD

Within the past several years, the profession of education has been shaken to its roots as national attention focused on education and on educators. Critics and friends have raised basic questions about the profession, including whether educational professionals have successfully met the challenges that the students and the schools present and even more fundamentally, if they are able to meet those challenges. Beginning with the highly publicized *A Nation at Risk*, seemingly endless and often contradictory criticisms, analyses, and recommendations have appeared from virtually every segment of contemporary American society.

The profession has not been silent. One highly acclaimed and somewhat controversial response is the Holmes Group, a consortium of leading American research universities who are committed to upgrading the profession of Teaching. Another major event has been the publication of the report on schools and education by the prestigious Carnegie Forum on Education and the Economy. Recently, we have seen the American Association of Higher Education take leadership in the issues of teaching and schooling with the well-known and well circulated "Kennedy Letter," in which Stanford University President Donald Kennedy calls for colleges and universities to take a major role in the advancement and improvement of pre-collegiate education.

In this recent explosion of concern for educational reform, we see a need for a general and national forum in which the problems of education can be examined in light of research from a range of relevant disciplines. Too often, analyses of very complex issues and problems occur within a single discipline. Aspects of a problem that are unfamiliar to those members of the discipline are ignored, and the resulting analysis is limited in scope and unsatisfactory for that reason. Furthermore, when educational issues are investigated by members of one discipline, there is seldom an attempt to examine related issues from other fields or to apply methods developed in other fields that might prove illuminating.

The national debate on educational reform has suffered from this myopia, as problems and issues are identified and analyses and solutions often are proposed within the limited confines of a single disciplinary boundary. In the past, national discussions have been ill-informed or uninformed by current research partly because there are far too few mechanisms for interdisciplinary analyses of significant issues.

The present series of volumes, the *Rutgers Symposium on Education*, attempts to address this gap. The series will focus on timely issues and problems in education, taking an interdisciplinary perspective. The focus of each volume will be a particular problem, such as a potential teacher shortage, the structure of schools, the effects of cognitive psychology on how to teach mathematics. There is an accumulating corpus of high quality educational research on topics of interest to practitioners and policy makers. Each volume in the series will provide an interdisciplinary forum through which scholars can disseminate their original research and extend their work to potential applications for practice, including guides for teaching, learning, assessment, intervention, and policy formulation. We believe that this work will increase the potential for significant analysis as well as the potential for positive impact in the domains of both practice and theory.

The initial volume in the series, *Research Perspectives on the Graduate Preparation of Teachers*, is a logical choice. The preparation of teachers is a national concern. Enrollments in schools of education are rising; more college students are electing to prepare themselves to be teachers. The question under consideration in the first volume is: Are graduate programs for teacher preparation more likely than undergraduate programs to prepare highly qualified, competent, reflective professionals? A significant effort has already now begun to identify the central issues and variables that will determine our ability to answer the question posed. The authors of the chapters in the first volume provide a complex, yet inconclusive answer. The evidence reviewed and presented in this volume leads us to some conclusions and many issues yet to be resolved by future research. The first volume will catalyze debate about the issue and help to clarify what the next steps for both research and training must be.

It is with great pleasure that we initiate this series of volumes on contemporary educational issues, the *Rutgers Symposium on Education*. Our expectation is that this series will serve as a seminal contribution to the literature in educational theory and practice.

Louise Cherry Wilkinson
Professor of Educational Psychology and
Dean of the Rutgers Graduate School of Education

PREFACE

The authors in this volume are concerned about the quality of teaching in our schools. They are researchers studying teacher preparation, classroom instruction, educational policy, the development of teaching expertise, student thinking, the philosophy of education, instructional psychology, and educational administration. Each agreed to look at the question of graduate teacher preparation from the perspective of his or her research area.

The project was launched with a set of key questions: What can we learn from the results of previous graduate preparation programs? What models of graduate preparation are currently in use and what are the direct and indirect effects of implementing these models? What are the possible implications for the profession and the society of a move to graduate teacher preparation? Are the research bases for graduate preparation different from those for undergraduate preparation? What can we learn from research in such areas as instructional psychology, teaching effectiveness, and teacher thinking? How do teachers' conceptualizations of the subjects being taught influence teaching and learning in their classrooms? What kind of academic preparation is necessary for teaching and how does the answer to this question affect student selection and program design in teacher education? What do teachers actually learn during each phase of their preparation (initial training, student teaching, first years of teaching) and who are the "teacher educators" during those times? How do novices become experts and what characterizes expertise in teaching? How and when do we evaluate teachers' competence?

The chapters in this book began as tentative answers to these questions circulated among the volume contributors. Then the contributors made presentations based on their analyses at a conference, the first Rutgers Invitational Symposium on Education. Finally, after much discussion and revision, the upcoming chapters were completed.

Even though this book was conceived as a collection about the graduate preparation of teachers, it grew into a larger project. As the authors wrote and discussed, we found that much of what we said applied equally to undergraduate preparation. In fact, the ideas and analyses in the following pages should be of interest to anyone who believes that the education of teachers should be informed by our best knowledge about teaching and learning.

Many people worked to make this project possible. Dean Louise Cherry Wilkinson established the Rutgers Invitational Symposium on Education and supported this first effort from inception to end. Judy Lanier, Virginia Richardson-Koehler, David Berliner, and Tom Good made valuable suggestions during the project's early planning stages. The conference was funded in part by a grant from the New Jersey Department of Higher Education. Carol Weinstein served as co-director of the conference. Jane Sherwood and C. J. Tarter worked diligently to organize the conference. Alison Gooding and Louise Cherry Wilkinson read every chapter along with me and helped to guide the authors in their revisions. Denise (Campbell) Crisci coordinated the entire project from the collection of drafts through the typing and revising of manuscripts, to the last detail of the book. Mary Araneo was the production editor at Prentice Hall. Susan Willig, editor-in-chief at Prentice Hall, encouraged us throughout our writing. To all these friends and colleagues, thank you.

Anita E. Woolfolk
Princeton, New Jersey

RESEARCH PERSPECTIVES ON THE GRADUATE PREPARATION OF TEACHERS

1

GRADUATE PREPARATION OF TEACHERS: THE DEBATE AND BEYOND

Anita E. Woolfolk

For several years educators and politicians have been debating how best to educate teachers. Plans for improving teacher preparation programs are included in the reports of the Carnegie Commission Task Force (1986) and the Holmes Group (1986). While the two reports reach different conclusions on some questions, they agree that professional education for teachers should be moved to the graduate level. Similar recommendations have been made by the Task Force on Extended Programs, established by the American Association of Colleges of Teacher Education (AACTE, 1983). Since these reports appeared, the debate has raged about the value of graduate preparation for teachers (see, for example, Howey & Zimpher, 1986; Soltis, 1987; Tom, 1986).

The authors of this book gathered for a conference to examine the idea of graduate preparation for teachers. In bringing this group together at Rutgers University, our goal was to consider such preparation from the perspective of research on teaching and teachers. We were less interested in debating policy and program design and more interested in stepping back from the debate to see if something important was being overlooked. The authors brought to this analysis their understanding of research on past and present graduate preparation programs, the development of expertise in teaching, classroom instruction, learning to teach, supervision of student teachers, and teacher assessment. Other conference participants pressed us to care-

I would like to thank Carol Weinstein for her many helpful comments on this chapter.

fully consider the implications of graduate teacher preparation for the profession and the larger society.

In this introductory chapter, I hope to provide a context for the analyses to come. Since many authors in this volume assume the reader has a general understanding of various models of graduate preparation and the arguments for them, the first section briefly describes these models and arguments for readers less familiar with the area. Next we turn to the central purpose of the book—looking beyond program configuration to issues and information that have been overlooked in the debate about graduate preparation. Thus, the last four sections of the chapter raise questions, some old, some new, about teacher preparation.

THE MODELS AND THE ARGUMENTS

Over the years and recently, many models have been developed for graduate teacher preparation (see AACTE, 1983 and Scannell, 1987 for a complete discussion of these models). As a brief introduction, let us consider two major categories of programs: integrated and postbaccalaureate.

In integrated programs, students begin their preparation gradually as undergraduates with a few courses in education. Often these courses include some field experiences to acquaint students with the profession. But the bulk of the undergraduate time is devoted to the academic disciplines, and students pursue a major, usually in some field other than education. Integrated programs may or may not include a full-fledged student teaching experience at the undergraduate level, though many do. During a fifth (and sometimes a sixth) year students concentrate on professional teacher education courses. These postbaccalaureate years usually include at least one internship experience. Even within this integrated model, many variations are possible. Internships may be paid or unpaid. The postbaccalaureate study may include additional courses in academic disciplines as well as professional education courses. Students may receive a bachelor's degree after four years and a master's (M.Ed. or M.A.T.) after the fifth or sixth year. Alternatively, students may receive both the bachelor's and the master's at the end of the entire program. In some programs, the postbaccalaureate work does not culminate in a graduate degree at all, but only in some limited number of graduate credits (for example, 15) or merely in eligibility for certification.

A second general category of models involves concentrating all the professional preparation at the graduate level. Thus students come with a bachelor's degree and spend one to several years preparing to teach. Again, there are many variations. Students may receive a master's degree (M.Ed. or M.A.T.) upon completion of the program, may receive no graduate degree but accrue a number of graduate credits, or may simply be eligible for certification. Additional course work in the academic disciplines may be part of the program, but often there is little time for such study. The program may be field-based with much of the time devoted to supervised internships and "hands-on" learning. Generally, these postbaccalaureate programs are offered by a college or university, but in some states "alternate routes" to certification make it possible for individuals with appropriate undergraduate degrees to attain certification without enrolling in a college program. These alternate routes usually involve some didactic preparation, but most of the training comes in the form of internships supervised by public school personnel.

Each approach has advantages and disadvantages. In integrated programs there can be more time to study and consider teaching. But it is difficult to transfer into these programs at the graduate level. Some schools insist that transfer students take the undergraduate courses they have missed, often for no credit, before they are allowed to begin the graduate section of the program. Postbaccalaureate programs simplify the problem of transfer students and allow individuals who had not considered teaching during their undergraduate years to enter the profession after graduation.

The chapters in this volume by Richardson-Koehler and Fenstermacher, Wise, Weinstein, and Zeichner include discussions of the arguments for and against extended preparation. Briefly, individuals favoring a move to graduate preparation suggest that such programs will allow more time for prospective teachers to master both the academic and the professional material necessary to teach well. Also, graduate preparation, it is argued, will help elevate the status of teaching and make it more akin to other professions, such as law and medicine. More academically talented students will consider teaching, since such a decision will not require them to take time away from a full undergraduate major in an academic discipline and, in many programs, will allow them to earn an advanced degree.

On the other side of the debate are educators who suggest that the content, not the timing, of teacher preparation is the real issue. Many critics believe that a move to graduate preparation will be expensive, discourage economically disadvantaged students from entering the profession, and actually narrow the pool of talented individuals who consider teaching.

BEYOND THE ARGUMENTS: QUESTIONS FOR ALL TEACHER EDUCATORS

Many different questions are raised by the authors of the upcoming chapters. The first question I will consider is "What are we trying to accomplish in initial teacher preparation?" In one sense, all of the researchers in this volume have something to say about the goals of teacher education. A number of chapters contain direct assertions about the characteristics of good teaching and the sort of teacher our preparation programs ought to produce. In other chapters an ideal is implied or assumed. The second question is "In what contexts should individuals learn to teach?" Again, many authors recognize and discuss the power of contextual influences on the neophyte teacher. The final question is "What do we know about graduate teacher preparation?" Authors examine historical precedent and contemporary practice. Each of these questions deserves a closer look.

What Are the Goals of Initial Preparation?

On one issue the authors of this volume tend to agree. Teacher preparation programs should educate but not necessarily certify their graduates. Several chapters make a case for a clearer separation between education and certification, assistance and assessment, formative and summative evaluation. These distinctions are especially pertinent in Peterson and Comeaux's chapter on teacher assessment, Borko's discussion of learning to teach, and Hoy and Woolfolk's examination of the optimal climate for supervision of student teaching experiences.

If we are to decide how best to assist and educate our teachers, we must first decide what kind of teachers we want.

Prestigious Teachers.   As noted earlier, many proponents of graduate preparation believe that this approach will elevate the status of teachers. As the status of teachers improves, so the argument goes, more able people will be drawn into and remain in the profession (see Chapter 10). Public support for education in general and teachers in particular will increase. Thus one goal of reformed teacher education might be to produce higher status, more respectable teachers. What exactly would it take to achieve this goal? Is graduate preparation necessary? Is it sufficient? Chapters by Zeichner and Weinstein about the effects of moving to graduate level preparation suggest that individuals associated with such programs perceive improvements in the academic quality of their students. And students in these programs seem to enjoy the elevated status that comes with earning a "real master's degree."

If teacher education becomes a more highly respected program of study, will this increased status carry over into the career of teaching? If not, the graduates of these more prestigious programs are likely to become disillusioned with their chosen career. We cannot raise the standards and expectations for prospective teachers and then assume they will be happy with an occupation that falls far below those expectations. But even if increased status for the profession follows improvements in teacher preparation programs, we may still have to face some unanticipated negative consequences. Can teachers become more respected and the teaching career more desirable without creating a psychological distance between teachers and their students, much like the distance between physicians or lawyers and their clients? This issue was hotly debated at the conference and no consensus was reached. The chapter by Richardson-Koehler and Fenstermacher describes a school that has adopted the hierarchical model of teaching advocated in the Holmes and Carnegie reports. In this school some teachers work only with students, while others—those with advanced training or experience—spend some of their time teaching and the rest supervising, planning, and administering the program. There is an emphasis on specialization. Richardson-Koehler and Fenstermacher believe that this has led to increased distance between students and teachers and, more fundamentally, that this approach presents an elitist, antidemocratic model to students. Their chapter challenges us to think carefully about our vision of the ideal professional in teaching.

Reflective Teachers.   Many of the authors in this volume are less concerned about perceptions of the status and professionalism of teachers and more interested in their competence, although obviously the two dimensions are related. The image of the ideal appearing over and over in this book is that of the reflective teacher. Almost every author makes reference to this ideal. Peterson and Comeaux, for example, include an extensive discussion of the reflective professional, noting the suggestions of the Holmes Group (1986) and the Carnegie Task Force (1986). They base their arguments on the burgeoning research in the areas of teacher planning, thinking, and decision making. "Recent scholarly research on teaching has provided support for the image of the teacher as a reflective professional. The research has documented that teaching is a complex and cognitively demanding process that requires professional knowledge in a wide variety of areas . . ." (see Chapter 8).

Thus, most authors in this volume would agree with Griffin's (1984) view that the ideal teacher is reflective, deliberate, and collaborative. Reflective teachers seek to understand why particular actions or strategies have particular effects within a given group of students. They can bring a number of perspectives to bear in this systematic analysis of their own and their colleagues' teaching. Their analysis and reflection are guided by a fairly coherent set of principles about teaching, learning, children, the dynamics of the classroom, and the contexts of schooling. They are self-critical, thoughtful, and perennially dissatisfied with their current level of expertise, always striving to know and understand more. They are not content simply to analyze and understand. These ideal teachers *act* in deliberate ways on their reflections. They plan and experiment with various methods of teaching. Finally, they prize the support and suggestions of their colleagues and freely give the same in return.

But this cannot be the whole story. If we are to set as a goal the preparation of reflective, deliberate, collegial professionals we must answer at least two remaining questions. What exactly do reflective teachers know that allows them to critically analyze teaching, in other words, what do thoughtful teachers think about? Second, a question that is central for teacher education: How do teachers learn to be reflective?

Knowledge for Reflection. In answer to the first question, "What do reflective teachers know that allows them to critically analyze teaching?", several authors in this volume turn to the work of Shulman (1986, 1987) on the range of knowledge required for good teaching. Shulman has proposed a model of professional knowledge that includes seven domains of knowledge: (a) subject matter; (b) curriculum; (c) general pedagogy or teaching principles, such as strategies of classroom management, that apply to all subjects; (d) teaching principles that are specific to a subject such as how to demonstrate or explain a particular concept so students will understand, called pedagogical content knowledge; (e) learners and their characteristics; (f) educational contexts (small groups, classroom, schools, etc.); and (g) goals and values of education. The chapter by Peterson and Comeaux uses Shulman's seven domains as a framework for designing the content and sequence of an extended assessment procedure for teachers based, in part, on the national examinations for physicians. Anderson's chapter focuses on the Shulman's domains of subject matter knowledge and pedagogical content knowledge.

Shulman's seven domains map the categories of professional knowledge but tell us little about the content of those categories. Another approach to answering the question "What do thoughtful teachers think about?" is to examine the research on expertise teaching. Results of investigations into the differences between experts and novices in fields such as physics problem solving (Chi & Glaser, 1982; Larkin, Mc-Dermott, Simon, & Simon, 1980), medical diagnosis (Patel, Frederiksen, & Groen, 1984), and chess (Chase & Simon, 1973) have encouraged educational researchers to use similar methods to study expertise in teaching. This research, though in its infancy, suggests that the knowledge of experienced teachers as well as the ways they organize and apply their knowledge differ from that of novice teachers. The research also tells us that expert knowledge is highly particularistic and situation-specific. It is constructed through experience in many different teaching situations. Thus, the development of such expertise takes time.

Can we design programs that better prepare our students to develop expertise as they gain experience? Can we set as one goal of initial preparation programs the development of "expertisable" teachers, individuals who have the knowledge and habits of mind to steadily improve throughout their early years in the classroom?

The authors in this volume believe we can. Carter and Doyle use the research on expertise in teaching as one basis for rethinking the teacher education curriculum. They suggest that the purpose of teacher education should be to develop in our students rich propositional and procedural knowledge about teaching. This knowledge ought to be structured by the commonly occurring events of teaching such as opening a class, establishing rules and procedures, explaining a concept, and so on. Teaching should be represented as problem solving. The problems to be solved are the common pedagogical events of schooling, and the procedures to be used are derived from knowledge in the seven domains identified by Shulman (1986, 1987). The curriculum of teacher education should thus give students knowledge for solving pedagogical problems, practice in applying the knowledge, and the chance to reflect on the solutions.

Becoming Reflective. The second question "How do teachers become reflective?; How do they apply knowledge to solve problems?" is more difficult to answer. Unfortunately, even though we are beginning to understand something about the character of expert knowledge in teaching, we know very little about how that knowledge actually develops, except that the development takes time and experience. There are no simple rules we can teach our students that will make them expert.

Discussions among the conference participants about the rough road to excellence in teaching uncovered another issue that sparked controversy: In addition to (or even before) emphasizing the ability to be reflective, should we attempt to give our students some "basic skills" for teaching? If so, what are they? Some educators suggest that the vast research on effective teaching has identified actions of "expert" teachers. This influential body of work has been touted by many as providing the sorely needed catalog of standard practices for teacher education. If we understand what effective teachers do to manage and instruct their students, so the argument goes, then we know how very good teachers have solved some of the common pedagogical problems of schooling, and we can pass these skills on to preservice teachers.

The chapter in this volume by Carter and Doyle raises very serious objections to this line of reasoning, suggesting that the direct teaching of these skills may not be desirable or even possible. The findings of research on effective teaching have a role to play in teacher preparation, but do not serve as blueprints for action. Carter and Doyle suggest that these findings are best used as frames or perspectives for thinking and reasoning about teaching.

Hoy and Woolfolk argue, however, that we must maintain a balance in teacher education between technical skills and reflection. In teacher preparation it may be essential to encourage both skill and reflection, since beginning teachers who do not have a minimal repertoire of management and instructional skills may come to overvalue those skills, adopt dysfunctional controlling strategies simply to survive, and never develop the habit or the appreciation of reflection. In his classic guide for beginning college teachers, McKeachie (1986) makes a similar point when explaining why he discusses educational theory only after he has provided 220 pages of guidelines for practice:

> I have found that most beginning teachers have too many immediate problems to worry very much about general questions of educational theory. It is only after you have mastered some of the day-to-day problems that you are able to sit back and wonder why some things work and others don't. (p. 221)

In order to educate beginning teachers to be technically competent, thoughtful, and prepared to develop expertise through experience, we must consider the contexts for learning to teach.

Contexts for Learning to Teach

As the conference participants presented and discussed their ideas, another set of questions began to emerge, generally about the contexts in which students learn to teach and their effects. Where do our students really learn to be teachers? In college classes? In the field placements? In the first full-time teaching position? Who are the most influential teacher educators? Professors? Cooperating teachers? Fellow teachers? Or even the teacher education student's former elementary and secondary teachers? When should teachers learn? In undergraduate school, graduate school, or both? During the first years of teaching? These questions brought us back again to perennial concerns about how best to design and coordinate didactic and experiential learning. While participants at the conference did not exhaustively examine all aspects of this dilemma, they did explore in some depth three issues: (a) the difficulties of developing a useful understanding of subjects to be taught given the typical undergraduate program of study, (b) the potential for field experiences to be both educational and miseducative, and (c) the dangers of becoming too focused on the question of graduate *versus* undergraduate preparation for teachers.

With respect to undergraduate education in the subjects to be taught, Charles Anderson's chapter makes a compelling case for a kind of disciplinary knowledge that is difficult to achieve, but that is none the less critical for success in teaching. Given the typical undergraduate experience of somewhat disconnected courses, frequent multiple-choice tests, few requirements or opportunities for writing, emphasis on the accumulation of facts and information, greater concern for answers than for questions, and little chance to integrate understanding across chapters in one course (much less across courses or fields), we must face the fact that much of what our students learn about their subjects is not useful in teaching those subjects. In other words, the context of the usual undergraduate program is not an ideal situation for learning to teach. Anderson's chapter also outlines the barriers that stand in our way if we decide to provide a more appropriate kind of disciplinary preparation for our students. To take this challenge seriously probably will require, at the very least, extensive changes in the way we teach curriculum and methods courses.

The authors in this volume recognize that without some form of practice, students of teaching will have difficulty turning knowledge into action. But many of the authors are also concerned about possible miseducative effects of experiential learning. While carefully supervised experiences seem to be one of the best contexts for learning to be both skilled and reflective, they are also among the most difficult to accomplish. To be successful, teacher education programs have always needed the cooperation of the many individuals who contribute to the prospective teacher's preparation—professors in the academic disciplines, professors of education, administrators in colleges and in the public schools, cooperating teachers, and university supervisors of student teaching. This cooperation is especially critical when it comes to designing, supervising, and monitoring effective student teaching experiences. However, chapters by Borko and by Hoy and Woolfolk question whether such cooperation is possible without radical changes in our current programs.

When the discussion at the conference turned to consider the timing of teacher education and the value of undergraduate *versus* graduate preparation, conference participants did not reach a consensus. Some cautioned that a move to graduate level preparation would be counterproductive if this means that professional education courses are simply pushed to the graduate level, thus not allowing students the time to assimilate information and move toward developing expertise. Many participants were concerned about one-year "crash courses" in teaching. Some feared designers of graduate preparation programs may assume that an undergraduate degree in a field is an indication of adequate disciplinary preparation for teaching. Thus, the development of the kind of disciplinary knowledge described by Anderson could be overlooked. Still other participants made the case that the quality and maturity of students attracted by graduate programs is the best argument for such programs. But even though debate on these questions was heated at times, the discussion during the conference quickly moved beyond this debate to other issues. There was general agreement that *what* and *how* prospective teachers learn it is more important than when. Participants also agreed that the entire debate should be informed by a more careful examination of past and present graduate level preparation programs.

What Do We Know about Graduate Teacher Preparation?

The chapter by Zeichner in this volume reminds us that graduate preparation for teachers has been attempted before. During the 1950s and 1960s literally millions of dollars of public funds and private foundation support were spent to establish innovative graduate level preparation programs. All the major variations in program design were attempted. Zeichner's search for evaluations of these programs uncovered material that few other researchers had located. His analysis suggests that some conclusions are warranted about the effects of graduate preparation for teachers, but many opportunities for learning about these programs were lost because evaluations of the programs were either severely flawed, incomplete, or nonexistent. His chapter is, in part, a cry for better, more thoughtful coordination of program design and evaluation procedures. We know the questions, but we seem to systematically avoid gathering the information that will allow us to answer them.

In writing her chapter for this volume, Weinstein visited graduate preparation programs at Austin College, the University of Kansas, and the University of Virginia. At the time of her visit, these programs had been in full operation for almost 20 years, for three years, and for only a few months, respectively. Weinstein spoke with faculty, administrators, and students in an attempt to determine the perceived and actual effects of the new graduate programs. She was able to reach some conclusions, but, like Zeichner, she found that data needed to answer many of the questions were not being systematically gathered or that appropriate comparison groups were not available.

CONCLUSIONS: WHAT SHOULD WE KNOW?

Many more issues and questions arise in the following pages, but one answer is clear. The very questions researchers identify as critical could be answered if thoughtful research and evaluation designs were incorporated into our teacher education programs. How does expertise develop in teaching? What kinds of students come to our programs? Do we attract different types of students when we move to graduate level preparation? What do students actually learn from our courses? from field experiences? What are the effects of different teaching approaches on the students' understanding of the subjects they will be teaching? Is it possible for teacher preparation programs to help students attain the kind of disciplinary knowledge described by Anderson as necessary for successful teaching? How do our students beliefs about their subjects, children, teaching, and learning change as they move through our programs and the first years of teaching? How do they think about teaching problems, make plans and on-line decisions? What perspectives or frames do they use when and if they reflect on their teaching? What are the sources of those perspectives? How do the teachers we educate justify what they do in classrooms? How does all this change with teaching experience? What distinguishes teachers who move toward expertise from those who leave teaching or who stay and seem only to stagnate?

How might we study these questions? We could conduct in-depth case studies following a few students from entry into our programs through several years of teaching. Valuable information might be obtained through interviews, observations, journals, or stimulated recall. We might conduct large-scale questionnaire studies establishing a data base on all our students, mapping characteristics and beliefs as they develop during preservice preparation and inservice experience. We might systematically compare different methods for teaching our courses or supervising our students. In all of these approaches, we must not forget to include examinations of the contexts in which our students learn and teach. We need to know how the climate, norms, and resources of a field placement or the characteristics of a cooperating teacher influence the development of our students. Institutions might share evaluations methods and procedures so comparisons can be made across program types or geographic regions.

If we decided to study these questions as an integral part of reforming the teacher preparation programs at our institutions, we could fill some of the most important holes in our understanding of how teaching expertise does and does not develop. In carefully and systematically examining these issues, we not only will make significant contributions to research on teaching, we also will come to understand our own students better. We will know their characteristics, beliefs, and values. We will learn what sense (or nonsense) they make of our courses. We will see what actually happens in supervision conferences and if this experience complements or conflicts with the preparation we have given our students. Substantive communication among all the teacher educators (university and public school) will be encouraged or even necessitated. We will be forced to pay attention to the long-term outcomes of our preparation programs. Finally, our students will feel the extent of our concern for them, their opinions, attitudes, and responses to their own education.

REFERENCES

AMERICAN ASSOCIATION OF COLLEGES OF TEACHER EDUCATION. (1983). *Educating a profession: Extended programs for teacher education.* Washington, DC: AACTE.

CARNEGIE TASK FORCE ON TEACHING AS A PROFESSION. (1986). *A nation prepared: Teachers for the 21st century.* New York: Carnegie Forum on Education and the Economy, Carnegie Foundation.

CHASE, W. G., & SIMON, H. A. (1973). Perception in chess. *Cognitive Psychology, 4,* 55-81.

CHI, M., & GLASER, R. (1982). *Knowledge and skill differences in novices and experts* (Tech. Rep. 7). Pittsburgh: Learning Research and Development Center, University of Pittsburgh.

GRIFFIN, G. (1984). Why use research in preservice teacher education: A proposal. *Journal of Teacher Education, 35*(4), 36-40.

HOLMES GROUP EXECUTIVE BOARD. (1986). *Tomorrow's teachers: A report of the Holmes Group.* East Lansing, MI: The Holmes Group.

HOWEY, K. R., & ZIMPHER, N. L. (1986). The current debate on teacher preparation. *Journal of Teacher Education, 37*(5), 41-50.

LARKIN, J., MCDERMOTT, J., SIMON, D. P., & SIMON, H. A. (1980). Expert and novice performance in solving physics problems. *Science, 208*, 1335-1342.

MCKEACHIE, W. J. (1986). *Teaching tips: A guide for the beginning college teacher* (8th ed.). Lexington, MA: D. C. Heath.

PATEL, V. L., FREDERIKSEN, C. H., & Groen, G. J. (1984). *Differences between experts and novices in a complex verbal task in a medical domain* (Rep No. CME 84-3). Montreal: McGill University, Center for Medical Education.

SCANNELL, D. (1987). Fifth year and extended programs. In M. Haberman and J. Baccus (Eds.), *Advances in teacher education* (Vol. 3, pp. 168-180). Norwood, NJ: Ablex.

SHULMAN, L. S. (1986). Those who understand: Knowledge growth in teaching. *Educational Researcher, 19*(2), 4-14.

SHULMAN, L. S. (1987). Knowledge and teaching: Foundations of the new reform. *Harvard Educational Review, 57*(1), 1-22.

SOLTIS, J. F. (Ed.). (1987). Reforming teacher education: A symposium on the Holmes Group Report [Special Issue]. *Teachers College Record, 88*(3).

TOM, A. (1986). *The case for maintaining teacher education at the undergraduate level.* St. Louis, MO: Coalition of Teacher Education Programs.

2

LEARNING FROM EXPERIENCE IN GRADUATE TEACHER EDUCATION

Kenneth M. Zeichner

One of the key recommendations in many contemporary proposals for the reform of teacher education in the United States is that the undergraduate education major be eliminated and that initial teacher certification be awarded following a period of graduate study ranging anywhere from a semester to three or more years. A variety of models for graduate or "extended" teacher education has been proposed in recent years by individual teacher educators (e.g., Gideonse, 1982; Joyce & Clift, 1984; Smith, 1980), by groups of teacher educators and/or deans of Schools of Education (e.g., American Association of Colleges of Teacher Education, 1983; The Holmes Group, 1986; Howsam, Corrigan, Denemark, & Nash, 1976), and by task forces and commissions that extend beyond the teacher education community in their membership (Carnegie Forum on Education and the Economy, 1986; National Commission for Excellence in Teacher Education, 1985).

This movement toward the elimination of undergraduate teacher education has not been without opposition. Tom (1986), Hawley (1986, 1987), Mehlinger (1986), and Travers and Sacks (1987) are a few of its most vocal critics. Almost no one has argued against the development of graduate level programs as one of a series of options for entry into teaching. Most, if not all, of the opposition is toward the idea of establishing graduate or "extended" preparation as the *only* option.

The author would like to thank Alan Tom (Washington University) and Alison Gooding and Anita Woolfolk (Rutgers University) for their helpful comments.

Proponents of graduate teacher education programs have offered a variety of rationales for moving beyond four years of preservice preparation. For example, Kerr (1983) and Clark (1986) have argued that the underfunding and low status of teacher education are due largely to the fact that teacher preparation occurs at the undergraduate level. Advocates of graduate teacher education see the establishment of graduate programs as a necessary step in the professionalization of teaching, one that they feel will eventually lead to the allocation of greater resources to teacher education, resources comparable to those directed toward other professional preparation programs. Many of the advocates of graduate teacher education have also offered the "inadequate time hypothesis" (Tom, 1986) as a justification for graduate programs. They've argued that more than four years are needed just to prepare teachers to a "safe level of beginning practice" (Denemark & Nutter, 1984), assuming that we also want these beginning professionals to be (a) as well educated in the liberal arts as other college students, (b) thoroughly grounded in the subject matter they will teach, and (c) in possession of a professional education that reflects our current knowledge about teaching and the increasing complexity of the teacher's role.

Opposition to the establishment of graduate teacher education[1] as the only route to certification has raised many serious questions about the desirability of eliminating undergraduate teacher education. For example, Tom (1986) has argued that this movement has encouraged an emphasis on procedural issues and has distracted attention from the reform of the substance of both the general and professional components of teacher education. Also, if the structure of teachers' work and the school as a workplace remain essentially unchanged, Hawley (1986, 1987) has argued that graduate teacher education will narrow rather than increase the quantity and quality of the talent pool for teaching. Finally, some critics speculate that the establishment of graduate programs will complicate an already existing ethical dilemma by further reducing access to teaching for low income and minority candidates (Cronin, 1983; Gallegos, 1981).[2]

Hawley (1986, 1987) has recently been critical of the current debate over graduate teacher education. He argues that much of the debate over this issue rests on unsubstantiated claims and assumptions. Hawley suggests that the quality of the debate could be greatly enhanced by more analysis of the costs and consequences of various teacher education improvement strategies. In addition to its reliance on unsubstantiated claims and on speculation, this debate also fails to attend to history. Despite the fact that millions of dollars have been spent in the development, implementation, and evaluation of graduate teacher education programs (the Ford Foundation alone spent over $70 million in the 1950s and 1960s), references to our previous experience with graduate teacher education in the current debate are scarce.

Contemporary critics and proponents of graduate teacher education routinely dismiss our prior experience with graduate programs and conclude, without explicit analysis, that there is no empirical evidence available in support of the idea of graduate teacher education. Cyphert & Ryan (1984) refer to graduate teacher education as a promising idea awaiting supporting data. Hawley (1987) concludes that "there is absolutely no evidence that extended preparation programs make teachers more effective as they enter the profession" (p. 276). Finally, Matthes and Duffy (1987) state that no studies exist that compare M.A.T. graduates[3] and graduates of conventional undergraduate programs on any dimensions.

This chapter will challenge the assumption of a lack of meaningful literature on graduate teacher education and will examine selected aspects of the history of graduate teacher education to determine if there are lessons to be learned that can inform the current debate. The analysis will focus on post-1950 graduate programs, particularly those sponsored by the Ford Foundation and its Fund for the Advancement of Education. The focus will be on empirical evidence related to the relative impact of graduate *versus* conventional programs on *recruitment* into teaching, *retention* in teaching, and the *quality* of teaching as well as on the reflections of those who have participated in graduate teacher education programs.

It will be argued that while the lessons to be learned from our prior experiences with graduate teacher education programs are important, they are also very limited because of weaknesses in the methods that have been used to assess program impact. Several suggestions will be offered for overcoming the limitations of past evaluation efforts so that useful information about the relative impact of different kinds of teacher education programs is not lost.

GRADUATE TEACHER EDUCATION IS NOT A NEW IDEA
AND COMES IN MANY VARIETIES

The concern about preparing teachers at a graduate level for their initial certification did not originate in the current debate on teacher education. Proposals and programs for graduate teacher education date back to the beginning of the century. As early as 1895 Brown University offered a program of practice teaching at the graduate level after completion of the undergraduate teacher education curriculum (Shaplin & Powell, 1964). The idea of five-year teacher preparation programs dates back to at least 1905 with California's actions regarding secondary teachers (Benjamin, 1933). Most of the early proposals for extended preparation programs were limited to secondary teachers, with the first proposal for extended preparation for elementary teachers appearing in 1934 (Von Schlichten, 1958). Prior to the 1930s, even before a four-year college degree was required in all states, discussions of graduate teacher education abounded. But few programs were actually established, mainly because of the intolerable economic burden it would have created for most students. The first Master of Arts in Teaching program was established at Harvard in 1936, a program that provided a model for many of the Ford-sponsored programs of the 1950s. Another significant event in the history of graduate teacher education occurred in 1961 with the passage of the Fisher Bill in California, which required a minimum of five years of teacher preparation for all elementary teachers (Hendrick, 1967).

Throughout the 1950s and 1960s the literature in teacher education was filled with arguments for the establishment of graduate teacher education as the norm for preservice teacher education. Articles contained descriptions of individual programs and testimonials to their success, guidelines for the establishment of similar programs, and some limited assessments of the impact of particular graduate programs on recruitment, retention, and teaching effectiveness.

An examination of this literature indicates clearly that there are many important differences among graduate teacher education program models, so many differences in fact that the term graduate teacher education applied to a program is almost meaningless without more information about the details of the program. One important distinction is between those programs that require five or more years prior to initial employment *versus* those that require five or more years as a condition for attaining full or final certification. In the latter case, individuals are permitted to teach with provisional certificates and the graduate or extended portion of their preparation occurs during the inservice period. Another critical distinction is between "extended" programs that include an integrated curriculum of general and professional education during both the undergraduate and graduate years and programs that save all professional education courses for the fifth year, after the completion of a full four-year undergraduate program. Some graduate programs include extensive, supervised internships (paid or unpaid), while other programs require only the typical and more limited student teaching experience. In some "extended" programs, graduates earn both a bachelor's and a master's degree, while other programs grant only the baccalaureate degree. Graduate teacher education programs vary in length from one semester to about three years beyond the baccalaureate.[4]

This chapter will focus on an analysis of some of the lessons to be learned from graduate teacher education programs sponsored by the Ford Foundation and other graduate programs (e.g., internship and M.A.T. programs) closely resembling the Ford models. The Ford Foundation sponsored several different kinds of graduate teacher education programs during the 1950s and 1960s. Financial support for many of these programs came from Ford's Fund for the Advancement of Education. By 1959 Ford had spent over $35 million on the initiation of over 70 programs, including $3 million alone on its first major venture in the state of Arkansas. During the 1960s Ford made an even greater commitment to funding programs that would help alter dominant practices in teacher education, such as the existence of teacher education as an undergraduate enterprise.[5]

Ford sponsored programs included fifth-year programs designed for liberal arts graduates without prior professional education, fifth-year programs specializing in teacher preparation for older liberal arts graduates, and M.A.T. programs (mainly for secondary teachers) that were jointly planned by education and arts and science faculties and included both professional and academic courses in the graduate portion of the program. The "Breakthrough" programs were a particular group of 43 programs funded in 1958 mostly within these categories (Bigelow, 1957; Stone, 1968; Woodring, 1957). Ford was not the only instigator of these programs. Many, including the National Teacher Corps (Corwin, 1973), were established without Ford funding, but often these efforts were modeled after significant aspects of the Ford projects of the 1950s and 1960s (Saxe, 1965).

The Ford projects were primarily directed at liberal arts graduates without prior professional training. Two main goals of many Ford projects were to attract bright and talented liberal arts graduates to careers in teaching and to involve liberal arts faculty in the tasks of teacher preparation—tasks that many of these faculty had successfully avoided. There was also speculation that some Ford officials had a third goal as well—that the success of the M.A.T. model would lead to the eventual demise of Schools of Education (Elisberg, 1981). The Ford programs were often presented in the literature as experimental tests of specific hypotheses about various patterns of teacher education. For example, the Arkansas project was presented as a test (on a statewide basis) that all professional education is best delayed until the fifth year. The M.A.T. model was offered as a test of the idea that the professional and academic components of a teacher's education can be planned as a single unit. Finally, the Cornell University program was presented as a test of the idea that classroom experience with closely related seminars can take the place of formal professional courses during a graduate fifth year (Woodring, 1957).

Much of the evaluation data related to these Ford-sponsored programs consists of institutional self-reports describing the strengths and weaknesses of particular program patterns and components (e.g., Cogan, 1955) or Ford-sponsored accounts or evaluations of the programs (e.g., Coley & Thorpe, 1986; Stone, 1968; Woodring, 1957). Recently, several independent studies have also been conducted of Ford-sponsored graduate preparation programs and of projects closely resembling the Ford prototypes (e.g., Elisberg, 1981; McDonald & Elias, 1980). Without taking a position on the desirability of eliminating the undergraduate major, this chapter will draw upon both published and unpublished sources, including the perceptions of program participants (Boyter, 1954), to identify some of the lessons we can learn from our experience with these graduate programs.

THE RELATIVE IMPACT OF GRADUATE TEACHER EDUCATION PROGRAMS ON TEACHER RECRUITMENT, RETENTION, AND EFFECTIVENESS

Three broad questions have been repeatedly posed in assessments of graduate teacher education programs. Have these programs been successful in attracting talented liberal arts graduates into teaching? How long do graduates of these programs stay in teaching compared to graduates of traditional programs? Are there any data on the relative teaching effectiveness of teachers prepared in graduate programs in comparison with graduates of four-year programs?

As early as 1958, teacher educators were critical of the quality of empirical evidence supporting the establishment of graduate teacher education programs.

> In no case has evidence been adduced to indicate that teachers with five years of preparation have in fact been proved superior to those with less preparation . . . . No significant body of research has resulted from the five years of initial preparation requirement which

provides evidence as to whether or not this requirement has produced better teachers. (Von Shlichten, 1958, pp. 49-50)

Although condemnation of the empirical literature has continued until today, as evidenced by the comments of Hawley (1987) quoted earlier, it is very rare to find criticisms, past or present, based on a systematic examination of studies conducted evaluating program models. All of the Ford-sponsored programs and many others as well have provided us with some data related to one or more of the three questions posed above. Although much of what exists is in the form of subjective self-assessments, systematic studies were also conducted and reported for some programs. Before rejecting out of hand the heuristic value of our accumulated experience with graduate teacher education, we need to carefully examine the studies conducted to date and explicitly assess the quality of the evidence. Even if the overall conclusion remains that there is no empirical support for the superiority of graduate programs, we may still be able to learn something about the conceptual and methodological problems involved in accumulating evidence about the impact of different programs that will help us to accumulate more useful evidence in the future.

The Quality of Teacher Education Students

One of the major goals of all of the Ford programs, and many others as well, has been to attract into teaching bright and talented students who might not otherwise choose to enroll in a teacher education program. As Coley and Thorpe (1986) have pointed out, many graduate programs invested heavily in the recruitment of high quality students, sometimes through the establishment of networks such as the Harvard 29 College Plan (Cartwright, 1961), and frequently offered students scholarships or paid internships as incentives. Efforts have been made to assess the quality of the graduates of these programs, often in comparison with graduates from traditional four-year programs at the same institutions.

If there is one conclusion that can be drawn about our experience thus far with graduate teacher education, it is that the students enrolled in these programs have been of uniformly high quality as measured by typical academic criteria. Two recent assessments of M.A.T. programs (Coley & Thorpe, 1986; Elisberg, 1981) and assessments of the Ford programs in general (e.g., Stone, 1968) have concluded that students in these programs have been consistently in the upper ranges of academic ability. "The M.A.T. programs provided some superior teachers who emerged from a pool of students whose academic ability and leadership potential were considerably above the average for the profession" (Elisberg, 1981, p. 129).

Although the relative proportion of our nation's teachers supplied by these programs has always been very small, the fact that graduate preparation programs have brought and continue to bring many talented people into teaching cannot be disputed. Whether graduate programs attracted people into teaching who would not have otherwise chosen to enter through some other route (had the graduate option not been available) still remains an open question in most cases. Some assessments of graduate programs (e.g., Coley and Thorpe, 1986) cite data related to the attractions that graduate programs held for these academically superior students (e.g., the ability to obtain a graduate degree and a teaching credential in a short period of time). Some data also exist indicating that liberal arts graduates would not have become teachers if the only route available had been the conventional one (Stone, 1968). Generally, however, further data are needed to support the conclusion that graduate programs are *necessary* for attracting these bright students into teaching.

It should also be noted that faculty associated with several contemporary extended teacher education programs have commented on significant changes in the academic capabilities of students in their programs after their schools implemented extended program structures. For example, Andrew (1984) identifies the academic characteristics of the students at the University of New Hampshire as one of the strongest indicators of its success. Faculty at the University of Florida have also noted improvements in the academic credentials of students after the initiation of PROTEACH (Zeichner, 1987). This increase in the quality of students may, however, be a result of the increased standards associated with program changes rather than a result of the graduate nature of the programs. Some educators such as Hawley (1987) contend that similar results can also be brought about by alternative strategies such as the radical reform of undergraduate teacher education programs and/or significant changes in the workplace of the school and the occupation of teaching. Although the evidence supports the view that graduate programs have been successful in bringing talented students into teaching, it does not support the view that this is the only or even the best way to achieve this important goal.

Two other kinds of claims appear in the literature related to the quality of students who have participated in graduate teacher education programs. First, there are many claims, most based purely on subjective observations, that teachers prepared by the graduate programs are especially sought after by the best school systems in the country (e.g., Cogan, 1955). There is very little specific data however, cited in support of these global assertions. There are also claims that M.A.T. programs and other types of graduate teacher education have supplied a disproportionate share of leaders (e.g., principals, professors, policy makers) for our educational system (Elisberg, 1981). Some evidence exists to support this assertion. For example, an evaluation of the Ford-initiated internship program at the University of Oregon concluded on the basis of an examination of the professional biographies of principals hired in the Eugene public schools that the internship program had supplied the system with a disproportionate number of principals who entered leadership positions more quickly than those who came into the system through conventional undergraduate programs.

Retention in Teaching

Teacher educators have long predicted that the increased time commitment and rigor associated with graduate teacher education programs would strengthen the holding power of the teaching profession for program graduates. For example, over 50 years ago, Hill (1932) asserted that "increased and exacting standards of admission to the profession of high school teaching will challenge men and women to enter upon training for such service with the expectation of making it a life career" (p. 431). This argument, usually coupled with an explication of the advantages of making teacher education look more like the education of other professionals, persists today. The only difference now is that contemporary commentators (e.g., Wise, Chapter 10) place more emphasis on the importance of coupling changes in teacher education with changes in the occupational structure and workplace characteristics of teaching.

There have been several assessments of the entry and retention rates for graduates of traditional four-year *versus* graduate teacher education programs. Almost everyone who has examined this issue is in agreement that graduate teacher education programs are at least comparable to and sometimes slightly better than traditional programs in terms of the proportion of graduates who enter the classroom and who then remain in teaching over time. This has been concluded with regard to the Ford programs in general (Spalding & Krathwohl, 1959; Stone, 1968; Woodring, 1957), the M.A.T. programs in particular (e.g., Coley & Thorpe, 1986; Elisberg, 1981; Matthes & Duffy, 1987), and for contemporary extended programs that have been around long enough for retention rates to be assessed (Andrew, 1986).

Some of the success of graduate preparation programs in placing their graduates is undoubtedly due to the teacher shortages that existed during the times these programs have been most prevalent. The finding that graduates of these programs tend to stay in teaching as long as graduates of conventional programs is particularly notable and appears to contradict some of the recent evidence that "the best and the brightest" leave the classroom sooner (e.g., Schlechty & Vance, 1981). One of the reasons for this counterintuitive finding may be related to the fact that many of the graduates of M.A.T. and other graduate programs have taught in suburban communities with students in the upper ranges of socioeconomic status (Coley & Thorpe, 1986). The high retention rates may be a reflection of the more favorable conditions of professional practice experienced by these teachers rather than of the type and quality of their training. Comparisons of retention rates under similar teaching conditions would be a useful addition to the literature on this issue.

Teaching Effectiveness

One of the most important comparisons that can be made between graduate and conventional undergraduate programs is in terms of the quality of teaching evidenced by program graduates. A careful reading of the literature reveals that, contrary to the popular belief that such comparisons have never been attempted, three kinds of studies have been conducted: (a) comparisons of teaching performance based on principals' and/or supervisors' ratings; (b) comparisons of teaching performance based on classroom observations by researchers; and (c) comparisons of teaching performance based on the subjective accounts of program personnel. Studies conducted at Yale in the 1950s (Holden, 1958) are representative of the first category. Here principals of 100 schools employing Yale program graduates were surveyed. By a vote of more than two to one, these principals rated the "M.A.T. Product" superior rather than average.

The M.A.T. graduates were rated superior rather than inferior by a vote of more than ten to one. When compared to teachers who graduated from traditional programs, the M.A.T. graduates were judged to be better in terms of their knowledge of subject matter, their ability to communicate information about and interest in a subject, and in their ability to cooperate with other teachers and administrators. The only areas in which traditional students were rated higher than M.A.T. graduates were discipline and classroom control. Similar reports of the relative superiority of the teaching of individuals from graduate programs, based on the comments of principals and supervisors, can be found in Elias & McDonald (1980) for the Temple University and University of Oregon internship programs and in assessments of the "Breakthrough Programs" (Stone, 1968). Only one instance could be located in which graduate trained teachers were rated below teachers educated in undergraduate programs. Woronoff (1958) conducted several studies of the University of Southern California's program and found negative results for the graduate program in one of these evaluations.

Woodring (1957) outlines many of the obvious limitations of relying on principals' ratings to assess program impact, but concludes that these ratings should not be ignored entirely. We clearly need to go beyond these kinds of ratings in our assessments of the impact of graduate teacher education on the quality of teaching.

Several studies exist in which classroom observations have been conducted to assess the effectiveness of teachers from graduate preparation programs. For example, Vollmer (1986) used the Georgia Teacher Performance Assessments Instruments to assess the growth in teaching competence of students in the University of Pittsburgh's M.A.T. internship program in Elementary Education. She found that 36 of the 45 competency indicators were significantly improved over the course of the internship experience and that the M.A.T. model does indeed have an important influence on the acquisition and growth of teacher competencies. The lack of a comparison group is an obvious problem with this and several similar studies.

Several studies also compare the teaching performance of teachers from graduate and undergraduate programs based on systematic classroom observations conducted by trained research assistants. For example, studies at Cornell University compared the teaching performance of graduates from its experimental fifth-year program in elementary education with that of graduates of several traditional four-year programs. On the basis of two half-days of classroom observation by researchers using the "Teacher Evaluation Record," the quality of teaching evidenced by 46 graduates of the special program was judged to be better than that of 103 graduates of four-year programs at several nearby campuses on a wide range of teaching performance measures (Cornell University, 1957).

Other studies have shown that teachers from graduate teacher education programs perform at least as well as but not necessarily better than teachers who complete conventional four-year programs. For example, evaluators of the Arkansas Experiment in Teacher Education concluded, on the basis of two half-days of classroom observation by researchers using "Ryan's Classroom Observational Record" that teachers from the graduate fifth-year programs outperformed the traditionally trained teachers on 21 of the 22 measures of effective classroom behaviors (Spalding & Krathwohl, 1959).

Mitzel (1958), in his criticisms of the Cornell program evaluations, raises a point that is fundamental to understanding the problems associated with attempts to accumulate classroom-based evidence about the impact of graduate teacher education. He argues that the comparison of Cornell students with those from nearby institutions is inappropriate and that observed differences in teaching performance might reflect nothing more than differences in program selection criteria. Cornell students underwent a much more stringent selection process than students at the other institutions (only 43 percent of qualified applicants were admitted over the life of the program), and the Cornell students who were admitted had higher scores on the National Teachers' Examination and on a test of professional knowledge than students in the comparison groups. Nothing in the Cornell study design enables one to attribute differences in teaching evaluations to differences in the structure and content of the various teacher education programs. This problem has been raised in relation to many other evaluations of the Ford-sponsored program as well. Stone (1968) claims that "a key question in program evaluation is whether these teachers are significantly different as a result of the program's new structure and content or because of a redirection of the flow of talent that the program sparked." Several assessments of the graduate program literature have concluded that selection differences rather than differences resulting from variations in program structure are likely to be causes of the observed differences in program outcomes.

> No study has been undertaken to determine whether the level of competence of some of the graduates was a result of who they were to begin with or what was done to them. . . . The data supporting the high quality of teaching by M.A.T. graduates has not been derived from a systematic evaluation of the effect of the training . . . real evidence that the M.A.T. idea actually improved teaching is lacking. (Elisberg, 1981, p. 130)

Thus, despite several studies that show that the quality of instruction evidenced by teachers from graduate programs is comparable to or superior to that of teachers from four-year programs,[6] weaknesses in the design of evaluation studies prevent us from attributing any of these findings to the character and quality of particular teacher education programs. Although the widely held conclusion about the lack of empirical support for the superiority of graduate programs has been upheld in this analysis, it is important to understand some of the reasons why, after the implementation of over 100 programs during the last 30 years, we have failed to accumulate clear evidence on this question.

Improving the Quality of Evidence Related to Graduate Teacher Education

Mitzel (1958) complained that only a very small portion of Ford program budgets were devoted to the documentation and evaluation of program impact. He argued that a much larger share of a program's budget needs to be devoted to evaluation activities. Stone (1968) voices a similar complaint in his evaluation of the Ford "Breakthrough Programs," a specific set of Ford programs initiated in 1958. He notes that

> budget items for "research," "evaluation," and "follow-up studies" were usually deleted when Breakthrough grants were made to colleges and universities. As a consequence few of those innovative efforts gathered substantive hard data about their students, their curricula, the success of their products or program impact. The Fund for the Advancement of Education and later the Ford Foundation's history of publishing material which reports as fait accompli that which project directors hoped to achieve is testimony to this report . . . . Ford's refusal to provide for scholarly and systematic evaluation of results of the Breakthrough demonstrations is questionable. In the long run, this must be recorded as the most significant deficiency of the efforts by seed money to promote change in higher education. (pp. 170- 171)

It is very clear that we must do a much better job in the future of documenting both the anticipated and unanticipated effects of a variety of program models. And these evaluations need to go beyond merely documenting the effects themselves. We need to design our evaluations to enable us to understand the relative impact of selection and socialization as well as the particular programmatic and contextual conditions related to the realization of specific outcomes. We also need to provide for the adequate financial support of evaluation activities. If the programs are externally funded, as many have been in the past, this may mean that foundations need to fund fewer programs so that those funded can be systematically studied. Institutions may also need to think about initiating small experimental programs rather than attempting to change all programs at once, again so those that are mounted can be carefully studied. It is inexcusable that we have learned so little from the millions of dollars allocated to graduate teacher education programs over the past 35 years. Careful study of the relative impact of a variety of teacher education program models, including graduate ones, is long overdue.

A recent assessment of the impact of 12 post-1980 alternative certification programs indicates that the problems evident in past evaluations of graduate programs may be recurring. In this study Adelman (1986) interviewed supervisors of 16 certification candidates in 12 programs and asked them to compare the teaching performance and subject matter backgrounds of these candidates in relation to traditionally trained teachers. Not surprisingly, Adelman found that the supervisors of the alternative certification candidates characterized their instructional skills as at least as good as, if not better than, those of traditionally prepared teachers (14 of the 16 were rated above average or superior) and judged the subject matter backgrounds of all of the candidates to be above the average for beginning teachers. Despite Adelman's appropriately cautious comments concerning the limits of generalizing from this preliminary study, we have reason to be concerned with this continuation of the evaluation of graduate teacher education programs in a manner that does not enable us to sort out the relative contribution of selection and socialization to the outcomes under investigation. If we do nothing to change this pattern of program evaluation, then we will be no further along after another 30 years than we are now in understanding the relative impact of different program models.

The complex design and analysis problems involved in evaluating the impact of different teacher education program models have been addressed in the general literature on educational research methodology. Cook and Campbell's (1979) discussions of the design and analysis of "quasi- experiments" in field settings clearly indicate how far research methodology has progressed beyond the overly simplistic methods evident in many studies of graduate teacher education programs. There are several examples in the teacher education literature of program evaluations and studies of teacher learning that can inform the design of studies of graduate teacher education. Romberg and Fox's (1975) use of "process-impact evaluation" to assess the effects of a particular component of the Teacher Corps and the current studies of the National Center for Research in Teacher Education on teacher learning in a variety of teacher education programs (National Center for Research on Teacher Education, 1987) are two examples of work within teacher education that has dealt somewhat successfully with the kinds of problems that emerge in the literature evaluating graduate teacher education programs.

These and other inquiries into the impact of teacher education programs have several characteristics in common. First, each study has attempted to document and describe the significant features of the teacher education programs under study. Evaluations of graduate teacher education programs have been concerned for the most part with determining the success of a program (e.g., whether or not certain outcomes occur and how these compare to outcomes of other programs). Few of these studies have directly investigated the programs themselves. There is a widespread belief, however, that these kinds of "program testing evaluations" (Corwin, 1973) are less useful in the long run than studies that help us learn how particular program components are related to certain results and under what conditions. "Unless the underlying features responsible for the outcomes are identified, the study cannot yield knowledge that will be applicable beyond the specific program being evaluated (Corwin, 1973, p. 345).

In order to successfully document the significant features of teacher education programs, studies must reflect the character and quality of the events under investigation. Tabachnick (1975) argues that teacher education programs are "dynamic events" that occur over time and that are embedded in a broader sociocultural context. Those who seek to capture the significant aspects of these dynamic events must do so longitudinally and attend to the broader contexts in which programs exist. If researchers followed this advice, we would be able to move beyond merely generating findings about which programs produce more effective teachers. We would begin to understand more than we do now about the specific contributions of particular teacher education program components to a variety of outcomes. We would also be less likely to draw misleading conclusions about the impact of teacher education programs, such as those described earlier about the relative retention rates of graduates of M.A.T. and conventional programs, that do not account for external contexts.

There are a variety of design possibilities and methods of analysis available to those who would conduct studies of graduate teacher education programs within these broad guidelines. Studies of graduate teacher education programs need to begin to reflect more of the complexity and sophistication evident in state of the art research and evaluation methodology.

THE REFLECTIONS OF PROGRAM PARTICIPANTS

In addition to what we can learn from an analysis of research and evaluation studies that have sought to assess the impact of graduate teacher education programs on teacher recruitment, retention, and effectiveness, there are also lessons we can learn from studying the reflections of faculty, teachers, administrators, and students who participated in the Ford-sponsored programs. Unfortunately, many of these reflections are not particularly helpful. The literature is filled with "lessons from experience" and with recommendations for practice that go little beyond stating the obvious. The importance of good relations between schools and universities and between education faculties and arts and science faculties are stressed over and over again in the literature. There are, however, many insights we can gain from examining the written reflections of participants in graduate teacher preparation programs that can inform the design of the next generation of programs. Several examples of these will now be described to illustrate the nature of the data that can be expected to emerge from a more thorough mining of this vast literature than was possible for this chapter.

First, the Ford programs' vigorous efforts to recruit talented students into teaching were generally successful. The past successes of these programs in their utilization of the media for recruitment and in the establishment of recruitment networks, which involved special efforts to recruit students into teaching from liberal arts colleges without teacher education programs, could be useful to those teacher educators who are now attempting to draw liberal arts majors into teacher education at the graduate level. Generally, graduate programs have placed a greater emphasis on extensive recruitment than is typical for most teacher education programs. Examples of successful recruitment practices include sending faculty to liberal arts colleges to make presentations about specific teacher education programs; using news releases, radio announcements, and local service organizations to publicize programs; and combining student recruitment with the other professional activities of faculty as they travel across the country.[7]

We also know from the experience of the Ford programs that some type of financial support, either through scholarships or paid internships, is important to the success of these recruitment efforts at the postbaccalaureate level. If teacher education is to compete favorably with other professions for some of the talented students it hopes to attract into graduate programs, then financial support is crucial. This point has been stressed repeatedly in analyses of Ford-sponsored programs (e.g., Cartwright, 1961; Cogan, 1955; Holden, 1958). Elisberg (1981) concluded, with regard to the M.A.T. model, that

> to compete for good students, financial subsidies must be offered to them. As the grants terminated, salaried internships became the only means to adequately subsidize programs. Without the salaried internship, there is little hope for the survival of M.A.T. programs because they will continue to cost more than institutions and school systems are willing to pay. Without outside financial support, programs of this nature will not be able to survive. (p. 132)

A few programs, like the Internship Program for College Graduates at Temple University, do not offer direct financial assistance of any type to students, but students in these cases are usually employed as full-time teachers and complete their course-work during the evenings and summers.

The availability of financial support, whether in the form of scholarships, internships, or regular paid teaching positions, may be especially important in determining the eventual impact of graduate programs on the access of minorities to teaching. There are many reasons other than the lack of financial support why minorities have not chosen or were not permitted to go into teaching in large numbers. The provision of such support in graduate teacher education programs by itself is not going to solve the problem. It is important, however, that the next generation of graduate teacher education programs does everything possible to provide incentives to bring talented minorities into teaching.

We have also learned from our experience with graduate teacher education programs that special attention must be given in the future to preparing teachers to teach diverse students in our urban centers. For the most part, the Ford programs and those like them have failed to respond to the needs of our inner city schools (Keppel, 1986). Many graduate programs, particularly those granting the M.A.T. (Coley & Thorpe, 1986), have prepared teachers to work primarily with white middle-class students who attend suburban schools. Only a few of the Ford programs (e.g., Syracuse University's Urban Teacher Preparation Program) and some others (e.g., Teacher Corps) have ever tried to employ a graduate model that prepares teachers for work in inner city schools. It would be very unfortunate if the next generation of graduate teacher education programs also failed to respond to this pressing need. Students in teacher education are generally reluctant to teach in inner city schools with low income and minority populations (Joyce, Yarger, Howey, Harbeck, & Kluwin, 1977). We need to bring talented people into the profession, but we must be equally concerned with where these talented individuals will teach and who will benefit from their expertise. Generating another set of elite, academically oriented programs that primarily serve the interests of the already most advantaged in our society is not a defensible course of action for the next generation of graduate programs to pursue, by default or otherwise. The issue of equity needs to be at the forefront in the design of the next generation of graduate programs, especially given the changing demographics, which project fewer and fewer minority teachers and larger and larger percentages of minority students in most of our urban centers (Dilworth, 1984).

Finally, there are many lessons we can learn from the past about how to conceptualize the design of particular program components. For example, one of the greatest concerns in graduate programs has been the quality of the internship experience. We've learned through many evaluations of these programs that the quality of the internship varies greatly across programs and cannot be taken for granted. The quality of supervision during the internship is one area of particular concern that needs to be addressed in the next generation of programs. Assessments of graduate programs clearly indicate a great deal of dissatisfaction in some cases with the quality of supervision (e.g., Coley & Thorpe, 1986). In these situations, according to Stone (1968), supervision often fell short of program rhetoric and lapsed into little more than pro forma contact. Shaplin and Powell (1964) concluded that "in many programs the internship remains an immersion into full time teaching with a minimum of preparation and the experience of the intern becomes a fight for survival" (p. 182).

We've learned from our experience with graduate teacher education programs that the internship by itself is no guarantee that clinical work will enhance the quality of teacher learning or teaching. Assessments of intern programs have alerted us to certain aspects of this experience, such as supervision that need to be carefully planned and supported. We should make use of the insights now available in accounts of graduate programs and in studies of clinical teacher education (e.g., Hoffman & Edwards, 1986) to ensure that the internship components in the next generation of graduate teacher education programs do not repeat the mistakes of their predecessors. Supervisors need to be carefully educated for their work with interns and given adequate time and resources to perform their roles. The experience of interns needs to be carefully structured and linked to the rest of the program's curriculum. Finally, the clinical sites in which interns work need to embody qualities such as the ones identified by Hoffman and Edwards (1986) and by McIntosh (1968) that facilitate teacher learning. (See Chapter 7 for a more complete discussion of supervision in teaching education.)

The quality of the internship as well as the quality of the other elements of graduate programs cannot be left to chance. Those who are now involved in the design of graduate teacher education programs need to carefully examine the insights provided by the faculty, students, and teachers who have participated in these programs in the past. It's time that our accumulated experience with graduate teacher education began to inform the current debate. This history will not tell us exactly what to do in the design of programs or resolve the question about whether graduate teacher education should become the norm, but it will help us to plan more intelligently those graduate programs that will inevitably emerge from the current debate.

NOTES

[1]The term graduate teacher education will be used throughout this chapter to refer to both postbaccalaureate and extended programs. See Chapter 1 for a discussion of the different graduate program models.

[2]See Chapter 1 for a more detailed discussion of the arguments for and against the establishment of graduate teacher education as the norm for preservice training.

[3]M.A.T. (Master of Arts in Teaching) refers to one popular model of graduate teacher education. This model as well as several others will be discussed shortly.

[4]See Chapter 1 for a more detailed discussion of the characteristics of different models of graduate teacher education.

[5]The Ford Foundation also funded a small number of four-year undergraduate teacher education programs.

[6]It should be noted that these studies have generally adopted an overly narrow view of teaching by focusing only on overt teacher behaviors. The assessment of other important dimensions of teaching such as decision-making capabilities (Chapter 8) and knowledge of subject matter (Shulman, 1986) needs to be incorporated into future comparisons of teaching quality.

[7]See Coley and Thorpe (1986) for more examples of recruitment practices used by graduate teacher education programs.

REFERENCES

ADELMAN, N. (1986). *An exploratory study of teacher alternative certification and retraining programs*. Washington, DC: U.S. Department of Education.

AMERICAN ASSOCIATION OF COLLEGES OF TEACHER EDUCATION. (1983). *Educating a profession: Extended programs for teacher education*. Washington, DC: AACTE.

ANDREW, M. (1984, October). *Restructuring teacher education: The University of New Hampshire's five-year program*. Paper presented to the National Commission on Excellence in Teacher Education. San Francisco, CA.

BENJAMIN, H. (1933). The five-year curriculum for prospective secondary teachers. *Educational Administration and Supervision, 19*(1), 1-6.

BIGELOW, K. (1957). New directions in teacher education appraised. *Journal of Teacher Education, 59*, 350-356.

BOYTER, M. E. (1954). A study of five-year programs. *Journal of Teacher Education, 5*(3), 194-197.

CARNEGIE FORUM ON EDUCATION AND THE ECONOMY. (1986). *A nation prepared: teachers for the 21st century*. Washington, DC: The Forum.

CARTWRIGHT, W. (1961). Fifth-year programs in teacher education. *Journal of Higher Education, 32*(6), 297-311.

CLARK, D. (1986). Transforming the structure for the professional preparation of teachers. In J. Raths & L. Katz (Eds.), *Advances in teacher education* (Vol. 2, pp. 1-20). Norwood, NJ: Ablex.

COGAN, M. (1955). Master of Arts in teaching at Harvard University. *Journal of Teacher Education, 6*(2), 135-142.

COLEY, R., & THORPE, M. (1986). *A look at the MAT model of teacher education and its graduates: Lessons for today*. Princeton, NJ: Educational Testing Service.

COOK, T., & CAMPBELL, D. (1979). *Quasi-experimentation: Design and analysis issues for field studies*. Chicago: Rand McNally.

CORNELL UNIVERSITY. (1957, July). *An exciting adventure in education: Fifth annual report of the Cornell experimental program for the preparation of elementary teachers.* Ithaca, NY: Cornell University.

CORWIN, R. (1973). *Reform and organizational survival: The Teacher Corps as an instrument of educational change.* New York: John Wiley and Sons.

CRONIN, J. (1983). State regulation of teacher preparation. In L. Shulman & G. Sykes (Eds.), *Handbook of teaching and policy* (pp. 171-191). New York: Longman.

CYPHERT, F., & RYAN, K. (1984). Extending initial teacher preparation: Some issues and answers. *Action in Teacher Education, 6*(1-2), 63-70.

DENEMARK, G., & NUTTER, N. (1984). The case for extended programs of initial preparation. In L. Katz & J. Raths (Eds.), *Advances in teacher education* (Vol. 1, pp. 203-246). Norwood, NJ: Ablex.

DILWORTH, M. (1984). *Teachers' totter: A report on teacher certification issues.* Washington, DC: Howard University Institute for the Study of Educational Policy.

ELIAS, P., & McDONALD, F. (1980). *Study of induction programs for beginning teachers* (Vol. 3). Princeton, N.J.: Educational Testing Service.

ELISBERG, J. (1981). *A study of selected Master of Arts in teaching programs in the U.S.* Unpublished doctoral dissertation, Northwestern University.

GALLEGOS, A. (1981). The dilemma of extended/five-year programs. *Journal of Teacher Education, 32*(1), 4-6.

GIDEONSE, H. (1982). The necessary revolution in teacher education. *Phi Delta Kappan, 64*, 16-21.

HAWLEY, W. (1986). A critical analysis of the Holmes Group's proposals for reforming teacher education. *Journal of Teacher Education, 37*(4), 47-51.

HAWLEY, W. (1987). The high costs and doubtful efficacy of extended teacher preparation programs: An invitation to more basic reforms. *American Journal of Education, 95*, 275-313.

HENDRICK, I. (1967). Academic revolution in California. *Southern California Quarterly, 49*(2,3,4), 127-166; 253-295; 359-406.

HILL, C. (1932). A five-year plan for the professional training of secondary school teachers. *Educational Administration and Supervision, 18*, 427-437.

HOFFMAN, J., & EDWARDS, S. (Eds.). (1986). *Reality and reform in clinical teacher education.* New York: Random House.

HOLDEN, W. (1958). The master of arts in teaching at Yale 1951-58. *Journal of Teacher Education, 9*(4), 393-400.

THE HOLMES GROUP. (1986). *Tomorrow's teachers.* East Lansing, MI: The Holmes Group.

HOWSAM, R., CORRIGAN, D., DENEMARK, G., & Nash, R. (1976). *Educating a Profession.* Washington, DC: AACTE.

JOYCE, B., & CLIFT, R. (1984). The Phoenix agenda: Essential reform in teacher education. *Educational Researcher, 13*(4), 5-18.

JOYCE, B., YARGER, S., HOWEY, K., HARBECK, K., & KLUWIN, T. (1977). *Preservice teacher education.* Palo Alto, CA: Stanford University Center for Educational Research.

KEPPEL, F. (1986). A field guide to the land of teachers. *Phi Delta Kappan, 67*, 18-23.

KERR, D. (1983). Teaching competence and teacher education in the U.S. In L. Shulman & G. Sykes (Eds.), *Handbook of teaching and policy* (pp. 126-149). New York: Longman.

MATTHES, W., & Duffy, W. (1987, April). *Teacher retention and satisfaction: A comparison of M.A.T. and B.S./B.A. graduates in teacher education.* A paper presented at the annual meeting of the American Educational Research Association, Washington, DC.

McDONALD, F., & ELIAS, P. (1980). *Study of induction programs for beginning teachers* (Vol. 1). Princeton, NJ: Educational Testing Service.

McINTOSH, R. G. (1968, February). *An approach to the analysis of clinical settings for teacher education*. Address presented to the annual meeting of the Association for Student Teaching, Chicago, IL.

MEHLINGER, H. (1986). A risky venture. *Phi Delta Kappan, 67*, 33-36.

MITZEL, H. (1958). Comments on the Cornell experimental program for the preparation of elementary teachers. *Journal of Teacher Education, 9*(4), 383-386.

NATIONAL CENTER FOR RESEARCH IN TEACHER EDUCATION. (1987). *Materials about the center and its role*. East Lansing, MI: Michigan State University.

NATIONAL COMMISSION FOR EXCELLENCE IN TEACHER EDUCATION. (1985). *A call for change in teacher education*. Washington, DC: AACTE.

ROMBERG, T., & FOX, G.T. (1975). Problems in analyzing dynamic events within teacher education. In G.T. Fox (Ed.), *Evaluating teacher education*. Madison, WI: U.S. Office of Education/Teacher Corps.

SAXE, R. (1965). Evaluating the breakthrough programs. *Journal of Teacher Education, 16*, 202-209.

SCHLECHTY, P., & VANCE, V. (1981). Do academically able teachers leave education? The North Carolina case. *Phi Delta Kappan, 64*(1), 106-112.

SHAPLIN, J., & POWELL, A. (1964). A comparison of internship programs. *Journal of Teacher Education, 15*, 175-183.

SHULMAN, L. (1986). Those who understand: Knowledge growth in teaching. *Educational Researcher, 15*(2), 4-14.

SMITH, B. O. (1980). *A design for a school of pedagogy*. Washington, DC: U.S. Department of Education.

SPALDING, W., & KRATHWOHL, D. (1959). *A report on the evaluation of the Arkansas experiment in teacher education*.

STONE, J. C. (1968). *Breakthrough in teacher education*. San Francisco: Jossey & Bass.

TABACHNICK, B. R. (1975). Describing dynamic events within teacher education. In G. T. Fox (Ed.), *Evaluating teacher education*. Madison, WI: U.S. Office of Education/Teacher Corps.

TOM, A. (1986). *The case for maintaining teacher education at the undergraduate level*. St. Louis, MO: Coalition of Teacher Education Programs.

TRAVERS, E., & SACKS, S. (1987). *Teacher education and the liberal arts: The position of the consortium for excellence in teacher education*. Swarthmore, PA: Swarthmore College.

VOLLMER, M. (1986, March). *Meeting the teacher shortage head on*. Paper presented at the annual meeting of the American Association of Colleges for Teacher Education, Chicago.

VON SCHLICHTEN, E. (1958). Idea and practice of a fifth-year requirement for teacher certification. *Teachers College Record, 60*(1), 41-53.

WOODRING, P. (1957). *New directions in teacher education*. New York: Fund for the Advancement of Education.

WORONOFF, I. (1958). Teacher education programs for liberal arts graduates. *Journal of Teacher Education, 9*(4), 359-362.

ZEICHNER, K. (1987). *Exploratory site visit: University of Florida PROTEACH*. Unpublished field notes. East Lansing, MI: National Center for Research in Teacher Education.

3

CASE STUDIES OF EXTENDED TEACHER PREPARATION

Carol Simon Weinstein

Not too long ago, a colleague noted ironically that teachers are referred to as professionals only when they go out on strike. The context of that reference, of course, is the statement that "professionals shouldn't strike." His observation captures the ambiguous status of teaching in our society. On the continuum from occupation to profession, teaching lies somewhere in between (Case, Lanier, & Miskel, 1986). Although it is clearly a service devoted to the public good, and thus meets one criterion of a true profession, teaching lacks most of the other characteristics: a recognized base of specialized knowledge; the autonomy of practitioners to apply that knowledge in diverse situations and to exercise independent judgment and discretion (Darling-Hammond, 1987); and the ability of the members to establish criteria for entry and standards for responsible practice.

Similarly, the preparation of teachers can hardly be considered professional. Teacher education is not guided by the basic concept that characterizes all recognized

This work was funded by the Rutgers Research Council and the New Jersey State Department of Higher Education. The opinions expressed in this paper do not necessarily reflect the position, policy, or endorsement of either organization. A version of this paper was presented at the Rutgers Invitational Symposium on Education, May 1987. The author wishes to acknowledge the cooperation and assistance of Bill Freeman, Austin College, Jerry Bailey, University of Kansas, and Jerry Moore, University of Virginia, as well as the faculty, administrators, students, and public school personnel who graciously shared their knowledge and impressions of five-year teacher preparation programs.

professions: the guarantee of "safe practice with clients" (Denemark & Nutter, 1984). Nor are the entry requirements equivalent; in most cases, licensure is granted automatically upon completion of an approved teacher education program, without a written examination, a performance test, or a closely supervised induction period (Wise, 1986).

Given this situation, it is not surprising that much of the current effort to professionalize teaching has emphasized the need for graduate level preparation. This proposal, however, has been the focus of considerable controversy. Indeed, a recent survey (Guyton & Antonelli, 1987) of institutions belonging to the American Association of Colleges of Teacher Education found that

> all of the common recommendations regarding teacher education are high priority items for educational leaders, except the recommendation that the professional education for teachers be moved to the postbaccalaureate level . . . and the findings of this survey indicate little interest or activity in that direction. (p. 48)

Why are educational leaders so wary of graduate level preparation? What are the issues at the heart of the debate? This chapter will begin by summarizing arguments culled from a review of the recent literature on graduate level preparation. (For a more complete discussion, see Howey & Zimpher, 1986.) The paper will then describe three cases of extended teacher preparation and examine the problems, issues, and questions that arise in the development and implementation of these new programs. Although there are numerous models of extended preparation (see AACTE, 1983), the chapter will focus on institutions that have established five-year integrated programs.

THE ARGUMENTS

The Need for Increased "Life Space"

Proponents of extended programs assert that four years is an insufficient period in which to provide prospective teachers with an extensive general education, an academic specialization, rigorous professional education, and significant clinical experience. Since teachers must be "learned persons" as well as professionals (Case, Lanier, & Miskel, 1986), a full liberal arts curriculum is considered essential. Ample time for professional education is also needed, however, to ensure that teachers acquire the specialized knowledge base of research on teaching and learning that is now available (Berliner, 1984) and to prepare them to deal with the demands of mainstreaming, multicultural education, health and family life education, and the urgent needs of a diverse, increasingly poor population (Denemark & Nutter, 1984).

Despite the apparent reasonableness of the argument for more time, it is not without its critics. Tom (1986), for example, argues that the key issue is quality, not quantity. Similarly, Gallegos (1981) contends that additional space might be available in the four-year structure if "worthless or duplicated instruction" were eliminated. For both of these educators, the major question is how to improve the curriculum provided to prospective teachers *within* a four-year time frame.

Enhanced Prestige

Schools, colleges, and departments of education constitute the "slums" of academia (Ducharme, 1986). Their faculty—especially those associated with undergraduate teacher education programs—suffer from a lack of resources and a lack of status. Their programs are often continued by institutions simply to provide a "holding company" for lower ability students (Lanier & Little, 1986). Their students must frequently overcome peer ridicule and family opposition in order to pursue a teaching career.

It is clear that the proposal for graduate level preparation is partly an attempt to reverse this situation and to increase the prestige associated with teaching. Graduate teacher education will make entry into the field more difficult and will assure that teachers are once again "ahead" of the general public in terms of educational status. Proponents argue that teaching will move toward the professional end of the continuum only when teacher preparation becomes comparable to that of recognized professions (Wise, 1986).

Even advocates, however, admit that graduate preparation alone will not professionalize teaching. At the inaugural meeting of the Holmes Group, for example, Albert Shanker, President of the American Federation of Teachers, warned that the efforts to require graduate teacher preparation could backfire unless they are accompanied by changes in the structure of the schools (Shanker, 1987). Clearly, graduate preparation will enhance the prestige of teaching only if it leads to greater public confidence in teachers and if this translates into greater willingness to increase salaries and to improve working conditions (Wise, 1986).

Quality and Supply of Students

A recent study of approximately 600 high school seniors ranking in the top half of their classes revealed that only 8 percent rated themselves as "very interested in teaching," while 63 percent reported that they were "not interested" (Kemper & Mangieri, 1987). Data like these confirm our worst fears; in the competition for the most talented students, teacher education is an obvious loser. Those who favor graduate level preparation argue that the enhanced prestige of teacher education will attract talented college students, while easy access to undergraduate programs compounds the problem of quality. As Sykes (1983) has observed, these easily accessible undergraduate programs actually serve as "disincentives to bright students, who shun association with a major stigmatized as anti-intellectual" (p. 90).

On the other hand, opponents of extended preparation maintain that undergraduate teacher education provides a larger pool of candidates from which the strongest can be selected; they suggest that graduate programs might dissuade students from entering teaching. Hawley (1986a), for example, predicts that the additional costs of graduate level teacher preparation will almost certainly decrease the number of students entering teaching, and most likely the quality as well, since talented students will choose other career options. Hawley calculates that the additional costs of graduate preparation could be as much as $20,000 when forgone earnings, tuition, and loan fees are taken into consideration. Although financial aid could offset the additional costs for students, such subsidies would detract from the pool of money that could be used to bring about more effective educational reforms (Hawley, 1986b).

The problem of quality and quantity becomes even more complex when the need for minority teachers is considered. All recent reform reports have emphasized the urgency of recruiting minority teachers, but there is substantial doubt that graduate programs in teacher education would be accessible to low-income and minority students. As Gallegos (1981) writes:

> Can anyone honestly doubt that such additional costs to students of teaching would eliminate a significant number of qualified low-income and minority students from the profession? Are there any guarantees anywhere that loans or scholarship funds will be available for these young people? Would school districts or the professional associations that would be part of a collaborative program contribute to such support? The obvious answer is—not likely. (p. 6)

Further exacerbating the problem of quantity is the probability of a teacher shortage in the immediate future. In the 1960s, appeals for extended programs were not persuasive because they coincided with increases in K-12 enrollments. As we near the 1990s, the same problem threatens to undermine the move to graduate preparation. It is questionable whether institutions can establish extended programs while school districts and states implement a "warm-body-in-every-classroom" policy (Wise, 1986, p. 4).

Economic Impact on the University

In addition to the financial impact on the student, the economic cost to the institution must be considered. Resources for four-year teacher preparation programs are based on large student-faculty ratios and on the assumption that courses will use an inexpensive lecture format. This is in sharp contrast to graduate programs that provide for small sections and carefully supervised laboratory and clinical experiences. At the University of New Hampshire, for example, the introductory course for the extended program is taught in sections of 15, obviously more expensive than the previous introductory course of 300-500 students in one large lecture. In addition, the full-year internship is both labor intensive and costly to the institution (Andrew, 1981). Will institutions be willing and/or able to provide the additional funding that will obviously be needed?

A recent article in *Newsweek* magazine (Rogers, 1987) described the ways in which interactive video simulations are being used to train police officers, soldiers, medical doctors, and astronauts to deal with real life contingencies (see Chapter 8). "Artificial reality" and other technologies hold unlimited promise for teacher preparation. In our teacher education "culture of poverty," however, funding is barely adequate to provide print materials and paper. As Berliner (1984) admits,

> it costs [Arizona] about $15,000 to educate a liberal arts undergraduate in, say, comparative literature, history, or psychology. To educate an individual for the vitally important profession of teaching, the state pays $2,000 less. I wonder what Arizona pays to train its medical doctors, nurses, computer scientists, and architects? I am afraid that Arizona, like the 49 other states engaged in teacher preparation, gets precisely what it pays for. (p. 96)

Unless institutions are willing to fund teacher education programs at a level adequate to allow for small courses, intensive supervision, the use of video equipment, microteaching, and interactive computer simulations, even five-year programs will not constitute true professional preparation.

THE METHOD AND THE QUESTIONS

In an attempt to gather information about these issues, data were collected during spring 1987 from three institutions committed to extended teacher preparation: Austin College in Sherman, Texas; the University of Kansas in Lawrence; and the University of Virginia in Charlottesville. These schools were chosen primarily for three reasons. First, they had established comparable five-year programs (in contrast to postbaccalaureate fifth-year programs). Second, they offered an opportunity to examine extended preparation in different contexts—at a small, private liberal arts college, a large state university, and a smaller state university characterized by faculty as a "private university with public funds." Finally, the programs represented different stages of development. At the time of the visits, the Austin Teacher Program (ATP) had been in operation for almost 20 years, the University of Kansas had just graduated its first five-year program students, and the program at the University of Virginia was in its first year of operation.

During three-day visits to each campus, faculty, administrators, students, and public school personnel were interviewed, and written materials (e.g., reports, program descriptions, catalogues, and handbooks) were examined. Data collection focused on the content and organization of the programs, the status of teacher education in the college/university community, the impact of the extended program on the quality of students and minority representation, and the economic consequences of the program for students and for the institution.

The unstructured nature of the interviews allowed respondents to discuss additional issues that were especially salient at each institution. These issues sometimes emerged as more important and problematic than those identified from the review of the literature and will be examined in a later section of this chapter.

THE CASES

Austin College

Planning for the ATP was initiated in 1966 by two members of the Department of Education who were disenchanted with their conventional program. According to a booklet describing the history and goals of the ATP, teacher education students of the late 1960s were critical of "boring education courses" and demanded "more participation, greater involvement, [and] opportunities to direct their own learning"; similarly, the college administration was encouraging faculty "to pioneer . . . to move to the 'cutting edge,' to 'dare to be different'" (Freeman, 1986, p. 6). Influenced by educators such as Combs, Postman, Weingartner, Holt, Rogers, and others, the education faculty launched a five-year program based on the following assumptions: (1) a thorough liberal arts education is essential for prospective teachers; (2) a quality program cannot be completed in the traditional four academic years; (3) students must assume an active role in their preparation and participate in the design and implementation of an individualized program of teacher preparation; and (4) the role of faculty is not merely to instruct, but to guide and direct students toward the goal of effective teaching and to create, coordinate, and facilitate activities that promote the individual's attainment of that goal.

Although the program has evolved over the last 15 years, it continues to embody these assumptions. Table 3-1 presents the general education and major requirements for ATP students.   Beginning in their freshman year, students take one "education lab" per year; the freshman lab receives no credit, the sophomore and junior labs are one credit each, and the senior lab receives four credits. These undergraduate courses consist of weekly seminars held on campus. Except for the junior year, field experiences are coordinated with the labs and are designed to engage students in a wide range of activities prior to the graduate teaching experience. Each field experience has specific objectives and is monitored by the seminar leader. By the end of the fourth year, students have accumulated 60 hours of teaching and 25 hours of observing. Thirty to fifty students enroll in the early education labs; approximately 20 to 25 complete the five-year program.

The bulk of professional education is delayed until the fifth, postbaccalaureate year, when students take graduate courses in "topics" (multicultural education, special education, and computers), curriculum and instruction, reading, and research methods and complete a full semester of student teaching or a paid internship, a situation where the intern is the sole teacher in the classroom (see Table 3-1 for a summary of requirements). Completion of the program culminates in a teaching credential and a master's degree.

The ATP has several distinctive features in addition to the graduate year that justify the "nontraditional" label assigned by faculty. Prospective elementary and secondary teachers attend all classes together, except for the courses in curriculum and instruction and reading given in the fifth year. There are no specific subject methods courses for elementary or secondary students; responsibility for methodol-

TABLE 3–1 Summary of Program Requirements

	AUSTIN COLLEGE	UNIVERSITY OF KANSAS	UNIVERSITY OF VIRGINIA
General Education	ATP students fulfill the general education requirements of Austin College, including specific courses in English, speech, American history, political science, psychology, science, math, computer science, and foreign languages.	Education candidates take 60 credits of general education, including 12 hours of language arts (literature, composition, public speaking, and children's literature), six hours of behavioral sciences, nine hours of social science, nine hours of arts and humanities, and 12 hours of science and math.	Education candidates fulfill the general education requirements of the College of Arts & Sciences, including courses in humanities (writing, literature, public speaking, foreign language), science/mathematics (one full year of a single science; mathematics; computers), social science (one year of western civilization; American history; and general psychology), and physical education. One semester of economics is also required for elementary teachers.
Academic specialization	ATP students must complete the academic specialization requirements of Austin College. Elementary students select one of the following specializations: art, biology, English, French, German, history, mathematics, music, physical education, Spanish, and speech. In addition, they must complete an academic specialization in a combination of subjects taught in the elementary school. Prospective secondary teachers need to have two teaching fields (except for those students in music, art, biology, business, chemistry, English, and math, where single teaching fields are permitted).	Teacher education students complete an academic specialization or "teaching field" that generally equals, and in some cases exceeds, the credits required in the regular liberal arts major. Prospective elementary teachers may have an academic concentration of one major (at least 36 credits) or two minors (at least 20 credits each); middle school teachers have two minors or a major and a minor; and secondary, one major or a major and a minor.	Teacher education students complete the normal requirements for a bachelor of arts degree in the College of Arts & Sciences. Elementary teachers complete a major from one of the following disciplinary groups: history and social sciences, language studies, sciences, or mathematics. In addition, a 15 semester-hour supporting field must be completed from a group other than the one including the major. Major requirements are not completed until the spring semester of the fifth year, when students take 6–9 credits of advanced courses in their major field.

TABLE 3-1 (Continued)

	AUSTIN COLLEGE	UNIVERSITY OF KANSAS	UNIVERSITY OF VIRGINIA
Admission requirements: Undergraduate Program	1. Satisfactory completion of freshman, sophomore, and junior "education labs"; 2. Approved degree plan; 3. Passing score on the Pre-Professional Skills Test; 4. Maintenance of 2.5 overall GPA and 2.65 GPA in field of specialization.	1. 60 hours of credit-bearing coursework; 2. Overall GPA of 2.5; 3. Passing score on the math and writing portions of the Pre-Professional Skills Test.	1. Satisfactory completion of sophomore year courses; 2. Minimum SAT scores of 1000; 3. Minimum 2.0 GPA.
Graduate Program	1. B.A. degree; 2. Satisfactory score on GRE (students who score less than 850 are considered on an individual basis); 3. Completion of all undergraduate requirements; 4. Approved graduate degree plan; 5. Approval by the Graduate and Teacher Education Advisory and Admissions Committee; 6. State ExCet test for certification.	1. B.S. in Education degree (awarded upon completion of 126 hours, all general education courses, all teaching field courses with at least a 2.5 GPA, and those professional education courses required for graduation with at least a 2.5 GPA); 2. 3.0 undergraduate GPA (students with a 2.75 to 2.99 are eligible to be admitted on a probationary basis).	1. Demonstrated competence in basic skills; 2. 2.7 overall GPA; 3. 3.0 GPA in academic major; 4. Recommendations from CAS and Curry School advisors; 5. Satisfactory performance in field experiences; 6. Satisfactory performance on GRE and NTE (target scores for the GRE are 1000, with any score less than 850 requiring special justification).
Degrees Awarded	B.A. at end of four years; M.A. at end of fifth year.	B.S. in Ed at end of four years; 15 graduate credits at end of fifth year.	B.A. from CAS and master's degree from Curry School of Education; both awarded at end of fifth year (proposal currently being considered to award a master's in teaching degree rather than a master's of education, in order to convey preservice nature of degree).

ogy has been shifted to supervising teachers in the public school classrooms. The five education faculty rotate course assignments and share the supervision of students and interns. The program emphasizes students' responsibility to help plan their education and to take an active role in their learning. Freshmen begin a "portfolio" that contains an autobiography, course evaluations, their thoughts on effective teaching, documentation of acquired teaching skills, lists of books read, and descriptions of field experiences. They are encouraged to transform this "empty manila folder" into a file "thick with material" by the time they graduate (*Austin Teacher Program*, 1986-87, pp. 17-18).

University of Kansas

The School of Education currently has approximately 100 faculty, 800 undergraduates, and 1900 graduate students. Examination of five-year teacher preparation programs was initiated by the former dean in 1975, but active discussion did not occur until 1979 when an anticipated drop in credit-hour production and declining state resources threatened the school's well-being. According to the dean, "the strongest and most comprehensive programs [in the state] would garner state support. The challenge to the School of Education was to develop such a program" (Hammond, 1986).

Later that year, a task force composed of faculty, public school personnel, and state education department representatives was established to develop a concept paper on new teacher education programs. The task force concluded that change was necessary because of (1) the expansion of knowledge [in education]; (2) an oversupply of teachers; (3) the increasing role of technology; (4) a growing emphasis on individualized instruction; (5) the discrepancy between research findings and teaching practices; and (6) the national trend to extend teacher preparation (Hammond, 1986). In 1980, the faculty approved the development of a new program, conferring a bachelor's degree in four years and certification plus 15 graduate hours at the end of an additional year of study. Another committee, composed of volunteers from each department, then set to work to develop the courses, activities, and admission and retention standards. The completed package was approved in 1982. The first students completed the five-year program in 1986.

Table 3-1 summarizes the general education and teaching field requirements of the new program, as well as admission standards. Professional education coursework begins in the first two years, focusing on career awareness, multicultural education, and child and adolescent development. During junior and senior years, students take the bulk of their professional education courses, concentrating on learning and development, communication, curriculum and instruction, student evaluation, methods, media and microcomputers, reading, and special education.

The fifth year consists of a six-week student teaching experience, 12 weeks of graduate courses in management, special education, school governance, history of education, and instruction, and a full-semester "internship," a more extensive student teaching experience. The overall distribution of credits is as follows: general education, 60; teaching field, 40–48; professional education, 54–62 (29–32 in the first four years; 25–30 in the fifth year, including 15 hours of graduate credit).

University of Virginia

The Curry School of Education has approximately 100 faculty, 200 under-graduate and 900 graduate students. The arrival of a new dean in 1983 signaled the initiation of a number of innovations, including one-year warranties for teacher education graduates, the appointment of public school teachers as clinical instructors, and the development of a five-year integrated teacher preparation program.

The Committee on Teacher Education Redesign, established in the fall of 1984, was chaired by the new dean and composed of representatives from each department. The development of a five-year program was not the initial aim of the Committee, but as members studied the recent literature on teacher education, examined reports of previous committees, and prepared their own position papers, they concluded that their goals could not be accomplished within a four-year time period. The Committee created the broad outline of a new program, requiring five years of study and culminating in the simultaneous awarding of a bachelor of arts degree from the College of Liberal Arts and Sciences and a master's degree from the Curry School of Education. The program went into operation in fall, 1986.

Over five years, students take approximately 40–45 semester hours in liberal arts (25 percent), 50–72 hours in their major and supporting fields (40 percent), 38–40 hours in professional education (25 percent), and 12–15 hours in clinical work (10 percent) (see Table 3-1). Professional education begins in the sophomore year and continues through the fifth. Teams of faculty have been established to design the generic courses required in each year of the program. Each team is chaired by a member of the original redesign committee and is composed of faculty from different Curry departments (including individuals who have never previously been involved in teacher education). Their task is to develop syllabi for generic courses and accompanying laboratory activities (microteaching, computer simulations, etc.) and to specify field experiences. The generic component is organized around four main topics: (1) teaching as a profession; (2) development, learning, and exceptionality; (3) curriculum, instruction, and assessment; and (4) social concerns and action research. Cutting across these topics are three major themes or "program threads"—special education, multicultural education, and educational technology. All committees have the task of infusing these themes into the courses they develop.

During the fifth year, students will do a full semester of student teaching (the "teaching associateship") in the fall and return to campus in the spring to complete their major, to take a graduate course in contemporary educational issues, and to carry out a field project in education.

ANALYSIS OF THE ISSUES

Content and Structure of Extended Programs

The development of all three programs is grounded in the conviction that a four-year period is insufficient to prepare both a well-educated person and a professional teacher. Yet, programs vary significantly in the way the additional life space provided by the fifth year is allocated. At Austin College, the undergraduate years are devoted entirely to liberal arts except for the seminars and field experiences that constitute the "labs" (and of these, three are for minimal or no credit). Brochures and handbooks proudly announce that the additional year has *not* meant any additional coursework in education. While the University of Kansas has also used the additional life space to increase credits in general education and academic concentrations, there have also been increases in the professional education component and in credit-bearing clinical experiences. Courses are now offered that were absent from the earlier programs (e.g., multicultural education; media and microcomputers; exceptionality; management, etc.). The University of Virginia now requires students to meet the general education and major requirements of the College of Liberal Arts and Sciences and has also increased the amount of field experience. All programs are now able to devote a full semester to student teaching.

The additional time represents a precious resource. Not surprisingly, decisions about how to allocate it are difficult and may evoke heated conflicts. Faculty in foundations see the extra year as an opportunity to teach the full three-credit courses in history, philosophy, and sociology that didn't fit in the old program; subject area specialists consider it imperative to increase the specific methods courses, while generalists argue that the additional time could best be used by adding courses in generic instructional skills; public school personnel want courses in classroom organization and management, while faculty cognizant of the standards of the National Council for the Accreditation of Teacher Education (NCATE) argue the need for courses in multicultural education, special education, and computers. And students, of course, are generally most interested in additional field experiences.

During the period of program development, faculty at all three institutions agreed on one issue: the new program couldn't be simply an extension of "the same old thing." This seems to have translated into a determination to avoid a proliferation of "methods" courses. Indeed, methods courses for elementary teachers were decreased in all three programs. When the ATP was first developed, faculty decided to have all methods taught by cooperating teachers during field experiences; only recently, because of state requirements, has the program included a graduate course in elementary or secondary curriculum and instruction. At the University of Virginia, the separate methods courses previously offered in the elementary program have been replaced by six-credit "blocs" in language skills (reading, language arts, children's literature, creative arts) and reasoning skills (mathematics, science, social studies, and creative arts). At the University of Kansas, state regulations mandate that elementary teachers take courses in the methodology of all elementary subjects. This conflicted with the faculty's plan to decrease specific methodology and increase coursework on topics such as growth and development, communication and counseling skills, classroom management, evaluation, and microcomputers. The problem was resolved by reducing methods courses from three credits to one credit each. The first cohort of students to experience this reduction was extremely dissatisfied, however, and faculty are considering a proposal to increase methodology once again.

Along with the decrease in specific subject methods has come increased work in generic instruction. There appear to be three reasons for this shift in emphasis. First, the research on teaching (e.g., academic learning time, Fisher et al., 1980; explicit instruction, Rosenshine & Stevens, 1986) now constitutes a core of knowledge with which all prospective teachers should be familiar. Second, despite a certain uneasiness, faculty at the three institutions feel a responsibility to introduce their students to the work of educators like Madeline Hunter (1982). A clear theme heard across campuses was the need to ensure that students would be aware of the effective schools/instructional skills approach dominating inservice education and would be prepared for the evaluation procedures they would be facing as first-year teachers (e.g., the Beginning Teacher Assistance Program used in Virginia). Third, faculty expressed a concern about unnecessary "redundancy." Although all students complain about duplication of coursework, students in five-year programs are particularly vigilant in this regard. Generic courses are perceived as being "efficient": they avoid the situation in which lesson planning, Bloom's taxonomy, and inquiry teaching are taught over and over again in every specific methods course and allow those courses to demonstrate applications and to focus on truly unique material.

Another common feature of these extended programs is the emphasis on field experiences that begin early, continue throughout the undergraduate years, and culminate in a semester of student teaching during the fifth year. Although faculty, students, and public school personnel all see these experiences as extremely desirable, the increased need for placements, cooperating teachers, college or university supervisors, and general coordination constitutes a challenge, if not an actual problem, at all three institutions. The size of the ATP permits faculty to monitor and supervise field experiences; in fact, one of the impressive aspects of the program is the extensive, shared knowledge that faculty have about students' performances in courses and field settings. The Austin College emphasis on teaching makes possible this increased time commitment on the part of faculty. At both Kansas and Virginia, however, the research orientation creates a disincentive to spend time supervising. "Clinical instructor" programs at both institutions serve as a partial solution to this problem (although such programs create another problem—see the discussion on "cost"). At Kansas, a cadre of 100 public school teachers have been appointed as "adjunct clinical instructors" to work with pre–student teachers; they receive $100 a year and an identification card that allows them to use the university's facilities. Thus far, they have been given no special training in supervision. At Virginia, clinical instructors also receive faculty privileges; in addition, they are paid $500 for student teaching and additional monies for pre–student teaching and for attending a one-week training program in the summer.

Prestige

Emerging clearly from the comments of faculty and students are the linkages among prestige, the liberal arts, and degree status. At Austin College and Virginia, teacher education students major in an academic area and receive a bachelor of arts degree. During conversations, numerous faculty indicated that this degree was extremely important to students at their institutions. One University of Virginia professor described how in the past the teacher education program had lost bright students who did not want to transfer to Curry and receive a bachelor's degree in education. Now that students receive a bachelor of arts degree from the College of Arts and Sciences, she predicts an increase in academically talented students entering teacher education.

Conferring a master's degree at the end of the fifth year (either a master's degree in education or a master of arts degree in education) also seems to enhance the prestige of teacher education. ATP and Virginia students were consistent in mentioning the master's degree as a major attraction of the program; in fact, they vehemently asserted that they would not want to invest the additional time if their programs did not culminate in a master's degree. They described how their friends were impressed by the fact that they were getting two degrees. One young woman put it succinctly: "My friends say, 'Wow, you're getting your master's!'" The fact that Virginia is considering a change from the M.Ed. to a Master of Teaching was a source of consternation to several students, primarily because "nobody ever heard of that degree."

It appears that an emphasis on liberal arts and the awarding of a master's degree increase a program's prestige because they are perceived as indicators of rigor. Similarly, admission and retention standards must be seen as competitive, and the professional education component must have a reputation for being intellectually demanding. If not, teacher education students will be ridiculed for "spending five years playing with crayons instead of four." One ATP student described the reactions of Austin College students to the five-year program: "Austin College is a big pre-med school. It's hard. Students don't see this as a 'real masters' at first. But then, if they know someone, they realize you do a thesis, and they say, 'Oh, it *is* a real masters.'" Similarly, a University of Kansas student shared the following impression: "*We* feel better; we know some students didn't make the 2.5 and others are sweating the 3.0. But I'm not sure my peers recognize this. . . . It'll take time."

Both comments indicate that internal awareness of change precedes public awareness; they underscore the importance of public relations, an aspect of program development often neglected in academia. One dean described his frequent contact with the institution's news service and admitted that the coverage was crucial to fostering positive perceptions of teacher education and the five-year program. A faculty member at the same institution astutely commented that "much of what is being done to improve teacher education is to make us feel better, to change the perception of teacher education. New students can believe they are part of an elite group, in a structurally different, better program; they can [enter teacher education and still] maintain their legitimacy." The challenge, of course, is not only to create the perception, but to make it accurate.

With an emphasis on liberal arts, preprofessional studies, extensive clinical experience, and graduate work, extended programs have many of the characteristics of true professional preparation. This should help to improve the status of teacher education and, eventually, of teaching itself. At the present time, however, there is a limit to the prestige that can be associated with programs that prepare individuals for a career not highly valued by society. Until teachers' working conditions and salaries improve, the decision to enter teacher education will not be hailed with enthusiasm or admiration. As one ATP student put it, "education is not considered the fast lane." Even at the three institutions studied, some faculty worry that their liberal arts colleagues are still warning the best students away from a career in teaching.

Enrollment Patterns

Faculty at all three institutions report that the quality of students in their five-year programs surpasses the quality of students in former four-year programs and that teacher education students now compare favorably with their noneducation peers. Unfortunately, this issue has not received consistent, systematic attention, and complete documentation is not always available.

At Austin College, an analysis of ATP students graduating in 1986 indicates the following group profile: college GPA=3.02; SAT (verbal)=490; SAT (quantitative)=500; GRE=930. Although this presumably indicates an improvement in the academic qualifications of teacher education candidates, the average composite SAT of the Austin College freshman class in 1981 was 1050, somewhat higher than the average for ATP students. On the other hand, a comparison between ATP students (fall 1981) and freshmen entering public universities across the country (fall 1980) reveals that ATP students generally received higher grades in high school and had higher class rank. Another indicator of quality is the fact that all ATP graduates (N = 19) passed the state's "Examination for the Certification of Educators in Texas" (ExCET) in the first year of administration (1986), the best record of the 65 Texas institutions with teacher education programs.

At the University of Kansas, mean ACT scores of teacher education students are somewhat higher than in previous years (scores of 19.76, 20.44, 21.32, and 22.17 for the years 1981, 1982, 1983, and 1985 respectively; Bailey, 1987; Hammond, 1986, p. 223), and juniors entering the School of Education have higher GPAs than their noneducation counterparts. Kansas also takes pride in the fact that nine Kansas students (with ACT scores of 30-32) received Congressional Teacher Scholarships this year out of 20 awarded statewide; this was the largest number received by any state institution.

The picture at the University of Virginia is similarly encouraging. For the former four-year students, SAT scores ranged from 1050 to 1080; this was lower than the average score of 1180 for the University as a whole. The first cohort of students entering the new five-year program had mean SATs of 1180; the mean SATs of the second group of students currently applying is 1220 (based on first 30 applicants).

While these increases may be partly due to the fact that talented students are attracted by extended programs, they are also a function of new admission, retention, and exit standards imposed either by the institution or the state (see Table 3-1). Higher admission and retention standards certainly screen out students with lower test scores and GPAs. However, we do not yet know whether programs are actually attracting greater numbers of academically talented students. This would require an analysis of the distribution of scores, not just an examination of means.

Not surprisingly, these new standards have had a negative impact on the number of minority students in teacher education. All three institutions express concern with the extremely low proportion of minorities in their programs, although they report that minority representation has always been low. Both Kansas and Virginia have been discussing strategies designed to recruit minorities. The recently appointed dean at Kansas, for example, has initiated large-scale fundraising for scholarships, has met with the Black Faculty Senate, and is planning to work closely with potential "feeder districts" and community colleges.

In terms of overall enrollment, the move to a five-year program does not appear to have produced any long-term negative consequences. At Austin College, faculty report that enrollment in teacher education "held steady" after the five-year program was implemented, and then actually increased even in spite of rising tuition. Kansas reports improvement in the most recent enrollment figures after a long period of decline. However, it is impossible to determine if this is due to the five-year program or to national trends in teacher supply and demand.

Students' reactions to the cost of the additional year varied across campuses and may be related to whether or not the program culminates in a master's degree. At the University of Kansas, students expressed concern over the fact that they would have to pay graduate fees in their fifth year, but would be ineligible to receive Pell grants. In contrast, students at Virginia did not feel the additional expenses would pose a hardship, although Curry has not yet determined whether students will have to pay graduate fees. ATP students also dismissed cost as "inconsequential," despite the fact that Austin College is a private institution and that ATP students tend to come from lower-income families than their noneducation counterparts (White, n.d.). One student remarked: "By the end of four years, you're so in debt, what's an extra year?" The important factor for students was that their master's degree would allow them to start higher and move faster through the salary scale. The possibility of a paid internship also eases the financial situation.

Economic Impact on the Institution

The cost to the school or department of education depends on the way in which additional time is allocated to coursework and field experiences, the number of students involved, and the arrangements made with districts for payment of cooperating teachers. At Austin College, for example, formal coursework in professional education was shifted to the fifth year, and no education courses were added. Thus, there was no need for additional faculty. Since the number of students is small, the three undergraduate field experiences can be monitored by seminar instructors. Moreover, cooperating teachers are paid by the state, not by the institution. All of these factors minimize the economic impact on the department.

The situation at the University of Kansas provides a dramatic contrast. Additional coursework in education and additional field experiences have increased the need for teaching time, supervision, and money. The school's budget officer calculates that the extended program costs approximately $60,000 more than the four year program; the bulk of this money goes to hire graduate assistants for instructional needs. These funds come from "shrinkage" (monies made available when faculty take sabbaticals, unpaid leaves, etc.) and would normally be used to purchase equipment, to fund travel, or to meet unexpected expenses. The newly appointed dean emphasized that institutions considering a five-year program should prepare a cost analysis early in the planning stage.

At the University of Virginia, it is anticipated that the additional teaching required by the program will be handled through the internal reallocation of faculty. Funds for the clinical instructor program ($500/semester for student teachers) were provided through a state grant during the first year of operation. The University subsequently identified the clinical instructor program as a "high priority in its budget request to the General Assembly. As a result, funding for the program was received in the amount of $196,000 for two years, and is now a regular part of the University's budget" (Comfort, Cooper, & Moore, n.d.).

Additional Issues

One of the interesting themes to emerge across all three institutions was the tension between the need to implement a coherent, well-structured program and the traditions of faculty autonomy and control by individual instructors over the courses they teach. At Austin College, faculty rotate through most courses, and decisions about content are made jointly. At Virginia, a faculty member involved in course development commented, "It used to be that the program was the person. . . . The particular content depended on who taught the course. We don't want that anymore." Teams of faculty are currently developing the objectives and syllabi for the courses in the generic sequence. While team members may also be involved in teaching the courses, at least initially, it is anticipated that other faculty will become increasingly involved. Kansas' program was developed in a similar fashion.

The advantages of "group ownership" are obvious; yet the potential for conflict and resentment must be recognized and confronted. University and college faculty are usually rewarded for individual accomplishment, and respect for "academic freedom" can work against the coherence and integration needed in a professional program.

The importance of establishing a commitment to group ownership of the program is crucial in another way also. Most academic programs are developed in departments, which assures that they will have the faculty support needed for implementation. If teacher education is seen as the responsibility of the whole school, not the province of a single department, and committees of departmental representatives make decisions about content and courses, the program becomes removed from the faculty who may be needed for instruction. Moreover, if the program is administered by a director who sits outside of the departments in an "office of teacher education," the ability of that person to administer effectively depends on the willingness of department chairs and faculty to participate in teacher education. This in turn depends on the resources the director controls (e.g., graduate assistants) and on other rewards that can be offered for participation (e.g., merit salary increases).

A second issue discussed on all campuses was the need to accommodate postbaccalaureate students returning for certification. It is clear that admission standards, liberal arts requirements, and procedures for completing undergraduate courses in professional education and field experiences must be carefully planned. At Kansas, the director of teacher education pointed out the difficulty of screening students who have not come through the earlier field experiences. Virginia has decided to require postbaccalaureate students to make up undergraduate work before proceeding to fifth-year courses; this will have the effect of making the postbaccalaureate program two years.

The consequences of condensing field experiences and coursework in professional education have not yet been examined. But the desire to give postbaccalaureate students access to teacher education seems to conflict with an assumption underlying extended programs; namely, that learning how to teach takes time. As Howey and Zimpher (1986) observe:

> The complex skills of effective teaching are not acquired quickly. A familiar contention is that the scope of a teacher's responsibilities along with the myriad daily interpersonal interactions calls for a repertoire of abilities more diverse if not more complex than in most other professions. In the extended baccalaureate approach, there can be anywhere from a three to five year span of time in which coursework and experiences could be systematically and developmentally programmed to allow the beginner in a reflective manner to acquire the knowledge, skills, and dispositions associated with teaching. (p. 45)

The intense programs experienced by postbaccalaureate students entering the fifth year of a five-year program certainly do not encourage the reflective development of "knowledge, skills, and dispositions." Resolving this dilemma will not be easy, however, especially in the context of an impending teacher shortage and the increasing establishment of alternative routes to certification.

A third source of tension concerns the question of whether five-year programs should culminate in a master's degree. On the one hand is the obvious need to make five-year programs both attractive to students and prestigious, as well as the belief that a fifth year of study justifies a graduate degree. On the other hand, there is concern for the "academic integrity" of graduate programs and advanced degrees. At Kansas, the dean's original proposal to award a master's degree was rejected by faculty concerned about this very issue. Thus, the student teaching experience receives undergraduate credit, and students accrue just 15 graduate credits for the formal coursework they take during the fifth year. At Virginia, the proposal to offer the Master of Teaching degree is an attempt to clarify the preservice nature of the fifth year and to distinguish it from the master's of education that inservice teachers would receive for advanced study.

At the heart of this issue are questions about the characteristics of true graduate education. If courses presented in the fifth year are not more intellectually demanding than undergraduate courses and do not require prior knowledge or experience, can they legitimately be considered graduate? What are the differences between a fifth year of study in an extended program and nondegree, postbaccalaureate certification programs? If preservice teachers are primarily concerned with "how to" issues and lack extensive clinical experience, can they deal meaningfully with material on a sophisticated level?

"Quality criteria" for master's degree programs, developed by the Tennessee Conference of Graduate Schools (Minkel & Richards, 1986), include the following characteristics: (1) a tutorial experience—personalized instruction, advisement, and guidance; (2) an advanced level of sophistication and intellectual rigor; (3) a core of planned coursework, as opposed to a mere collection of courses and credits; (4) tool/technique/methodology requirements; (5) a research component; (6) extradisciplinary experience; (7) a culminating experience such as an advanced seminar, thesis, practicum, or internship; and (8) a comprehensive examination. With careful planning, all of these characteristics can be incorporated into extended teacher education programs. Even so, it is still no simple matter to design graduate-level courses that meet the needs and address the concerns of preservice teachers. One approach may be to have students complete a full semester of student teaching prior to taking graduate coursework. In this way, they can develop a real-world context for further study and develop the "felt need" that will make the additional study meaningful.

CONCLUDING THOUGHTS

The three extended programs reviewed in this paper present an interesting study in contrasts. The ATP has been in existence for almost 20 years, graduating about 25 students per year. The professional component emphasizes practical classroom experiences throughout the five-year period; formal coursework is limited and concentrated in the fifth year. The five faculty involved in the program are proud of the reputation the program has earned and are devoted to its continual improvement and refinement.

At the University of Kansas, the School of Education itself enrolls more students than all of Austin College. The increased complexity and bureaucracy make innovation considerably more difficult. The five-year program, initiated by the former dean and implemented in 1983, has generated faculty conflict, redirected energy away from research and scholarship, and created financial problems. Yet the School remains committed to the concept. The new dean has recently suggested a process for refining the program and is hopeful that revisions in the content and sequence of the professional component can be completed without delay. The first students to complete the extended program graduated in 1986; the School is now in a position to "fine tune" the program based on the experiences of this first cohort. Faculty are pleased with the liberal arts emphasis of the new program, the quality and commitment of the students, and the closer University-public school relationship that has been fostered by the clinical instructor program.

Since the extended program at Virginia is in its first year of operation, this case study has had to focus on the planning process and on written documents that outline what is still to come. It is impossible to predict with certainty the future of the program, but the atmosphere at Virginia is definitely optimistic. In general, faculty are extremely enthusiastic about the extended program. Whereas the Curry School had previously faced the possibility of severe cutbacks and even "dissolution," the five-year program has brought a good deal of favorable publicity to the School and has helped to enhance its stature within the University and the state. Under the leadership of the new dean, teacher education has become the number one priority for the School of Education and is now viewed as the program with "pizzazz."

According to Levine (1981), the profitability of an innovation ultimately determines its institutionalization. The future of extended teacher preparation programs depends upon several factors: the quality and numbers of students attracted to the programs; economic impact on students and the institution; enhanced prestige; administrative support; the establishment of close working relationships with the public schools; the societal context (the teacher supply and demand situation, the existence of alternative routes to certification, the opportunity to provide paid internships, state certification regulations); and the ability of the institution to create a situation in which involvement in teacher education is compatible with faculty's roles, responsibilities, and expectations for reward.

Ultimately, of course, proponents of teacher education must adopt a cost-benefit perspective and address the question of program effectiveness (see Chapter 2). Cooper (1983) cites a number of fundamental questions that must be examined in any evaluation of teacher education programs. These include: (a) What is the effectiveness of the program's graduates initially, over time, and in different settings? (b) To what extent do the program's graduates attribute their effectiveness to experiences received during the training program? (c) What effect does the program have on the characteristics, knowledge, skills, and attitudes of trainees? (d) How long do graduates of the program stay in teaching? (e) How do graduates of the program perceive it? and (f) How do significant others (supervising teachers, principals, personnel directors) perceive the program and its capabilities? The data collected in the present case studies provide a basis for cautious optimism. It is essential, however, that individual institutions conduct continuous, systematic evaluations of their programs in order to determine the congruence between original intentions and current realities.

REFERENCES

AMERICAN ASSOCIATION OF COLLEGES FOR TEACHER EDUCATION. (1983). *Educating a profession: Extended programs for teacher education.* Washington, DC: AACTE.

ANDREW, M. D. (1981). Five year teaching program: Successes and challenges. *Journal of Teacher Education, 32*(3), 40-43.

AUSTIN TEACHER PROGRAM. (1986-87). *The Latest Word.* Sherman, TX: Austin College.

BAILEY, J. (1987). Personal communication.

BERLINER, D. C. (1984). Making the right changes in preservice teacher education. *Phi Delta Kappan*, 66(2), 94-96.

CASE, C. W., LANIER, J. E., & MISKEL, C. G. (1986). The Holmes Group Report: Impetus for gaining professional status for teachers. *Journal of Teacher Education*, 37(4), 36-43.

COMFORT, R. E., Cooper, J. M., & Moore, J. R. (n.d.). *Clinical instructor: An expanded role for teachers in teacher education*. Unpublished manuscript.

COOPER, J. M. (1983). Basic elements in teacher education program evaluation: Implications for future research and development. In K. R. Howey & W. E. Gardner (Eds.), *The education of teachers: A look ahead*. New York: Longman.

DARLING-HAMMOND, L. (1987, January). *The requirements and benefits of responsible professionalism*. Paper presented at The Holmes Group Inaugural Meeting, Washington, DC.

DENEMARK, G., & NUTTER, N. (1984). The case for extended programs of initial teacher preparation. In L. G. Katz and J. D. Raths (Eds.), *Advances in teacher education* (Vol. 1, pp. 203-246). Norwood, NJ: ABLEX Publishing Corporation.

DUCHARME, E. R. (1986). The professors and the reports: A time to act. *Journal of Teacher Education*, 37(5), 51-56.

FISHER, C. W., BERLINER, D. C., FILBY, N. N., MARLIAVE, R., CAHEN, L. S., & DISHAW, M. M. (1980). Teaching behaviors, academic learning time, and student achievement: An overview. In C. Denham & A. Lieberman (Eds.), *Time to learn* (pp. 7-32). Washington, DC: U. S. Department of Education.

FREEMAN, B. (Ed.). (1986). *Exploring new frontiers in teacher education. The Austin Teacher Program*. Sherman, TX: Austin College.

GALLEGOS, A. (1981). The dilemma of extended programs. *Journal of Teacher Education*, 32(1), 4-6.

GUYTON, E., & ANTONELLI, G. (1987). Educational leaders' reports of priorities and activities in selected areas of teacher education reform. *Journal of Teacher Education*, 38(3), 45-49.

HAMMOND, M. F. (1986). Teacher education and the research university. *The Review of Higher Education*, 9(2), 193-227.

HAWLEY, W. D. (1986a). A critical analysis of The Holmes Group's proposals for reforming teacher education. *Journal of Teacher Education*, 37(4), 47-51.

HAWLEY, W. D. (1986b). Toward a comprehensive strategy for addressing the teacher shortage. *Phi Delta Kappan*, 67(10), 712-718.

HOWEY, K. R., & ZIMPHER, N. L. (1986). The current debate on teacher preparation. *Journal of Teacher Education*, 37(5), 41-50.

HUNTER, M. (1982). *Mastery teaching*. El Segundo, CA: TIP Publications.

KEMPER, R. E., & MANGIERI, J. N. (1987). America's future teaching force: Predictions and recommendations. *Phi Delta Kappan*, 68(5), 393-395.

LANIER, J., & LITTLE, J. W. (1986). Research on teacher education. In M. C. Wittrock (Ed.), *Handbook of research on teaching* (pp. 527-569). New York: MacMillan.

LEVINE, A. (1981). *Why innovations fail*. Albany, NY: State University of New York Press.

MINKEL, C. S., & RICHARDS, M. P. (1986). *Components of quality in master's degree programs*. Knoxville, TN: Tennessee Conference of Graduate Schools.

ROGERS, M. (1987, February 9). Now, 'Artificial Reality.' *Newsweek*, pp. 56-57.

ROSENSHINE, B., & STEVENS, R. (1986). Teaching functions. In M. Wittrock (Ed.), *Handbook of research on teaching* (3rd ed., pp. 376-391). New York: Macmillan.

SHANKER, A. (1987, January). *Needed changes in professional practice.* Paper presented at The Holmes Group Inaugural Meeting, Washington, DC.

SYKES, G. (1983). Contradictions, ironies, and promises unfulfilled: A contemporary account of the state of teaching. *Phi Delta Kappan, 65*(2), 87-93.

TOM, A. R. (1986). The Holmes Report: Sophisticated analysis, simplistic solutions. *Journal of Teacher Education, 37*(4), 44-46.

WHITE, J. (n.d.). *Project report: The Austin College student* (Addendum). Sherman, TX: Austin College, Department of Education.

WISE, A. E. (1986). Graduate teacher education and teacher professionalism. *Journal of Teacher Education, 37*(5), 36-40.

4

CLASSROOM RESEARCH AS A RESOURCE FOR THE GRADUATE PREPARATION OF TEACHERS

Kathy Carter and Walter Doyle

In this chapter we discuss the graduate preparation of teachers from the perspective of curriculum. In particular, we analyze research-based sources for defining the content of clinical teacher preparation and attempt to connect this analysis to issues of when and how teacher education should occur. At issue, then, is not comparative data (see Chapters 2 and 3). Rather, we are concerned with the conceptual foundations for understanding and predicting consequences of teacher education at whatever level it occurs.

It is our contention that questions of *when* and *how* in teacher preparation can only be answered within a framework that specifies *what* teacher education is. To this end, we outline the rudiments of a framework for defining the content of teacher education. It turns out that this framework also establishes the foundation for a research agenda in teacher education, an agenda that promises to inform the enterprise of clinical teacher preparation in ways that have not been done in the past.

The chapter is divided into three major sections. In the first section, we examine the contributions of research on effective teaching to curriculum in teacher education. The limitations of this research tradition for capturing operational and situational aspects of teaching practice are discussed. In the second section, an alternative approach is described, one that focuses on teaching ability as situated cognition. Studies on the tasks of teaching in classrooms, teacher comprehension, and expert-novice differences in cognition are reviewed as they relate to an understanding of teachers' knowledge structures and comprehension processes. In the final section, it is noted that few attempts have been made to extend research on teacher cognition to studies of how expertise is acquired. Nonetheless, some general understanding of how expertise develops is emerging from existing studies, and the expert-novice design provides a framework for organizing inquiry and curriculum deliberation. Examples of how this framework might apply to curriculum construction and research in teacher education are given. The chapter concludes with a discussion of implication of a curriculum perspective for issues in the graduate preparation of teachers.

RESEARCH ON EFFECTIVE TEACHING[1]

Over the years several attempts have been made to define a knowledge base for teacher education grounded in research (e.g., Howsam, 1976; Smith, 1983; Smith, Cohen, & Pearl, 1969). In most recent versions of this exercise, research on effective teaching is seen as a central resource for curriculum content in teacher education. In this section we review this research tradition and assess the adequacy of its contributions to teacher preparation curricula.

Process-Product Research

Substantial progress has recently been made in our knowledge about teaching effects in classrooms, especially in the basic skill subjects of reading and arithmetic in the early elementary grades and mathematics in the junior high school (for reviews, see Brophy & Good, 1986; Rosenshine & Stevens, 1986). This knowledge has accumulated from convergent findings of several large-scale correlational and experimental studies of teaching practices in actual classrooms and the relation of these practices to outcomes such as student achievement. Many have argued that this knowledge provides a resource of major significance for improving teaching (Gage, 1978, 1985), and several attempts have been made to incorporate this knowledge into programs of clinical teacher education and staff development (Griffin, 1983; D. Smith, 1983).

Studies of teaching effects generally take the form of "process-product" research (Gage, 1978). This label simply means that investigators study teaching effects by attempting to relate measures of the amount and quality of teaching processes to class mean scores on measures of students' achievements, usually scores on standardized tests of curriculum content. The logic of this approach is clear and compelling: Classes that differ in achievement must differ on dimensions of teaching processes. The researcher's task is to trace these patterns of difference to identify the classroom processes that reliably predict achievement. It is important to emphasize that within a teaching effects framework, one thinks about teaching primarily in terms of outcomes rather than in terms of classroom processes or issues involved in conducting lessons in complex environments. From a process-product perspective, in other words, teaching is a means to an end, not an end in itself.

[1]Portions of this section were adapted from Doyle (1987).

What has been learned from this research tradition? A summary of the major findings from teaching effects research can be organized into two broad categories: (a) time and curriculum; and (b) instructional quality.

Time and curriculum. One of the significant advances introduced into research on teaching in the 1970s was a focus on "pupil pursuits" (Harnischfeger & Wiley, 1976), often measured by such indicators as time-on-task or student engagement rate (Denham & Lieberman, 1980). The study of time produced two important findings. First, large differences in the amount of time students spend in various curriculum areas often occur across classrooms, schools, and school systems. Second, these differences in instructional time are frequently associated with corresponding differences in student achievement. Student achievement is influenced, that is, by the way time is allocated by teachers and used by students in classrooms. It follows that interventions affecting instructional time are likely to affect achievement.

But time alone is not the measure of quality in teaching. Simply increasing the available time, by lengthening the school day or year, will not improve achievement unless attention is also given to how time in classrooms is filled and what teachers do to affect the quality of the time students spend engaged with subject matter. At the very least, then, our conception of time in classrooms must include a dimension of curriculum.

Curriculum most often shows up in studies of teaching as *content covered and/or opportunity to learn.* The most sophisticated form of this measure is "academic learning time," or the time students spend working successfully with content measured on the criterion achievement test (Fisher, Berliner, Filby, Marliave, Cahen, & Dishaw, 1980). In thinking about instructional time, then, it is necessary to consider not only whether students are paying attention, but also what they are doing—solving word problems, answering comprehension questions, writing expository essays—and whether these "pursuits" are related to the curriculum being tested. When alignment occurs, in other words, when instruction includes and emphasizes the content tested, students achieve (Walker & Schaffarzick, 1974). Opportunity to learn, then, is a fundamental condition for student achievement.

Dimensions of instructional quality. Given comparable emphases on content, differences among classes in student achievement will result from differences in the quality of instruction, that is, the design of assignments, the clarity of explanations, the chances students have to practice, and the availability and accuracy of feedback. A complete picture of effective teaching must include, therefore, dimensions of instructional quality.

Classroom studies of teaching effects have generally supported a direct and structured approach to instruction (Brophy & Good, 1986; Rosenshine & Stevens, 1986). That is, students usually achieve more when a teacher:

1. Emphasizes academic goals, makes them explicit, and expects students to be able to master the curriculum.

2. Carefully organizes and sequences curriculum experiences.

3. Clearly explains and illustrates what students are to learn.

4. Frequently asks direct and specific questions to monitor students' progress and check their understanding.

5. Provides students with ample opportunity to practice, gives prompts and feedback to insure success and correct mistakes, and allows students to practice a skill until it is overlearned or automatic.

6. Reviews regularly and holds students accountable for work.

From this perspective, a teacher promotes student learning by being *active* in planning and organizing instruction, explaining to students what they are to learn, arranging occasions for guided practice, monitoring progress, providing feedback, and otherwise helping students understand and accomplish work (Good, 1983).

The findings on teaching effects reviewed here are based, in large measure, on the teaching of basic literacy and computational skills in elementary and junior high schools. But the emphasis is definitely not on rote memorization or mindless drill and practice. Direct instruction simply means that students are told explicitly what they are to learn and shown how to use specific cognitive operations to accomplish work. For example, students are told in direct instruction how to select the main idea of a passage or how to formulate a cause-and-effect argument. Indeed, many have argued that direct teaching is appropriate, in principle, for comprehension, problem solving, and other complex forms of academic work for which the underlying processes can be explained or demonstrated by teachers and practiced by students (Brophy & Good, 1986; Rosenshine & Stevens, 1986).

Translations into Teacher Education Practice

Some have argued that findings from research on teaching effects are best seen as sources of *guidelines* for teaching that teachers can apply directly in their classrooms. Good and Grouws (1979), for example, constructed a model format for fourth grade mathematics lessons that specified the order and approximate time allocations for such activities as review, development of new concepts, guided practice, seatwork, and homework. Emmer, Sanford, Evertson, Clements, and Martin (1981) made specific suggestions for organizing rooms, choosing and communicating rules and procedures, managing student work, and maintaining appropriate student behavior. Anderson, Evertson, and Brophy (1979) wrote 22 specific "principles" for teaching first grade reading groups (e.g., "The teacher should have the children repeat new words or sounds until they are said satisfactorily").

The results of the field experiments demonstrated clearly that guidelines or rules for practice based on research findings can be successfully communicated to teachers with a reasonably small investment of time and resources. In an extension of this work, Griffin, Barnes, O'Neal, Edwards, Defino, and Hukill (1983) were able to show that findings from research on teaching effects, when combined with knowledge about effective school leadership and change, could be used successfully by staff developers to change teacher practices in classrooms. It appears, then, that findings from research on teaching effects can be translated into usable knowledge for teachers.

Process-Product Research and the Teacher Education Curriculum

Despite these recent advances in process-product research and its application to staff development, the approach has several deficiencies as a source for teacher education curriculum, especially in the area of initial teacher preparation.

Many of the deficiencies in process-product research as a source of teacher education curriculum are implicit in the field experiments that have been used to demonstrate the strength and the practicality of findings from this research tradition. The field experiments described above demonstrated only that experienced volunteers were able to use some of the information contained in the treatment materials to modify their classroom practices. Not all of the information provided was used, especially when the suggestions involved substantial changes in existing practice. Moreover, novice teachers were less able than their experienced colleagues to make use of what they learned from the treatment materials (Clements, 1985). This result is not surprising, given that findings do not translate into unambiguous prescriptions or blueprints for action to be followed mechanically by teachers. All propositions derived from research findings (or any other source, for that matter) must be interpreted in light of particular conditions and connected to specific occasions for application. Findings, in other words, must be translated into practices applicable to specific circumstances.

Second, the field experiments did little to illuminate the processes by which teachers in experimental groups used the information provided in treatment materials. How did they react to and digest the guidelines derived from research on teaching effects? A recent study by Driscoll and Stevens (1985) sheds some light on this issue. These investigators found that experienced teachers tended to view research-derived propositions as information to inform their own planning and decision making rather than as prescriptions or rules for direct application in their classrooms. In line with recent analyses by Fenstermacher (1986), Tom (1984), and Zumwalt (1982), teachers appear to use information about teaching effects (as well as other types of information about teaching) to activate their own deliberations about events in their classrooms and to modify their own practical reasoning about teaching. Moreover, teachers probably filter their reception of guidelines through the schema they typically use to comprehend classroom events and processes (Carter, 1985, 1986). If, for example, a teacher understands classroom management in terms of the effectiveness of reprimands rather than as a process of guiding a complex activity system through time and space, information about the consequences of different activity structures for classroom order is likely to be seen as irrelevant to management success.

This analysis points to basic shortcomings of process-product research as a source for teacher education curriculum. In essence, process-product findings generate predictors of student achievement, in other words, information about the classroom conditions associated with students' performance on standardized tests. By themselves, these predictions contain little information about *contexts*, about how these conditions are established and maintained in classroom environments. And, despite the acknowledgement of curriculum-related variables, little information is provided about *content*—the character of the subject matter being taught or the tasks the students actually work on in the classes. Finally, process-product predictions give little insight into the knowledge structures and comprehension processes teachers use to interpret classroom scenes, translate subject matter into a classroom curriculum, or plan strategic actions to establish and sustain classroom events.

In the field experiments, however, the experimenters relied on experienced teachers' expertise in the areas of contexts, content, and cognition to carry research-based principles to their classrooms. As a staff development model, then, the experimental treatments of process-product research have a narrow utility. The approach is likely to work best with those who need the least amount of external support to modify their practices on the basis of new knowledge. Few such individuals are students in initial teacher preparation programs.

Teaching Ability as Situated Cognition

The perspective outlined here on how experienced teachers use information to solve teaching problems underscores two important aspects of teaching ability. First, effective teaching clearly requires *specialized knowledge structures* that teachers can use to interpret situations, identify relevant information resources, plan appropriate strategies, and enact these strategies in classrooms. These knowledge structures are generative (Wittrock, 1974): they enable teachers to recognize unencountered instances and create novel solutions to problems. Second, teachers' knowledge is richly *particularistic and situational*, thus enabling them to connect what they know to specific circumstances.

It is precisely in these areas, however, that process-product research is especially weak. As noted earlier, teaching in the process-product tradition is a means to an end. Little attention is given in this research to how teachers understand observed conditions of effective teaching, how these conditions are established in classroom situations, or how effective teachers acquired their abilities. Process-product researchers study the consequences of teaching acts, not the conditions of teaching or the processes of learning to teach. Moreover, knowledge about correlations between teaching practices and student achievement does not provide direct information about what teacher educators should do to make that knowledge available and usable to teacher education students. But these issues, which fall outside the purview of research on teaching effects, are basic to curriculum in teacher education. Despite the intrinsic value that findings from research on teaching appear to have, their application to teach education requires a translation into knowledge about classroom practice and about the conditions that foster these practices in teacher education students.

Clearly a broader framework is needed to consider fundamental issues of curriculum in teacher preparation, a framework that focuses less on identifying predictors of standardized test scores and more on the conceptual and behavioral processes of teaching in classroom environments. Fortunately such a perspective is beginning to emerge from recent extensions of inquiry in teacher cognition (Carter, 1985, 1986;

Carter & Doyle, 1987). Emphasis in this emerging framework is placed on the *tasks* teachers accomplish in classroom settings and on the *knowledge structures* that enable this task accomplishment to occur. A "task" has three basic elements: a goal to be achieved, a set of circumstances or "givens" under which the goals are to be achieved (i.e., a problem space), and a set of resources that can be used to reach the goal. Tasks are accomplished successfully by interpreting the problem space accurately (e.g., discovering what the problem of achieving order is in a particular class) and organizing resources (activities, rules, physical space) in ways that "fit" or account for the features of that problem space. Within this framework, actions are *situated*. The appropriateness or effectiveness of a particular teacher action (praise, question, reprimand) depends upon its role in the task being accomplished.

From this perspective, teacher education can be viewed as experiences designed to develop expertise in accomplishing classroom tasks. Curriculum proposals for teacher education can then be judged for their contributions to this overall purpose. The research base for this enterprise, in turn, is broadened beyond process-product correlations to include studies that illuminate the nature of classroom tasks, the knowledge structures that underlie accomplishment of these tasks, and the processes by which these knowledge structures are acquired.

To explicate this emerging framework, we examine two important lines of research. The first line consists of studies of processes and effects in classrooms and the task systems embedded in these settings (Doyle, 1983, 1986a; Doyle & Carter, 1984). Such studies identify and examine the situational demands that teachers must consider as they plan for and orchestrate classroom events. The second line of research consists of studies of teacher knowledge structures and comprehension processes, including studies of expert-novice differences among teachers (Carter & Doyle, 1987). We have restricted our attention primarily to pedagogical knowledge and to classroom studies that have implicit or explicit implications for understanding contexts, content, and cognition in teaching. There are, of course, other knowledge sources for teacher preparation, including knowledge in the specific subject matter areas that make up the curriculum. These knowledge sources are discussed in more detail in Chapters 6 and 8.

CLASSROOM TASK SYSTEMS AND TEACHER KNOWLEDGE

Teachers face two interrelated tasks in classrooms: (a) establishing and maintaining social order; and (b) representing and enacting the curriculum. Teachers must, in other words, achieve the cooperation of students in their classrooms and carry their students through a curriculum by designing academic work and engaging students in the intellectual processes required to understand and do that work. Because both of these tasks are jointly constituted by teachers and students, teachers must be able to form functional mental images of classroom reality in order to interpret complex events, recognize problems, and set about solving them.

Classroom Management

Traditionally, classroom management has meant discipline, that is, what teachers do to stop misbehavior after it occurs. Following the seminal work of Kounin (1970), management has been seen as conditions teachers establish to achieve order in classroom environments. Central to this view of classroom order is a *work system* consisting of (a) activities that organize students for working, such as large group presentations and recitations, small group discussions, and seatwork segments; and (b) rules and procedures that specify actions for routine events, such as obtaining materials, sharpening pencils, and turning in assignments. The most important feature of the work system for a class is the *programs of action* that define the nature of order for particular segments of time and pull students along specified paths. For example, during whole-class presentations, students are to attend to the teacher, follow along with examples, and respond to occasional questions. During discussions, in contrast, students are to attend to one another and the teacher and talk when an appropriate turn occurs. When a program of action is not established or breaks down because of disruptions, for example, when students talk out of turn during a discussion or exchange materials during a presentation, orderliness has no situational foundation. In such circumstances, reprimands intended to restore order are likely to be successful for only a few moments at a time.

The teacher's role in management has at least three dimensions. First, successful managers, defined by indicators of orderliness and achievement, *design* sensible and context-sensitive work systems for their classes. In other words, they prepare in advance for how students as a group will be organized to accomplish work and what rules and procedures will govern movement around the room and routine access to resources and distribution of materials. Second, successful managers *communicate* their work systems clearly to students through explanations, written materials, rehearsals, and sanctions. Especially at the beginning of the year, they make the work system a curricular event in the class: They teach the work system, as they would any lesson, with explanations, examples, practice, and feedback. Finally, successful managers *monitor* classroom events to make sure that the work system is operating within reasonable limits and to notice early signs of potential disruptions. By monitoring the flow of classroom activity, they reduce the need for frequent reprimands and other interventions to restore order and they maximize the opportunity for students to work with the curriculum being offered.

Carter (1985, 1986) examined detailed narrative records of classes taught by junior high school English teachers who differed on indicators of classroom management success. The focus in these studies was on identifying the interpretive frameworks teachers used to comprehend the problem of order and devise management solutions to this problem. These studies have suggested that experienced and effective teachers solve the problem of classroom order by devoting their attention to directing and sustaining classroom activities and by focusing on work systems in classrooms. Effective teachers understand, in other words, the importance of keeping work systems alive in classrooms. Indeed, reaction and action patterns of expert teachers can be accounted for by their emphasis on sustaining a program of action of academic work.

Academic Work

Studies have also focused on the academic work students are required to do in classrooms (Doyle, 1986b; Doyle & Carter, 1984; Doyle, Sanford, Schmidt-French, Emmer, & Clements, 1985). In these studies it was found that assignments with different cognitive and procedural complexity for students were enacted in very different ways in the classrooms and that these differences had substantial consequences for classroom management and for the nature of the work students actually accomplished. Familiar, routinized, and simple work was accomplished with ease. Explanations were clear and precise, students' misunderstandings were minimal, and work began quickly and proceeded efficiently. Moreover, there was a high congruence between the announced work and the final products students handed in. The teacher's criteria for evaluating products were consistently and often rigorously applied. On the other hand, complex assignments, in which students encountered novel information or problem types and were required to make decisions in order to generate products, were much more difficult to enact. Explanations were longer, students frequently failed to grasp key points, and work sessions seldom flowed smoothly. Moreover, assignments drifted—over time the teacher often became more explicit about product specifications and the scope of students' decisions were narrowed. In writing assignments, for example, teachers often introduced model sentences or paragraphs for students to emulate when they had difficulty generating acceptable essays on their own. As a result, the announced or intended work and the work students actually accomplished were often quite different.

This line of research suggests that tensions exist between management and curriculum because the work students do is implicated in classroom order (Doyle, 1986a). Work that places intellectual demands on students, such as assignments involving higher-order thinking, is often difficult to manage in classrooms. In turn, order can be achieved by simplifying cognitive demands for work and reducing consequences of failure to complete assignments adequately. In some instances, this set of conditions can drive the curriculum out of the classroom and eliminate opportunities for students to learn important aspects of the curriculum. Management, therefore, does not stand alone; it must always be seen in the context of curriculum decisions.

Summary

Research on management and academic work clearly suggests that curriculum and teaching are embedded in a complex array of classroom events (Carter & Doyle, 1987; Carter & Richardson-Koehler, in press). It would seem to follow that an expert teacher's knowledge is similarly event-structured. A teacher must, in other words, come to understand pieces of curriculum and instructional actions in terms of the events (e.g., activities, texts, assignments, students' mistakes and performance) associated with their enactment under real-world classroom conditions (Leinhardt & Greeno, 1986; Putnam, 1987).

UNDERSTANDING EXPERTISE IN TEACHING

Systematic attention to the nature of expertise in teaching has occurred only recently. Much of this early work has been informed by studies of expert-novice differences in semantically rich domains such as medical diagnosis (Patel, Frederiksen, & Groen, 1984), political cognition (Fiske, Kinder, & Larter, 1982); physics problem-solving (Champagne, Gunstone, & Klopfer, 1983; Chi & Glaser, 1982; Larkin, McDermott, Simon, & Simon, 1980); and games such as chess or bridge (Chase & Simon, 1973; Engle & Bukstel, 1978).

The Essential Character of Expert Knowledge

For present purposes, two important generalizations concerning the character of experts' knowledge can be drawn from this literature:

1. *Specialization and domain-specific.* Expertise is not simply a matter of being efficient in using general problem-solving strategies (e.g., problem analysis, hypothesis formulation, and testing). Experts appear, rather, to have detailed and highly specialized knowledge in their domain of expertise. This knowledge is "episodic"—it is embedded in previously encountered and remembered "cases" or "events" in the domain of interest. As a result, experts' knowledge is conditional and situational. Expert medical diagnosticians, for example, know the conditions under which a particular symptom, such as an elevated body temperature, is significant or epiphenomenal (Patel, Frederiksen, & Groen, 1984). This conditional feature of experts' knowledge enables them to rapidly apply what they know to specific cases. Experts' knowledge is also thought to be task-specific. Removed from their task environment, experts often appear to "lose" their expertise. Thus, an expert at diagnosing lung diseases will not necessarily be proficient in diagnosing brain tumors.

2. *Organized for interpretive capacity and efficiency.* In their task environment, experts have access to powerful analytical tools for interpreting situations and making executive decisions. Their knowledge of domain-specific scenes, patterns, and procedures is organized around fundamental interpretative concepts and propositions. The knowledge of novices, in contrast, is often organized around discrete objects or surface features of events and problems. Expert physics problem solvers, for example, begin by mapping the semantic or propositional structure of a problem, whereas novices often attempt prematurely to apply computational algorithms to the quantities expressed in the problem statement. Principle-oriented knowledge structures enable experts to process information from their environment efficiently, direct their attention to significant aspects of a case, sense gaps in their existing knowledge and understandings, and revise their knowledge as necessary by incorporating new cases. In addition, they can function easily with a larger quantity of readily available information and procedures. This interpretive capacity is especially useful for solving novel problems. In such instances, experts typically devote considerable energy to constructing a semantic model of a problem before searching for procedures to compute an answer. An expert researcher, for example, is likely to spend time trying to understand the theoretical relationship among variables in a domain before selecting a statistical design.

In summary, experts in a domain, in contrast to novices in the same situation, think differently about different things. In particular, experts are able to use richly elaborated conditional knowledge to interpret situations, bring a variety of information and procedures to bear on the case, and reflect constructively on their experience. Although experts' procedures and patterns of thinking are often routinized and even automatic, their methods are not formulaic. Rather they can adapt flexibly to a wide variety of standard and novel circumstances in their domain of expertise.

Experts in Teaching

In the past few years, serious attempts have been made to understand pedagogical expertise. Ways have been found to identify and describe the information processing of expert teachers (Carter, Sabers, Cushing, Pinnegar, & Berliner, 1987; Housner & Griffey, 1985; Leinhardt & Greeno, 1986) and to model ways of thinking as expert teachers accomplish instructional (Doyle, 1983, 1986b) and managerial tasks in classrooms (Carter, 1985, 1986).

Teachers' information processing.   As indicated earlier, to solve the problem of social order in classrooms, teachers must organize groups of students, establish rules and procedures, elicit students' cooperation in classroom activities, and sustain order in designated blocks of time across several months. This task requires complex, cognitive problem solving on the part of teachers. What is known about the nature of expert knowledge of this task? What solution strategies result from experts' problem-solving activities? How do expert and novice teachers differ in their understandings of this task and their task accomplishment?

Recent studies by Carter, Sabers, Cushing, Stein, & Berliner (1987); Carter, Cushing, Sabers, Pinnegar, & Berliner (in press), and Griffey & Housner (1985) have begun to explore these questions. Using a simulated teaching task that required subjects to prepare to take over a class in mid-year, Carter et al. (1987) examined expert/novice differences in processing and using information about students. One major finding from this study was that the routines experts reported for organizing and managing instruction were comparatively more rich and rehearsed than those of novices. Protocols obtained in the study suggested that experts, when preparing to assume responsibility for a class that had been taught previously by another teacher, gave considerable attention to getting the students "to work." Experts were anxious to "start fresh" with the class and to organize the group of students so that they could move through the curriculum. In coming to understand what needed to be done, experts were also able to make clear inferences about the previous teacher's practices. Much of this expert thinking was guided by routines and action plans drawn from their prior experience in the classroom. Novices were much less specific in interpreting what the previous teacher had done and in describing changes they might want to make in class routines and assignments.

In a task designed to uncover expert and novice differences in visual information processing, Carter et al. (in press) discovered a related focus on classroom work systems. Indeed, "work" appeared to be a salient organizing concept for experts as they viewed a series of classroom slides presented to them. Their comments suggested that they saw classrooms as moving systems and that they reacted quickly to visual stimuli indicating whether or not students were "working" well within that system. Novices' protocols did not reveal the same level of attention to work-related actions of students.

In this study, experts also showed a sense of "typicality" about classroom scenes and individual student's behavior. Once experts assessed a situation as "typical," they had little more to say. If situations or behaviors depicted in the same slides appeared to be unusual, however, experts spent considerable time attempting to make sense of anomalies. It appears, then, that experts' responses to management-related visual stimuli in classrooms are driven, at least in part, by their perceptions of what is "typical" vs. "atypical" in classroom scenes. This sense of "typicality" was notably rare in novice protocols.

In another study designed to examine expert/novice differences in teaching, Griffey and Housner (1985) found that expert physical education teachers constructed elaborate managerial plans for implementing activities and tasks for their students. Novices, in contrast, planned logically well-formed activities for teaching motor skills or exercise routines but gave considerably less attention than experts to how these events would be carried out under classroom conditions.

In summary, these studies suggest that experts draw on richly elaborated knowledge structures derived from classroom experience. Teachers' understandings are tied to the tasks they accomplish and are organized around classroom events. Expert teachers know the common forms of activities (recitations, seatwork, discussions) and academic assignments as classroom occurrences. Moreover, they are familiar with "typical" behaviors, interactions, and situations associated with such events. It is event-structured knowledge that likely helps expert teachers make highly accurate predictions about what can and may go on in classrooms.

Research on classroom tasks and teachers' knowledge does not nullify process-product research. Rather, the analysis suggests that process- product findings are best seen as *analytical categories* that inform the deliberative processes teachers use to interpret situations and plan actions. Information about the association between time and achievement, for example, can sensitize teachers to how time is spent in their classrooms and then be combined with information about managing classroom activities and constructing academic tasks to help design structures and processes to maintain or increase the quality of time use by students.

BECOMING AN EXPERT: THE CONTENT
OF TEACHER EDUCATION

Despite the progress made in our understanding of the character of expertise and particularly expertise in teaching, considerably less is known about how novices become experts. Indeed, few investigators have actually attempted to trace the processes by which one becomes an expert. Although the path to expertise is largely uncharted, the research summarized in this chapter provides a perspective for thinking about the content of teacher education as well as specific suggestions concerning the features the teacher education curriculum should embody.

Program Features

At least three major implications for teacher education curriculum can be drawn from research on experts' pedagogical knowledge. First, expert knowledge is situation and task specific. Expert teachers come to understand the settings in which they work and the ways in which those settings are organized by tasks of management and curriculum enactment. Second, the literature suggests that much of what experts learn is tacit knowledge. Such knowledge does not readily lend itself to formalization and direct instruction. Simon (1979) notes, for example, that experts in semantically rich domains such as chess and physics are estimated to have command of "some thousands or tens of thousands" of what are called "productions" (i.e., knowledge of patterns or action-situation connections) in their domains of expertise. In chess, however, only about 1300 of these productions have been formalized enough for programming on a computer. Similarly, in physics the typical introductory textbook chapter contains only about a dozen or so productions. It appears, then, that the gap between novice and expert is substantial, and much of the content of this gap cannot be specified very clearly. The acquisition of expertise can be explained, therefore, by the *construction* or invention of knowledge from experience. Finally, the acquisition of expertise appears to require repeated experience of accomplishing tasks in a domain. As a result, novices generally appear to require a large quantity of experience over a relatively long period of time to acquire the richly elaborated knowledge structures necessary to interpret situations and think productively about them. In other words, it takes time to become an expert.

Program Content

These features of expert knowledge suggest that teacher education experiences must have a high degree of situation and task validity. Moreover, the content of teacher education cannot be formalized into a set of specific skills or preset answers to specific problems. The purpose, rather, must be to develop rich propositional and procedural knowledge structured by the commonly occurring events of teaching in classrooms. To achieve this effect, teaching must be represented to teacher education students as a cognitive, problem-solving activity organized around the common pedagogical events teachers face in their occupational lives. In addition, teacher education must provide occasions to practice analysis and reflection concerning teaching events as well as opportunities for conversations with practicing experts. Finally, the development of event-structured knowledge of teaching is likely to take a long time. Teacher education students need time to construct their knowledge from experience with the rhythms and textures of teaching situations. Thus, teacher education should be conceived of as a long-term process.

Program Processes

This characterization of teacher education programs does not mean, of course, that teaching can only be learned by apprenticeship in field settings. Data on novices suggest that "natural" settings can be quite confusing, and novices may well direct their attention to irrelevant aspects of the stream of action. Constructed and guided experiences designed on the basis of an analytical understanding of teaching events are often more instructive than "natural" settings because the essential cognitive dimensions are more easily accessible. Such experiences, in turn, provide the cognitive foundation for knowledge construction in more natural environments.

Processes used to deliver teacher education content to novices must not only reveal pedagogical problems, they must bring out ways of thinking about these problems and provide opportunities for novices actually to practice problem solving. Several observers (e.g., Carter, 1986; Carter & Richardson-Koehler, in press; Doyle, 1986c; Shulman, 1986) have recently suggested that the use of cases may hold promise for achieving these ends. Simulations of teaching (Doak, Hipple, & Keith, 1987) may also be useful in representing teaching action associated with guiding a moving system through time and space. If properly constructed, simulations provide a controlled setting for "real-time" reasoning about commonly occurring clinical situations (Copeland, 1987).

In sum, research on experts' pedagogical knowledge suggests that teaching is much more than skills and technical performance on the one hand and artistry and personality on the other hand. Moreover, such limited representations of teaching are ultimately misleading. Teaching laboratories, when combined with long-term experience in field settings and with expert supervision, render the structure of teaching comprehensible so that novices can begin the path toward expertise.

Implications for Graduate Teacher Preparation

The central argument advanced here is that the curriculum of teacher education should be organized to foster expertise in the knowledge structures and procedures that underlie classroom teaching. This framework does not carry with it an argument for professional preparation at either the graduate or undergraduate level. Rather, it suggests content and processes that could be appropriate for either level. The central issue is not so much when teacher education should occur but what should be learned. Indeed, there is some evidence to suggest that the development of expertise is quite similar regardless of when one begins (Sternberg, 1985).

One important consideration, however, is the time devoted to teacher education. As noted, it takes time to learn to teach. Initial teacher preparation in clinical knowledge within graduate programs, however, is typically compressed into one year. Clinical preparation at the undergraduate level, in contrast, typically occurs over two years. If properly utilized for simulations, cases, and guided field practice, this extra time is likely to establish a much more solid foundation for constructing expert knowledge in teaching.

It is important, however, to avoid creating the expectation that expertise is the proximal goal of initial teacher preparation. As indicated, experts develop their rich understandings and functional problem-solving capacities because of the experience they have acquired over time with classroom events and their ability to reflect productively on this experience. Moreover, it is difficult for teacher candidates to learn some aspects of teaching without the "need to know" that comes from being confronted with complete responsibility. It is unlikely, therefore, that the pathway from novice to expert will end concurrently with the completion of coursework in teacher education.

From this perspective, the issues of graduate teacher education center on the continuing education of teachers. For the most part, graduate schooling for continuing teacher education has been driven by considerations of credentialing and academic degrees. Considerable imagination is needed to adapt graduate programs to the growing expertise of teachers in clinical settings. Perhaps participation in teacher education is one of the major avenues through which practicing experts can enrich their understanding of teaching and contribute to the growing expertise of the profession.

One final note: The expert framework proposed here would seem to have considerable heuristic value for thinking about the curriculum in teacher education. Nonetheless, considerably more research is needed to understand the basic event structure of teaching and the knowledge expert teachers use to understand and operate within classroom settings. Moreover, a large amount of basic research is needed on how teachers learn to teach (see Chapter 5), and substantial resources need to be invested in the development of teacher education processes that foster this understanding in novices.

REFERENCES

ANDERSON, L., EVERTSON, C., & BROPHY, J. (1979). An experimental study of effective teaching in first-grade reading groups. *Elementary School Journal, 79,* 193–223.

BROPHY, J. E., & GOOD, T. L. (1986). Teacher behavior and student achievement. In M. C. Wittrock (Ed.), *Handbook of research on teaching* (3rd ed., pp. 328–375). New York: Macmillan.

CARTER, K. (1985, April). *Teacher comprehension of classroom processes: An emerging direction in classroom management research.* Paper presented at the annual meeting of the American Educational Research Association, Chicago.

CARTER, K. (1986, April). *Classroom management as cognitive problem solving: Toward teacher comprehension in teacher education.* Paper presented at the annual meeting of the American Educational Research Association, San Francisco.

CARTER, K., CUSHING, K., SABERS, D., STEIN, P., & BERLINER, D.C. (in press). Expert-novice difference in perceiving and processing visual classroom information. *Journal of Teacher Education.*

CARTER K., & DOYLE, W. (1987). Teachers' knowledge structures and comprehension processes. In J. Calderhead (Ed.), *Exploring teachers' thinking.* London: Cassell PLC .

CARTER, K., & RICHARDSON-KOEHLER, V. (in press). The process and content of initial year of teaching programs. *Elementary School Journal.*

CARTER, K., SABERS, D., CUSHING, K., PINNEGAR, S., & BERLINER, D. C. (1987). Processing and using information about students: A study of expert, novice, and postulant teachers. *Teaching and Teacher Education, 3,* 147–157.

CHAMPAGNE, A. B., GUNSTONE, R. F., & KLOPFER, L. E. (1983). *A perspective on the differences between expert and novice performance in solving physics problems.* Pittsburgh: Learning Research and Development Center, University of Pittsburgh.

CHASE, W. G., & SIMON, H. A. (1973). Perception in chess. *Cognitive Psychology, 4,* 55–81.

CHI, M., & GLASER, R. (1982). *Knowledge and skill differences in novices and experts* (Tech. Rep. 7). Pittsburgh: Learning Research and Development Center, University of Pittsburgh.

CLEMENTS, B. S. (1985). *Beginning teachers' use of classroom management training* (R & D Rep. 6019). Austin, TX: University of Texas, Research and Development Center for Teacher Education.

COPELAND, W. D. (1987). Classroom management and student teachers' cognitive abilities: A relationship. *American Educational Research Journal, 24,* 219–236.

DENHAM, C., & LIEBERMAN, A., (Eds.) (1980). *Time to learn.* Washington, DC: National Institute of Education.

DOAK, E. D., HIPPLE, T., & KEITH, M. (1987). *Simulation and clinical knowledge in teacher education: Prologue to the future.* Proceedings from a National Invitational Symposium, November 13–14, 1986. Knoxville, TN: College of Education, University of Tennessee.

DOYLE, W. (1983). Academic work. *Review of Educational Research, 53,* 159–199.

DOYLE, W. (1986a). Classroom organization and management. In M. C. Wittrock (Ed.), *Handbook of research on teaching* (3rd ed., pp. 392–431). New York: Macmillan.

DOYLE, W. (1986b). Content representation in teachers' definitions of academic work. *Journal of Curriculum Studies, 18,* 365–379.

DOYLE, W. (1986c, April). *The world is everything that is the case: Developing case methods for teacher education.* Paper presented at the annual meeting of the American Educational Research Association, San Francisco.

DOYLE, W. (1987). Research on teaching effects as a resource for improving instruction. In M. Wideen & I. Andrews (Eds.), *Staff development for school improvement: A focus on the teacher,* (pp. 91–102). London: Falmer Press.

DOYLE, W., & CARTER, K. (1984). Academic tasks in classrooms. *Curriculum Inquiry, 14,* 129–149.

DOYLE, W., SANFORD, J. P., SCHMIDT-FRENCH, B. S., EMMER, E. T., & CLEMENTS, B. S. (1985). *Patterns of academic work in junior high school science, English,and mathematics classes: A final report* (R & D Rep. 6190). Austin, TX: University of Texas, Research and Development Center for Teacher Education.

DRISCOLL, A., & STEVENS, D. (1985, April). *Classroom teachers' response to the research on effective instruction.* Paper presented at the meeting of the American Educational Research Association, Chicago.

EMMER, E. T., SANFORD, J. P., EVERTSON, C. M., CLEMENTS, B. S., & MARTIN, J. (1981). *The Classroom Management Improvement Study: An experiment in elementary school classrooms* (R & D Rep. No. 6050). Austin, TX: University of Texas, Research & Development Center for Teacher Education.

ENGLE, R. W., & BUKSTEL, L. (1978). Memory processes among bridge players of differing expertise. *American Journal of Psychology, 91*, 673–689.

FENSTERMACHER, G. D. (1986). Philosophy of research on teaching: Three aspects. In M. C. Wittrock (Ed.), *Handbook of research on teaching* (3rd ed., pp. 37–49). New York: Macmillan.

FISHER, C., BERLINER, D., FILBY, N., MARLIAVE, R., CAHEN, L., & DISHAW, M. (1980). Teaching behaviors, academic learning time, and student achievement: An overview. In C. Denham & A. Lieberman (Eds.), *Time to learn* (pp. 7–22). Washington, DC: National Institute of Education.

FISKE, S. T., KINDER, D. R., & LARTER, W. M. (1983). The novice and the expert: Knowledge-based strategies in political cognition. *Journal of Experimental Social Psychology, 19*, 381–400.

GAGE, N. L. (1978). *The scientific basis of the art of teaching*. New York: Teachers College Press.

GAGE, N. L. (1985). *Hard gains in the soft sciences: The case of pedagogy*. Bloomington, IN: Center on Evaluation, Development, and Research, Phi Delta Kappa.

GOOD, T. L. (1983). Classroom research: A decade of progress. *Educational Psychologist, 18*, 127–144.

GOOD, T., & GROUWS, D. (1979). The Missouri Mathematics Effectiveness Project: An experimental study in fourth grade classrooms. *Journal of Educational Psychology, 71*, 355–362.

GRIFFIN, G. A. (1983). Implications of research for staff development programs. *Elementary School Journal, 83*, 414–425.

GRIFFIN, G. A., BARNES, S., O'NEAL, A., EDWARDS, S., DEFINO, M. E., & HUKILL, H. (1983). *Changing teacher practice: Final report of an experimental study* (R & D Rep. No. 9052). Austin, TX: University of Texas, Research & Development Center for Teacher Education.

HARNISCHFEGER, A., & WILEY, D. E. (1976). Teaching-learning processes in elementary schools: A synoptic view. *Curriculum Inquiry, 6*, 5–43.

HOUSNER, L. D., & GRIFFEY, D. C. (1985). Teacher cognition: Differences in planning and interactive decision-making between experienced and inexperienced teachers. *Research Quarterly for Exercise and Sport, 56*, 45–53.

HOWSAM, R. B. (1976). *Educating a profession*. Washington, DC: American Association of Colleges for Teacher Education.

KOUNIN, J. S. (1970). *Discipline and group management in classrooms*. New York: Holt, Rinehart, and Winston.

LARKIN, J., MCDERMOTT, J., SIMON, D. P., & SIMON, H. A. (1980). Expert and novice performance in solving physics problems. *Science, 208*, 1335–1342.

LEINHARDT, G., & GREENO, J. (1986). The cognitive skill of teaching. *Journal of Educational Psychology, 78*, 75–95.

PATEL, V. L., FREDERIKSEN, C. H., & GROEN, G. J. (1984). *Differences between experts and novices in a complex verbal task in a medical domain* (Rep No. CME 84–3). Montreal: McGill University, Centre for Medical Education.

PUTNAM, R. T. (1987). Structuring and adjusting content for students: A study of live and simulated tutoring of addition. *American Educational Research Journal, 24*, 13–48.

ROSENSHINE, B., & STEVENS, R. (1986). Teaching functions. In M. C. Wittrock (Ed.), *Handbook of research on teaching* (3rd ed., pp. 376–391). New York: Macmillan.

SHULMAN, L. S. (1986). Those who understand: Knowledge growth in teaching. *Educational Researcher, 15*(2), 4–14.

SIMON, H. A. (1979). Information processing models of cognition. *Annual Review of Psychology, 30*, 363–396.

SMITH, B. O., COHEN, S. B., & PEARL, A. (1969). *Teachers for the real world.* Washington, DC: American Association of Colleges for Teacher Education.

SMITH, D. C., (Ed.). (1983). *Essential knowledge for beginning educators.* Washington, DC: American Association of Colleges for Teacher Education.

STERNBERG, R. (1985). *Beyond IQ: A triarchic theory of human intelligence.* New York: Cambridge University Press.

TOM, A. R. (1984). *Teaching as a moral craft.* New York: Longman.

WALKER, D., & SCHAFFARZICK, J. (1974). Comparing curricula. *Review of Educational Research, 44,* 83–111.

WITTROCK, M. C. (1974). Learning as a generative process. *Educational Psychologist, 11,* 87–95.

ZUMWALT, K. K. (1982). Research on teaching: Policy implications for teacher education. In A. Lieberman & M. McLaughlin (Eds.), *Policy making in education.* Eighty-first Yearbook of the National Society for the Study of Education (Part 1). Chicago: University of Chicago Press.

5

RESEARCH ON LEARNING TO TEACH: IMPLICATIONS FOR GRADUATE TEACHER PREPARATION

Hilda Borko

This chapter focuses on the process of learning to teach and the implications of this process for the preparation of teachers. Any discussion of learning to teach is grounded, either implicitly or explicitly, in a view of what teaching is. The view adopted in this chapter is that teaching is a complex cognitive activity that requires the construction of plans and the making of rapid, on-line decisions (Borko & Shavelson, in press; Leinhardt & Greeno, 1986). Learning to teach entails the learning of cognitive skills such as decision making, problem solving, and reflection, as well as a set of observable teaching behaviors.

Learning to teach is not synonymous with teacher education. Rather, it is an ongoing process that ideally extends throughout a teacher's career. Because the intent of this book is to provide suggestions for the graduate preparation of teachers, the chapter focuses on learning-to-teach experiences typically included in graduate programs for preservice teachers; that is, pedagogical coursework and student teaching. These experiences comprise what Feiman-Nemser (1983) refers to as the preservice phase of learning to teach. (For a discussion of learning to teach as a career-long process and the phases of learning to teach, see Feiman-Nemser, 1983).

The issue of graduate *versus* undergraduate preparation of preservice teachers is not one that has been addressed by the research on learning to teach. And this research does not provide empirical evidence for the superiority of either graduate or undergraduate programs. Therefore, while this chapter emphasizes learning during pedagogical coursework and student teaching and presents patterns of findings and implications particularly relevant to the design of graduate teacher preparation programs, it does not focus exclusively on postbaccalaureate preservice teachers. Nor does it make the case that preservice teacher preparation should be the domain of graduate programs.

The chapter is divided into three sections. In the first, I make a case for the importance of designing teacher preparation programs that take into account the thinking and actions of novice teachers and the process of learning to teach. Based on research identifying differences between expert and novice teachers, I suggest that programs grounded exclusively in what is known about the teaching of effective, experienced teachers are inadequate. In the second section, I describe four major programs of research on the preservice phase of learning to teach. The third section presents patterns of findings from these studies and suggests implications of these patterns for preservice teacher preparation programs.

RESEARCH BASES FOR TEACHER PREPARATION PROGRAMS

Many colleges of education nationwide are currently engaged in revising and redesigning their preservice teacher education programs. They are turning to the effective teaching research for guidance in these reform efforts, encouraged by the fact that this knowledge base has increased substantially over the past 20 years. Much has been learned about the teaching behaviors of effective experienced teachers (for recent reviews see Brophy & Good, 1986; Rosenshine & Stevens, 1986) and about their thought processes (for recent reviews see Borko & Niles, 1987; Clark & Peterson, 1986; Shavelson & Stern, 1981). In reflecting on the effective teaching research and its potential role in teacher education, Gage (1984) suggests that we have, for the first time, a body of research-based knowledge to include in teacher preparation programs.

However, research within the field of cognitive psychology suggests that the application of teacher effectiveness research to teacher preparation may not be as straightforward as one might initially think. Specifically, recent research on the nature of expertise indicates that there are qualitative differences in the thinking and actions of experts and novices (cf. Berliner, 1986; Reed, 1982). For example, novices and experts use different strategies for solving problems (Fredericksen, 1984; Larkin et al., 1980). Information that is useful for experts may hold little meaning for novices (deGroot, 1965; Egan & Schwartz, 1979).

Recently, educational researchers have turned their attention to the nature of expertise in teaching. The growing body of research on this topic suggests that the characteristics of expertise identified in other cognitively complex domains are shared by expert teachers as well. To summarize briefly, expert teachers have more pedagogical and subject matter knowledge than novices and better developed conceptual systems (cognitive schemata) for organizing and storing this knowledge. As a result of their more extensive and better organized knowledge systems, expert teachers are more efficient than novices in their processing of information during both the planning and interactive phases of teaching (e.g., Leinhardt & Greeno, 1986; Leinhardt & Smith, 1985; Peterson & Comeaux, 1987).

Expert teachers do more of their planning in their heads than do novices, making mental scripts to guide the direction of their lessons. Experts' plans, or agendas, are more detailed and richer in interconnectedness than the agendas of novices. They include a greater number of student actions, teacher instructional moves, and routines for common classroom activities (e.g., Housner & Griffey, 1985; Leinhardt, 1986; Leinhardt & Greeno, 1986). Leinhardt (1986, p. 19) captures many of these differences by characterizing an expert's agenda as "a conceptual road map that keeps the lesson flowing in a particular direction. . . ."

Experts' interactive teaching is characterized by greater use of instructional and management routines than novices'. These routines are mutually known by the teacher and students, and their implementation requires little or no explanation or monitoring. Because they can be carried out with little conscious attention, routines reduce the cognitive demands on the teachers. Experts are able to further reduce the cognitive load during interactive teaching by being more selective than novices in the information to which they attend, focusing only on aspects of the classroom that are relevant to instructional decision making. By reducing cognitive demands in these ways, experts free themselves to focus on the important and/or dynamic features of the lesson content and on information from students about how the lesson is progressing. Further, because the sequence of behavior in routines is familiar to students, they too are able to concentrate on the content of the lesson without worrying about procedures or lesson structure (e.g., Berliner, 1987; Calderhead, 1981, 1983; Carter, Sabers, Cushing, Pinnegar & Berliner, 1987; Carter, Cushing, Sabers, Stein & Berliner, in press; Housner & Griffey, 1985; Warner, 1987) (for further discussion of teachers' subject matter expertise and pedagogical expertise see Chapters 6 and 4, respectively).

These differences in the thinking and actions of expert and novice teachers suggest that it may be quite inappropriate to educate novice teachers by presenting them with information about how expert teachers think and act and then expect these novices to adopt the routines or actions of experts. As is the case in other cognitively complex domains, novice teachers do not have the necessary knowledge and skills (e.g., repertoires of well-practiced instructional and management routines, cognitive schemata for common instructional techniques such as explaining and questioning) to simply imitate the complex patterns of teaching activities displayed by experts. To provide appropriate educational experiences, teacher preparation programs must take into account what is known about the thinking and actions of novices (as well as experts) and the process by which novices become experts. These programs must incorporate experiences designed for novices at various stages in the process of learning to teach and sequence those experiences to ensure a match between learner readiness and task demands.

As recently as three or four years ago, this recommendation would have been very problematic, as we knew little about the process of learning to teach (Feiman-Nemser, 1983) or the thinking and actions of novice teachers (Tabachnick & Zeichner, 1984). However, the educational research community can now happily report results of several recently completed or in-progress programs of research to address these issues. These research programs, and their implications for the preparation of teachers, are examined in the remaining two sections of this chapter.

LEARNING TO TEACH

The body of research on learning to teach is very diverse. Studies have been conducted from a variety of theoretical perspectives including teacher socialization, teacher development, and knowledge acquisition. Investigations also differ with respect to the phase of learning to teach they address. While the majority focus on the student teaching experience, there are studies of all components of the learning-to-teach process, from pretraining (i.e., experiences and influences prior to formal pedagogical coursework) to inservice or staff development (Feiman-Nemser, 1983). The thread that ties these studies together is a common concern for understanding how a person learns to teach and improves in teaching over time.

As mentioned above, the focus of this chapter is limited. In keeping with the book's intent to formulate recommendations for graduate teacher preparation, I concentrate primarily on the research that addresses the preservice phase of learning to teach. I also briefly explore extensions of three research programs into the induction phase, because the experiences and reactions of beginning teachers offer valuable insights regarding how best to prepare novices for their first year in the profession.

Four research programs serve as the basis of the discussion. These programs were selected using the following criteria: longitudinal (multiyear) examination of learning to teach; conducted in actual university and public school settings; and employing a combination of data collection strategies. They include Ken Zeichner and Robert Tabachnick's study of the development of teacher perspectives conducted at The University of Wisconsin, Madison; my work with colleagues at Virginia Tech and The University of Maryland examining novice teachers' planning, conduct, and evaluation of instruction; the program of research on the development of subject matter knowledge by Lee Shulman and colleagues at Stanford University; and the project coordinated by Sharon Feiman-Nemser at Michigan State University that explores preservice teachers' acquisition of pedagogical knowledge.

The Development of Teacher Perspectives

Tabachnick and Zeichner (1984, 1985; Zeichner & Tabachnick, 1985) conducted a two-year longitudinal study of the development of teaching perspectives in a small group of beginning teachers. Using Becker and colleagues' (1961) definition of perspectives as "a coordinated set of ideas and actions a person uses in dealing with some problematic situation, to refer to a person's ordinary way of thinking about and acting in such a situation" (p. 34), they examined the impact of student teaching and the first year of teaching on participants' teaching perspectives. During the first year of the study, they identified the teaching perspectives of 13 student teachers in relation to four specific categories: teacher's role, teacher-pupil relationships, knowledge and curriculum, and student diversity. They also traced changes that took place in participants' teaching perspectives during the 15-week student teaching experience and identified the various individual and institutional factors that were related to the development of these perspectives. They interviewed each student teacher a minimum of five times during the student teaching semester, observed them while teaching a minimum of three times, interviewed their cooperating teachers and university supervisors, and examined journals and transcripts of their weekly student teaching seminars.

Tabachnick and Zeichner (1984) concluded based on their first-year data that student teaching did not significantly alter the substance of participants' teaching perspectives. Rather, most participants ". . . became more articulate in expressing, and more skillful in implementing, the perspectives which they possessed in less developed forms at the beginning of the experience." Further, ". . . most student teachers grew increasingly comfortable with their initial positions, more confident in their abilities to handle a classroom in their preferred styles. . . ." (p. 33). Tabachnick and Zeichner note that these student teachers were expected to reflect about their classroom behavior, explaining and justifying it in journal entries and during seminars and supervisory conferences. They also actively participated in the selection of their student teaching placements. They were able to purposefully select themselves into situations with teachers who seemed to share their perspectives. Given these program characteristics, it is not surprising that the student teachers' perspectives solidified during the experience.

In the second phase of the study, Zeichner and Tabachnick (1985) followed four of the novice teachers into their first year of teaching to examine the impact of the first-year experience on their teaching perspectives and identify factors that influenced the continued development of these perspectives. They spent three one-week periods in each of the teacher's schools. During each visit they observed in the teacher's class on a daily basis and interviewed her about her plans for instruction and reactions to what had occurred. They also conducted in-depth interviews with each teacher about her professional development in relation to the four categories of perspectives, talked with six target students in each class to determine how they experienced classroom life, and interviewed the principal and two other teachers concerning their views of institutional pressures at the school.

Analysis of these data, combined with data from the student teaching year, resulted in "the construction of four case studies which describe the journeys of each teacher and the individual and social influences on their development from the beginning of student teaching to the end of the first year" (Zeichner & Tabachnick, 1985, p. 8). Despite initial similarities in their teaching perspectives the journeys of the four teachers differed. One continued to develop her teaching perspectives in a manner consistent with her development during student teaching, with the support and encouragement of people in her school. A second significantly changed her perspectives in response to organizational demands. Two were able to maintain perspectives in conflict with the dominant organizational cultures in their schools. However, one was more successful than the other in having her perspectives and behaviors accepted by the school. This differential success was due to a variety of factors, including personal characteristics such as political sensitivity and strength with which teaching perspectives were held and institutional factors such as the degree of contradiction between formal and informal school cultures.

Zeichner and Tabachnick interpret patterns across the cases as evidence that, for these four teachers, the interaction of the formal and informal cultures within their schools determined the organizational constraints and opportunities presented to them. The teachers' own interests and abilities played an important role in determining which constraints would be accepted or resisted and which opportunities would be realized or lost. Based on this analysis, Zeichner and Tabachnick conclude that the transition from student teacher to teacher appears to be highly person- and context-specific. There is no one explanation that can describe the entry of beginning teachers into the teaching role or the changes they experience during the induction year. The researchers suggest that this study offers teacher educators the challenge to find ways of creating and maintaining conditions within schools that will enhance the individual expressions of teaching perspectives encouraged in teacher preparation programs.

Novice Teachers' Preactive and Interactive Teaching

My work with colleagues at Virginia Tech and The University of Maryland (Borko, 1985; Borko, Lalik, Livingston, Pecic, & Perry, 1986; Borko, Lalik, & Tomchin, 1987; Borko, Livingston, McCaleb, & Mauro, in press) has many parallels to that of Zeichner and Tabachnick. However, while they examine general perspectives about teaching, we focus more specifically on novice teachers' thoughts about specific instructional events. Like Tabachnick and Zeichner, we followed novice elementary teachers through their final year of an undergraduate teacher preparation program and first year of teaching.

During the first year of the study, we analyzed the journals kept by seven stronger and seven weaker student teachers throughout their year-long professional field experience. This experience, the final year of their program, included seven university courses and four clinical field placements. In biweekly journal entries, student teachers described and evaluated their most successful and least successful lessons for the week. At the end of each field placement, they answered a set of questions about their professional development during the experience. We also selected four student teachers, two weaker and two stronger, to participate in an in-depth study of the planning and evaluation of reading lessons. We observed and videotaped each participant teaching a reading lesson once during each field placement. Before each observation we interviewed the student teacher about her planning for the lesson. Following the observation, we asked her to evaluate the lesson.

Data from the first year of our project indicated that stronger and weaker student teachers had similar conceptions of successful lessons. These conceptions, like the more general perspectives studied by Zeichner and Tabachnick, did not change over the course of the year-long field experience. All student teachers recorded similar descriptions of successful lessons in their journal entries. And the four participating in the intensive study of reading instruction adopted similar approaches to modifying and supplementing basal reading lessons. Stronger and weaker student teachers' journal entries about unsuccessful lessons did differ. Weaker student teachers taught more lessons that they considered to be unsuccessful, and their unsuccessful lessons seemed to be more discrepant from the shared conception of successful teaching.

Another factor that differentiated stronger and weaker student teachers was their planning. Journal entries indicated that stronger student teachers had a broader view of planning, which included anticipatory problem solving as well as the identification of teaching activities and learning or reviewing of lesson content. Interviews with the subsample of four student teachers confirmed this pattern. The stronger student teachers planned in more detail, considered more aspects of the lessons in their planning, and used a problem-solving approach in which they anticipated problems and made plans to lessen or circumvent them. For example, one student teacher developed a set of notecards containing instructions for small group work. Before students in her class began their first cooperative small group assignment, the student teacher distributed the instruction cards in an attempt to minimize students' off- task behavior. Thus, our data suggest the critical role that planning can play in the success of a student teacher. Careful, detailed planning conducted within a problem-solving framework may increase the probability that the novice teacher's lessons will match his or her conception of successful instruction.

We followed two stronger student teachers into their first year of teaching to examine how they planned, implemented, and evaluated their reading/language arts programs; what factors influenced these instructional programs; and what factors influenced their professional development (Borko et al., 1986). (For logistical reasons, we were unable to follow teachers who participated in our initial intensive study of student teachers.) We made three one-week visits to each teacher's class, at the beginning, middle, and end of the school year. During each visit, we conducted daily observations and interviews about reading instruction, as well as more general interviews about their reading programs, professional development, and influences on their first-year experiences. We also interviewed persons they identified as influential to their instructional programs and professional development in general.

Experiences of the two first-year teachers taught us primarily about factors that facilitate or impede entry into the profession. For both teachers, the first year was one of choices and compromises. For example, for a variety of reasons including their limited knowledge of the curriculum, limited time and energy, and school policies and expectations, both teachers relied on basal reading programs to a greater extent than they expected or liked. A major difference between the two teachers was in their personal assessments of success. One was comfortable with her compromises and viewed her first year as a success. The other assessed her first year much more negatively. Several aspects of their experiences as beginning teachers help explain these differences. The more satisfied first year teacher had a very positive relationship with an experienced "buddy teacher." To a much greater extent than the second teacher, she was treated as a professional decision maker and received support from school administrators and colleagues.

In a subsequent study conducted at The University of Maryland (Borko et al., in press), we examined the planning and postlesson reflections of secondary student teachers from a variety of content areas as well as elementary student teachers. Because of a greater number of participants (eight in secondary education and four in elementary education), we were able to observe and interview each student teacher for a period of only two consecutive days.

Patterns in the data revealed four factors related to participants' planning and lesson reflections: subject matter and pedagogical knowledge, content area influence, teaching multiple sections of the same course, and student teacher responsibility and control. The importance of strong content preparation was illustrated by the relationships between subject matter knowledge and (a) amount of time and effort required for daily planning; (b) focus of attention in planning (e.g., learning of content, planning of instructional strategies); (c) flexibility in planning and teaching; and (d) self-confidence as a teacher. The content area influenced the relative impact of the textbook, curriculum guides, and personal knowledge and experience on classroom instruction. Secondary students made differential use of the opportunity created by teaching multiple sections of the same course, with maximum benefit being derived from using this opportunity to obtain the cooperating teacher's feedback and revise instruction between sections. Finally, student teachers who perceived themselves as responsible for, and in control of, classroom events more frequently took active steps to correct problem situations and improve their teaching.

Several factors associated with success in learning to teach were evident across the studies within our research program: careful, detailed planning that incorporates strategies for minimizing potential problems; strong subject matter preparation to enable novice teachers to focus planning energies productively; and a perception (shared by the novice teacher and colleagues and administrators) that the novice teacher is responsible for, and in control of, classroom events.

Knowledge Growth in Teaching

The "Knowledge Growth in Teaching" research project conducted by Shulman and colleagues at Stanford University focuses primarily on novice teachers' subject matter knowledge (Grossman, 1987; Grossman & Reichert, 1986; Ringstaff & Haymore, 1987; Shulman, 1986, 1987; Wilson, Shulman, & Richert, 1987). Specifically, "... our project focuses on what teachers know about their subject matter, where and when they acquired that knowledge, how and why that knowledge is transformed during teaching or teacher education, and how knowledge is used in classroom instruction" (Wilson, Shulman, & Richert, 1987, p. 110). Participants were 21 student teachers enrolled in three fifth-year teacher preparation programs in California during the 1984-1985 academic year, representing the subject areas of English, social studies, biology, and mathematics. Twelve of the participants were followed into their first year of full-time teaching.

During the first year of the investigation, researchers conducted a series of interviews with participants that focused on their intellectual histories, general knowledge of their subject area, knowledge of the specific courses they were assigned to teach, general pedagogical knowledge, and pedagogical knowledge of their content area. They also conducted a series of planning-observation-reflection data collection cycles. Each cycle included a planning think-aloud, a planning interview focusing on knowledge of content and what they wanted the students to learn about the content, and an interview about the observed teaching to detect changes in the teachers' knowledge of subject matter and pedagogy as well as the perceived sources of those changes. Participants followed into their first year of teaching were observed during teaching and interviewed about the observed lessons. Interviews prior to the observations focused on their plans for the lessons. After each observation, teachers were asked to reflect on the lesson, student performance, and their own teaching.

Based on the first-year data, Shulman and colleagues developed two theoretical frameworks to describe central components of teaching and learning to teach (Shulman, 1987; Wilson, Shulman, & Richert, 1987). The first framework describes the knowledge bases for teaching. It identifies seven categories of knowledge that teachers draw upon when planning and teaching: subject matter knowledge, general pedagogical knowledge, curricular knowledge, knowledge of learners, knowledge of educational aims and purposes, knowledge of other content, and pedagogical content knowledge. The second framework describes the process of pedagogical reasoning. It includes five sets of activities that teachers cycle through to transform content for instruction: comprehension, transformation, instruction, evaluation, and reflection. Major findings associated with these frameworks are presented below.

In analyzing the first-year data, the research team paid particular attention to subject matter knowledge and pedagogical content knowledge. They found that student teachers' level of subject matter knowledge influenced both their planning and their teaching. For example, in mathematics a student teacher with stronger subject matter knowledge taught more "conceptually," while the teaching of a student teacher with weaker content knowledge was more "rule-based." Similarly, biology student teachers with stronger subject matter knowledge saw richer, more complex relationships among biological concepts and planned to teach from general concepts to specific information. Student teachers less knowledgeable about the discipline saw biology as involving simpler relationships among concepts and planned to focus on specific information while teaching.

Pedagogical content knowledge was of particular interest because it is a type of knowledge unique to teaching. As Shulman (1987) explains, "It represents the blending of content and pedagogy into an understanding of how particular topics, problems, or issues are organized, represented and adapted to the diverse interests and abilities of learners, and presented for instruction" (p. 8). Pedagogical content knowledge was a new type of knowledge for the student teachers. They all struggled with the issue of how to present subject matter to their students. In their searches for ways to explain the content of their disciplines, they sometimes generated representations or transformations to facilitate students' developing understandings. These representations took a variety of forms, including analogies, metaphors, examples, and illustrations.

In addition to developing a new type of knowledge, the student teachers developed new ways of thinking that helped them to generate subject matter transformations. Shulman and colleagues labeled this thinking "pedagogical reasoning" and described it as the process of taking what one already understands about content and teaching material and making it ready for effective instruction. They characterized the student teachers' struggles to find ways of presenting content to their students as attempts to use their developing pedagogical reasoning skills and pedagogical knowledge to transform their own knowledge of the discipline into "learnable" forms.

Following the second year of data collection, members of the research team used the frameworks for knowledge bases of teaching and pedagogical reasoning to develop and compare case studies of several of the participants, based on data from their student teaching and first year of teaching. These case study comparisons confirmed findings from the first year that teachers' subject matter knowledge could not account for many of the differences in their pedagogical reasoning and actions. Other factors such as their perceptions of students, self-perceptions as teachers, educational philosophy, beliefs about content, and disciplinary perspectives affected both their goals for and conduct of teaching. Based on these conclusions, the researchers suggest that teacher education programs must help student teachers to develop and integrate multiple types of knowledge and reasoning and to become aware of the roles that their knowledge and values play in shaping their teaching.

In an attempt to provide some direction to teacher education programs, Grossman and Richert (1986) analyzed data from the first year to determine the impact of coursework and fieldwork on the development of different categories of knowledge. The four categories of knowledge mentioned most frequently by the student teachers were conception of the subject for teaching, general pedagogy, student understanding, and topic-specific knowledge. Of all references to teacher education, 45 percent focused on coursework and 55 percent on fieldwork. Coursework was mentioned somewhat more frequently as influencing student teachers' conceptions of the subject for teaching and general pedagogy. Fieldwork was mentioned much more frequently as influencing their knowledge of student understanding. The two types of experiences were perceived as having approximately equal influence on topic-specific knowledge. The authors conclude that while novice teachers usually identify their fieldwork as the place where they learn how to teach, pedagogy can be (and is perceived to be) learned in university-based teacher education courses as well as in the field.

Knowledge Use in Learning to Teach

"Knowledge Use in Learning to Teach," the research program coordinated by Sharon Feiman-Nemser at Michigan State University, examines preservice teachers' learning experiences during formal preparation and how these experiences help and hinder the transition to "pedagogical thinking" (Ball & Feiman-Nemser, in press;

Feiman-Nemser, & Buchmann, 1986, 1987, in press). Feiman-Nemser and colleagues define pedagogical thinking as thinking about teaching that focuses on students and what they need to know rather than on oneself as the teacher or on the subject matter alone. (Note the similarity between this concept and pedagogical reasoning, as defined by Shulman and colleagues.) To understand the transition to pedagogical thinking, they describe and analyze what preservice teachers learn in relation to what they are taught, in both coursework and fieldwork. They also attempt to determine if and how the experiences that comprise preservice teacher education add up to preparation for teaching.

Between 1982 and 1984, members of the research team followed six elementary education students through two years of undergraduate teacher preparation. The students were in two contrasting programs: the Academic Program, which emphasized theoretical and subject matter knowledge and stressed teaching for understanding and conceptual change, and the Decision-Making Program, which emphasized generic teaching methods and research-based decision making.

Participants in the study were interviewed each semester about what they learned in their courses and field placements and how they thought these experiences would help them in their teaching. Researchers also observed a core course in each program (a course developed specifically for the program), taking field notes about content, activities, and interactions. During student teaching, which occurred in the second year of teacher preparation, the researcher paired with each student teacher visited weekly to observe and document the student teacher's activities and to talk informally with the student teacher, cooperating teacher, and university supervisor. Formal interviews also were conducted with each participant before and after student teaching. Reports of the research focus primarily on two cases from the first year and two cases from the second.

University coursework dominated the first year of formal teacher preparation. Both participants experienced difficulty making the transition to pedagogical thinking due, at least in part, to their limited knowledge of both subject matter and pedagogy. For example, one participant was given a group assignment to develop a spiral curriculum on a topic. Her group focused on poetry. Members of the group interviewed several students to determine their preconceptions and prior knowledge relevant to the unit; however, they ignored what the children said when completing the assignment. They apparently did not know how to translate this information into guidelines for instruction.

Coursework in the teacher preparation programs did not remedy participants' subject matter knowledge deficits. Nor did it provide enough "teacher education" (instruction, supervision, practice, and reflection) to sufficiently enhance their pedagogical knowledge. As a result, both participants attempted to compensate for limited subject matter and pedagogical knowledge by relying on textbooks, their own schooling, and practical experience in learning to teach.

The theme of the transition to pedagogical thinking also surfaced in the second year case studies, which focused on two participants' student teaching experiences. Both student teachers experienced difficulty in recognizing the differences between going through the motions of teaching (e.g., checking homework, talking at the board, giving assignments) and connecting these activities to what students should be learning over time. A bookmaking project conducted by one student teacher illustrates this difficulty. The student teacher focused on the technique of bookmaking rather than storywriting. She did not structure the project to help students understand the connection between making books and learning to write. Nor did she recognize the opportunity for learning that could be created by having the students share their books with each other. Unfortunately, even though her cooperating teacher was very good at capitalizing on potential academic learning experiences, he did not share his expertise with her.

Because of the central role of textbooks and teacher's manuals in elementary education, Ball and Feiman-Nemser (in press) considered separately the issue of what preservice elementary teachers learn and what they need to know about these curricular materials. Both the academic and the decision-making programs gave the message that textbooks should be used only as a resource and that following the text is an undesirable way to teach. Neither program showed students how to use the textbooks and teacher's manuals thoughtfully, by choosing and modifying suggestions and activities. However, like the first-year teachers in our study (Borko et al., 1986), student teachers in both programs ended up using basals and manuals in their teaching—some because of external pressure to maintain classroom practice and some because they were overwhelmed by the demands of the student teaching experience. And since they were never shown positive ways of using these curricular materials, they were unprepared to do it well.

Based on their research findings, Feiman-Nemser and colleagues conclude that, without guidance, preservice teachers will have difficulty making the transition to pedagogical thinking. By themselves, they can rarely see beyond what they want or need to do, or what the setting requires. They cannot be expected to critically analyze their beliefs about children, the knowledge they draw upon in making instructional decisions, or their reasons for these decisions while trying to cope with the demands of the classroom. The researchers suggest that teacher educators (university personnel and cooperating teachers) take an active role in guiding preservice teachers' pedagogical thinking and actions; for example, by demonstrating teaching actions and verbalizing pedagogical thinking, and by stimulating preservice teachers to analyze and discuss their actions and decisions.

PATTERNS AND IMPLICATIONS

Despite the diverse perspectives represented in these research programs, several patterns in the learning-to-teach process are evident. These patterns include: (a) the impact of content area preparation on teaching; (b) difficulties in learning the cognitive skills of teaching; (c) the central role of the textbook in novices' teaching; and (d) the influence of the cooperating teacher and university supervisor. Each of these patterns will be discussed, and implications for teacher preparation examined. In keeping with the focus on experiences that typically comprise graduate teacher preparation, suggestions for pedagogical coursework and student teaching will be emphasized.

Content Area Preparation

Findings from several of the research programs confirm the importance of strong preparation in one's content area prior to student teaching. Without adequate preparation, student teachers will spend much of their limited planning time learning content, rather than thinking about how to present content in a way that will facilitate student understanding. Student teachers with strong content preparation are more likely than those with weaker content preparation to be flexible in their teaching and responsive to students' needs. Their teaching tends to be conceptually based, with greater emphasis on the organization of knowledge within the discipline and less on the provision of specific information. Further, student teachers without adequate content area preparation are likely to lack confidence in their ability to teach well.

Content area preparation is not the responsibility of graduate teacher preparation programs. Rather, these programs typically assume that entering students have strong disciplinary backgrounds. To ensure that this is the case, colleges of education should establish criteria for content area preparation, and should adhere closely to these criteria when making admission decisions. Completion of a bachelor's degree in an appropriate field, even with a strong record of academic performance, is not always sufficient. For example, people seeking secondary social studies certification may have degrees in a number of specializations including history, political science, anthropology, and sociology. Given the wide variety of classes they can expect to teach, some diversity in coursework within their programs should be expected. Students with strong, but narrowly focused, backgrounds are likely to need additional coursework to provide a broader knowledge base for teaching. (See Chapter 6 for a much more extensive treatment of the role of content area preparation.)

Cognitive Activities of Teaching

Patterns in three cognitive activities of teaching—pedagogical thinking about content, planning, and evaluation of instruction—suggest areas of focus for teacher preparation programs. One of the most difficult aspects of learning to teach is making the transition from a personal orientation to a discipline to thinking about how to organize and represent the content of that discipline in ways that will facilitate student understanding. Preservice teachers in at least three of the research programs experienced difficulty in making this transition to pedagogical thinking about content. Perhaps even more troublesome is the fact that in several instances, evidence suggests that these teachers did not even realize they were having problems.

As Shulman (1987) reminds us, the capacity to transform content knowledge into forms that are pedagogically powerful and adaptive to particular groups of students is at the core of successful teaching. Since learning to make these transformations is such a difficult aspect of learning to teach, it needs more attention in teacher preparation programs than it typically receives. Coursework, for example, methods courses, should explicitly address the issue of how to represent the discipline—its content and thinking processes—to students of various ages and ability levels. Studies of pedagogical expertise can provide guidance in designing learning experiences. For example, Leinhardt's analyses of the content of explanations address the issue of how to present new material to students in ways that will facilitate their understanding (e.g., Leinhardt, 1986; Leinhardt & Greeno, 1986).

Another cognitive activity of teaching that warrants additional attention in teacher preparation programs is planning. Our research program at Virginia Tech and The University of Maryland was the only one that specifically examined preservice teachers' planning skills. However, the relationship we found between planning (e.g., amount of detail, use of a problem-solving approach) and success in student teaching is supported by several studies of pedagogical expertise. For example, experts' plans are more detailed and richer in interconnectedness than those of novices and include a greater number of teacher and student actions. As was the case for pedagogical thinking about content, we can look to the research on experts' planning when designing learning experiences. Experts' written plans are typically very brief and do not provide appropriate models for novice teachers. However, preservice teachers can use experts' verbal descriptions of their plans—from either published research or personal conversations—as guidelines when developing plans for their own teaching.

Teacher preparation programs must also help preservice teachers learn to critically analyze their own teaching. Several of the research programs indicate that without explicit guidance in this area, student teachers often do not realize when their teaching breaks down and students are not learning the intended lesson. A number of factors probably contribute to this situation. When teaching, student teachers' attention is so focused on keeping the lesson moving that they probably do not notice many student cues about understanding. Afterwards, they do not have the needed information to analyze the lesson and are often unclear about the kinds of criteria to use (Calderhead, 1987). One way to remedy this situation is for a university supervisor or cooperating teacher to videotape the student teacher's lesson and then analyze the videotape with him or her. The videotape enables the student teacher to watch the dynamics of the teaching-learning situation without the pressure of on-line decision making. Also, the supervisor or cooperating teacher can provide assistance in identifying and applying appropriate evaluation criteria.

Microteaching laboratories, in which preservice teachers are videotaped teaching lessons to a small group of peers, are another experience well suited to the development of the cognitive skills of teaching. In the laboratory setting, preservice teachers can practice planning, teaching, and then critically analyzing their planning and teaching, with the assistance of teacher educators and the ability to repeatedly view videotaped instructional segments.

Use of Textbooks and Teacher's Manuals

The issue of what preservice teachers should be taught about the appropriate use of textbooks and accompanying teacher's manuals and workbooks is particularly salient to elementary teacher preparation programs. Textbooks tend to dominate elementary instruction, and often they are poor. Many teacher educators believe that teaching can be improved by preparing professionals who develop their own curriculum rather than following a textbook. They give student teachers the message that following a textbook is an undesirable way to teach. Unfortunately, this message often is not accompanied by instruction on alternatives to reliance on the text. Further, even when such instruction is provided, this may not be an appropriate approach to take with novice teachers.

In two of the research programs, student teachers and first-year teachers found themselves relying on textbooks to a much greater extent than they initially intended. They did so for a variety of reasons, including limited time and energy, weaknesses in pedagogical knowledge of the content, insufficient knowledge of the curriculum to make sound decisions about alternatives, and a perceived need to teach in accord with standard operating procedures at the school. These patterns suggest that, given their stage of development, novice teachers should be encouraged to take advantage of the guidance provided by textbooks and teacher's manuals. Rather than categorically dismissing these resources, teacher educators should help novices learn to use them thoughtfully, by showing them how to select and modify content and activities, and providing guided practice (e.g., course assignments) in appropriate textbook use. They should also help novices to learn *from* textbooks and teacher's manuals, so that they can move toward increased independence from these materials as they gain in pedagogical expertise.

Cooperating Teachers as Teacher Educators

Patterns in several of the research programs alert us to the important role of the cooperating teacher in the learning-to-teach process. For student teaching to be more than practice teaching, and for student teachers to improve their abilities to teach and to think about their teaching, cooperating teachers must take an active role. They must model pedagogical thinking by demonstrating and then explaining to student teachers how they transform subject matter in ways that facilitate student understanding. They must also stimulate student teachers to talk about their reasons for doing things and provide constructive feedback based on observations on a regular, frequent basis.

However, as Feiman-Nemser and Buchmann (1987) note, cooperating teachers do not always have the expertise to be teacher educators. "Just as becoming a classroom teacher involves making a transition from person to professional, so too becoming a mentor involves making a transition from classroom teacher to teacher educator. Classroom teachers need time and commitment to develop the necessary understandings, skills and orientations and schools must broaden the scope of what teachers do and what they are rewarded for to include teacher education" (p. 272). The issue of resource allocation to teacher education should not be minimized. Without a reduced teaching load and time dedicated to working with student teachers, and without recognition and rewards for their efforts, there is little incentive for cooperating teachers to commit themselves to the role of teacher educator.

The Role of the University Supervisor

Another central player in the education of student teachers is the university supervisor. Much has been written about university supervisors' role in the learning-to-teach process (cf. Feiman-Nemser & Buchmann, 1987; Zeichner & Liston, 1987; Zeichner & Tabachnick, 1985) and about impediments to their effectiveness as teacher educators (cf. Calderhead, 1987). An in-depth analysis of the supervisory role is beyond the scope of this chapter; however, a few suggestions derived from the research on learning to teach are appropriate.

University supervisors serve the unique role of bridging the gap between the university and the public school. In this role, they can help student teachers apply knowledge derived from the scholarly literature on schooling, teaching, and learning to the realities of classroom life. By demonstrating the connection between scholarly knowledge and specific actions and decisions in the classroom, they can help student teachers develop cognitive skills that are grounded in the knowledge bases of teaching. To succeed in this role, university supervisors must act in concert with cooperating teachers and be seen as educators, rather than assessors, of preservice teachers.

CONCLUSION: AN ORIENTATION TO TEACHER PREPARATION

The research reported in this chapter clearly points out that learning to teach is a complex process, one that includes changes in cognition as well as observable behavior. Particularly difficult is the learning of cognitive skills such as planning, evaluation, and the transformation of subject matter knowledge for teaching. The research also provides evidence of limitations in learning that occur during the final stages of preservice preparation—pedagogical coursework and the student teaching experience. Students, even in some of the top colleges of education in the country, complete their teacher preparation programs with a limited ability to engage in the cognitive processes of teaching and with little change in their perceptions and conceptions of teaching.

In the previous section of this chapter, I offered several suggestions for modifying preservice teacher preparation in order to improve the learning-to-teach process. However, there is a fundamental issue that must be addressed prior to attempting these modifications, that of participants' general orientation to the teacher preparation experience and its capstone experience of student teaching. Specifically, several prominent researchers in education and teacher education have suggested that the view of student teaching as an apprenticeship, which is prevalent in teacher education programs both in the United States and abroad, serves as a major impediment to learning the cognitive skills of teaching (cf. Calderhead, 1987; Stones, 1984; Zeichner & Liston, 1987). Within an apprenticeship model, student teaching is viewed as an occasion to imitate and practice the behaviors modeled by the cooperating teacher and to demonstrate one's knowledge and skills to the university supervisor. The priority placed on proving one's instructional competence defines student teaching as an assessment task and the university supervisor as an assessor. This view of student teaching stresses the importance of observable behaviors and going through the motions of teaching, while undermining attempts to focus on inquiry and reflection.

This line of reasoning suggests that the first step in implementing a teacher education program (graduate or undergraduate) designed to facilitate learning to teach is to ensure that participants share a conception of student teaching as an occasion for learning the cognitive activities of teaching as well as the behaviors. This shared conception, unlike the apprenticeship model, must also foster an attitude of risk taking and experimentation, encouraging student teachers to try out new ideas and critically evaluate them, without worrying about the impact of their experiments on grades or formal evaluations within the program. With such a common orientation, participants from the university and public schools can work together to create an environment and a set of experiences designed to facilitate learning to teach and improving one's teaching over time. (See Chapter 7 for a discussion of this orientation toward the student teaching experience.) The suggestions offered above regarding content preparation, cognitive skills of teaching, use of textbooks, and the role of the cooperating teacher and university supervisor could aid in achieving these goals.

REFERENCES

BALL, D. L., & FEIMAN-NEMSER, S. (in press). The use of curricular materials: What beginning teachers learn and what they need to know. *Curriculum Inquiry*.

BECKER, H., GEER, B., HUGHES, E., & STRAUSS, A. (1961). *Boys in white*. Chicago: University of Chicago Press.

BERLINER, D. C. (1986). In pursuit of the expert pedagogue. *Educational Researcher, 15*(7), 5-13.

BERLINER, D. C. (1987). Ways of thinking about students and classrooms by more and less experienced teachers. In J. Calderhead (Ed.), *Exploring teachers' thinking* (pp. 60-83). London: Cassell Educational Limited.

BORKO, H. (1985). Student teachers' planning and evaluations of reading lessons. In J. Niles & R. Lalik (Eds.), *Issues in literacy: A research perspective. Thirty-fourth yearbook of the National Reading Conference*. New York: National Reading Conference.

BORKO, H., LALIK, R., LIVINGSTON, C., PECIC, K., & PERRY, D. (1986, April). *Learning to teach in the induction year: Two case studies*. Paper presented at the annual meeting of the American Educational Research Association, San Francisco.

BORKO, H., LALIK, R., & TOMCHIN, E. (1987). Student teachers' understandings of successful teaching. *Teaching and Teacher Education, 3*, 77-90.

BORKO, H., LIVINGSTON, C., MCCALEB, J., & MAURO, L. (in press). Student teachers' planning and post-lesson reflections: Patterns and implications for teacher preparation. In J. Calderhead (Ed.), *Teachers' professional learning*. London: Falmer Press.

BORKO, H., & NILES, J. (1987). Descriptions of teacher planning: Ideas for teachers and researchers. In V. Richardson-Koehler (Ed.), *Educators' handbook: A research perspective* (pp. 167–187). New York: Longman.

BORKO, H., & SHAVELSON, R. J. (in press). Teachers' decision making. In B. Jones & L. Idols (Eds.), *Dimensions of thinking and cognitive instruction.* New Jersey: Erlbaum.

BROPHY, J. E., & GOOD, T. L. (1986). Teacher behavior and student achievement. In M.C. Wittrock (Ed.), *Handbook of research on teaching* (3rd ed., pp. 328–375). New York: Macmillan.

CALDERHEAD, J. (1981). A psychological approach to research on teachers' decision making. *British Educational Research Journal, 7,* 51–57.

CALDERHEAD, J. (1983, April). *Research into teachers' and student teachers' cognitions: Exploring the nature of classroom practice.* Paper presented at the annual meeting of the American Educational Research Association, Montreal, Canada.

CALDERHEAD, J. (1987, April). *Cognition and metacognition in teachers' professional development.* Paper presented at the annual meeting of the American Educational Research Association, Washington, DC.

CARTER, K., CUSHING, K., SABERS, D., STEIN, P., & BERLINER, D. (in press). Expert-novice differences in perceiving and processing visual classroom stimuli. *Journal of Teacher Education.*

CARTER, K., SABERS, D., CUSHING, K., PINNEGAR, S., & BERLINER, D. (1987). Processing and using information about students: A study of expert, novice and postulant teachers. *Teaching and Teacher Education, 3,* 147–157.

CLARK, C. M., & PETERSON, P. L. (1986). Teachers' thought processes. In M. C. Wittrock (Ed.), *Handbook of research on teaching* (3rd ed., pp. 255–296). New York: Macmillan.

DEGROOT, A.D. (1965). *Thought and choice in chess.* The Hague: Mouton.

EGAN, D. E., & SCHWARTZ, B. J. (1979). Chunking in recall of symbolic drawings. *Memory and Cognition, 7,* 149-158.

FEIMAN-NEMSER, S. (1983). Learning to teach. In L. S. Shulman & G. Sykes (Eds.), *Handbook of teaching and policy* (pp. 150–170). New York: Longman.

FEIMAN-NEMSER, S., & BUCHMANN, M. (1986). The first year of teacher preparation: Transition to pedagogical thinking? *Journal of Curriculum Studies, 18,* 239–256.

FEIMAN-NEMSER, S., & BUCHMANN, M. (1987). When is student teaching teacher education? *Teaching and Teacher Education, 3,* 255–273.

FEIMAN-NEMSER, S., & BUCHMANN, M. (in press). Describing teacher education; A framework and a longitudinal study of six students. *Elementary School Journal.*

FREDERICKSEN, N. (1984). Implications of cognitive theory for instruction in problem solving. *Review of Educational Research, 54,* 363–408.

GAGE, N. L. (1984). What do we know about teaching effectiveness? *Phi Delta Kappan, 66,* 87–93.

GROSSMAN, P. L. (1987, April). *A tale of two teachers: The role of subject matter orientation in teaching.* Paper presented at the annual meeting of the American Educational Research Association, Washington, DC.

GROSSMAN, P. L., & RICHERT, A. E. (1986, April). *Unacknowledged knowledge growth: A reexamination of the effects of teacher education.* Paper presented at the annual meeting of the American Educational Research Association, San Francisco.

HOUSNER, L. D., & GRIFFEY, D. C. (1985). Teacher cognition: Differences in planning and interactive decision making between experienced and inexperienced teachers. *Research Quarterly for Exercise and Sport, 56,* 45–53.

LARKIN, J., MCDERMOTT, J., SIMON, D. P., & SIMON, H. A. (1980). Expert and novice performance in solving physics problems. *Science, 208,* 1135–1142.

LEINHARDT, G. (1986, April). *Math lessons: A contrast of novice and expert competence.* Paper presented at the annual meeting of the American Educational Research Association, San Francisco.

LEINHARDT, G., & GREENO, J. G. (1986). The cognitive skill of teaching. *Journal of Educational Psychology, 78,* 75–95.

LEINHARDT, G., & SMITH, D. (1985). Expertise in mathematics instruction: Subject matter knowledge. *Journal of Educational Psychology, 77,* 241–247.

PETERSON, P. L., & COMEAUX, M. A. (1987). Teachers' schemata for classroom events: The mental scaffolding of teachers' thinking during classroom events. *Teaching and Teacher Education, 3,* 319–331.

REED, S. K. (1982). *Cognition: Theory and applications.* Belmont, CA: Brooks/Cole Publishers.

RINGSTAFF, C., & HAYMORE, J. (1987, April). *The influence of subject matter background on planning and instruction: An English teacher and science teacher teach Cannery Row.* Paper presented at the annual meeting of the American Educational Research Association, Washington, DC.

ROSENSHINE, B., & STEVENS, R. (1986). Teaching functions. In M. C. Wittrock (Ed.), *Handbook of research on teaching* (3rd ed., pp. 376–391). New York: Macmillan.

SHAVELSON, R. J., & STERN, P. (1981). Research on teachers' pedagogical thoughts, judgments, decisions, and behaviors. *Review of Educational Research, 51,* 455–498.

SHULMAN, L. S. (1986). Those who understand: Knowledge growth in teaching. *Educational Researcher, 15*(2), 4–14.

SHULMAN, L. S. (1987). Knowledge and teaching: Foundations of the new reform. *Harvard Educational Review, 57,* 1–22.

STONES, E. (1984). *Supervision in teacher education.* London: Methuen.

TABACHNICK, B. R., & ZEICHNER, K. (1984). The impact of the student teaching experience on the development of teacher perspectives. *Journal of Teacher Education, 35,* 28–42.

TABACHNICK, B. R., & ZEICHNER, K. (1985). The development of teacher perspectives: Conclusions from the Wisconsin studies of teacher solicitation. *Dutch Journal of Teacher Education, 3,* 117–124.

WARNER, D. R. (1987). *An exploratory study to identify the distinctive features of experienced teachers' thinking about teaching.* Doctoral dissertation, The University of New England, Armidale, NSW 2351, Australia.

WILSON, S. M., SHULMAN, L. S., & RICHERT, A. E. (1987). "150 different ways" of knowing: Representations of knowledge in teaching. In J. Calderhead (Ed.), *Exploring teachers' thinking* (pp. 104–124). London: Cassell Educational Limited.

ZEICHNER, K. M., & LISTON, D. P. (1987). Teaching student teachers to reflect. *Harvard Educational Review, 57,* 23–48.

ZEICHNER, K., & TABACHNICK, B. R. (1985). The development of teacher perspectives: Social strategies and institutional control in the socialization of beginning teachers. *Journal of Education for Teachers, 11,* 1–25.

6

THE ROLE OF EDUCATION IN THE ACADEMIC DISCIPLINES IN TEACHER EDUCATION

Charles W. Anderson

INTRODUCTION

A large portion of every preservice teacher preparation program—graduate or undergraduate—occurs outside Colleges of Education in the academic departments. A key function of academic courses is to provide prospective teachers with the disciplinary knowledge they need to teach well. In general, though, we in teacher education are not very clear about what that knowledge might be. We require courses, count credits, and award credentials without either a serious discussion of what disciplinary knowledge prospective teachers need or an analysis of how they use that knowledge.

The need for earnest dialogue involving professors inside and outside the Colleges of Education as well as others involved in the training and certification of teachers is obvious. Achieving such a dialogue, however, will not be easy. Communication about the academic preparation of teachers has been limited not only by institutional and organizational factors, but also by the absence of a common intellectual framework that could serve as a basis for communication. Professors in education often differ substantially from colleagues in academic departments in their views

The author would like to acknowledge the helpful comments on an earlier draft of this chapter and suggestions for revision by Suzanne Wilson, Bill McDiarmid, Deborah Ball, Walter Doyle, and Anita Woolfolk.

of disciplinary knowledge, teaching, and the relation between the two. These differences can stymie attempts at serious communication.

The purpose of this chapter is to outline some of the key issues that educators and academic professors could discuss productively and to suggest some elements of a framework that might encourage thoughtful analysis of those issues. The first section of the chapter briefly describes a view of good subject matter teaching, including an analysis of how successful teachers of academic content use disciplinary knowledge. Based on this picture of successful teaching, the next section considers the nature of the disciplinary knowledge that teachers need for such instruction. To make this knowledge available to prospective teachers will be difficult, however. The reasons for these difficulties are explored in the third section of the chapter. Finally, I suggest some implications of the issues discussed for the graduate education of teachers.

THE USES OF DISCIPLINARY KNOWLEDGE IN GOOD TEACHING

To begin our discussion, we must establish some basic premises about the nature of good teaching and the role that disciplinary knowledge plays in it. If mere survival in a classroom is the goal, then teachers don't need to know very much about the content that they are teaching. There are patterns of practice in which disciplinary knowledge plays a relatively unimportant role (cf. Hollon & Anderson, 1987; Olson, 1983; Smith & Sendelbach, 1982). Teachers following such patterns can—and do—keep their students busy and out of trouble without knowing much more than the students about the subjects they are teaching. Some students even learn in such classrooms. If we are satisfied with this type of teaching, then we can call off the dialogue about academic preparation and concentrate on other issues.

We have good reason not to be satisfied with this level of teaching practice, however, and to believe that students of such teachers are missing something important. This section uses Bereiter and Scardamalia's (1987) idea of "an attainable form of high literacy" and Wilson, Shulman and Richert's (1987) discussion of knowledge transformation in teaching to develop an account of successful teaching practice in which disciplinary knowledge plays a critical role.

Teaching for an Attainable Form of High Literacy

Bereiter and Scardamalia (1987) contrast high literacy, necessary for sustained analytical efforts or the production of original work, with low literacy, the skills and knowledge necessary for basic functioning in our society. Although Bereiter and Scardamalia focus on reading and writing in their article, this contrast can be extended to other school subjects, as in Table 6-1.

Bereiter and Scardamalia argue that the schools are currently faced with a dilemma. Traditionally, high literacy has been taught to a small elite through a curriculum

TABLE 6-1   Functions of Low and High Literacy in Different Subjects

SUBJECT	FUNCTION OF LOW LITERACY	FUNCTION OF HIGH LITERACY
Reading (cf. Palincsar & Brown, 1984; Bereiter & Scardamalia, 1987)	Obtaining information from text, personal entertainment	Development of functional, productive knowledge, literary appreciation
Writing (cf. Bereiter & Scardamalia, 1987; Florio-Ruane & Dunn, 1985)	Filling out forms, personal letters	Development and communication of personally significant knowledge and beliefs
Mathematics (cf. Romberg, 1983; Hiebert, 1984; Skemp, 1978)	Basic measurement, calculations using basic facts	Mathematical abstraction, invention, proof, application
Science (cf. Eisemon, undated; Anderson, 1987)	Trust in science, knowledge of facts about the world	Scientific description, explanation, prediction, control of natural phenomena
Social studies (cf. Anyon, 1981)	Social and political conformity, knowledge of facts about history, geography	Ability to analyze and influence political, social, and economic systems

based on the classics and the traditional disciplines, while the vast majority of students have attained low literacy, and some have remained functionally illiterate.

There is a rhetoric that justifies a low literacy curriculum for nonelite students. Such students are described as needing more work on "basic skills" before they are ready to engage in "higher order thinking." In general, however, their basic skills are always found to be wanting, so they are exposed to a low-literacy curriculum throughout their academic careers. In contrast, even very young students in elite schools are taught the knowledge and skills needed for high literacy (cf. Anyon, 1981; Erickson, 1984). Social reconstructionist curriculum theorists argue that this is a basic mechanism by which schools help to maintain the class structure of our society.

Although such an arrangement is clearly inequitable, there have been some important ways in which it has always "worked." The elite schools prepared professionals and managers, while most students acquired socially useful and economically valuable skills that prepared them adequately for lower level occupations. The economy is changing, however. Jobs demanding mastery of basic low literacy skills such as computation or spelling are being automated out of existence at the same time as there is a greater need for workers who are prepared for jobs requiring intelligent decision making. Thus considerations of economics as well as equity demand that we help more students attain some form of high literacy.

This goal presents a considerable challenge. The traditional discipline-and-classic-based curriculum is embedded in an elite culture that is not shared by most students. We are therefore faced with a task that Bereiter and Scardamalia describe as "cultural bootstrapping," in which we must develop a curriculum and methods of instruction that embody "an attainable form of high literacy," one which empowers non-elite students to engage in the activities of high-literate people.

As a society, presently we have not been very successful at attaining this goal; doing so will involve much more than the reform of teacher education. However, we clearly should be trying to educate teachers who are part of the solution rather than part of the problem. This suggests a definition of "good teaching." Good teachers are those who are adequately prepared to help their students achieve an attainable form of high literacy.

The Transformation of Disciplinary Knowledge in Teaching

We can argue on intuitive grounds that teachers who are going to help their students achieve an attainable form of high literacy need to be highly literate in the subjects they are teaching. Such an argument provides little curricular guidance, however, for the educators of prospective teachers. *What* exactly do prospective teachers need to know about their disciplines, and *how* will they use that knowledge. Wilson, Shulman, and Richert (1987) suggest answers to both the "what" and the "how" questions. In this chapter I wish to accept and extend their answer to the "how" question while suggesting an alternative to their description of the nature of the disciplinary knowledge needed for successful teaching.

In response to the "how" question, Wilson, Shulman, and Richert suggest the model of the activities of teaching reproduced in Figure 6–1. Teaching is portrayed as a cyclical process, beginning with *comprehension* of the content to be taught, followed by *transformation* of the content into a form that makes it accessible to students, then *instruction*, *evaluation*, and *reflection*, leading to new comprehension and another teaching cycle at a higher level of understanding and performance. This cycle is not an all-purpose model of teaching. It might make as much sense, for example, to portray teachers as starting by setting up classroom routines and activity structures or as starting from consideration of students and their needs. However, this chapter will use Wilson, Shulman, and Richert's model because it focuses attention on just those planning and teaching processes that make the heaviest demands on teachers' disciplinary knowledge (see Figure 6-1).

In particular, Wilson, Shulman, and Richert emphasize the importance of the *transformation* of knowledge in teaching. Good teachers, teachers who are helping their students attain some form of high literacy, must take their disciplinary knowledge and transform it into curriculum, that is, a plan for learning that makes disciplinary knowledge accessible to students and helps them to master it.

Thus, transformation plays a key role in Wilson and Shulman's answer to the "how" question posed above. Successful teachers use disciplinary knowledge by transforming that knowledge into something that students can understand (as well as for other activities of teaching, including comprehension, instruction, evaluation, and

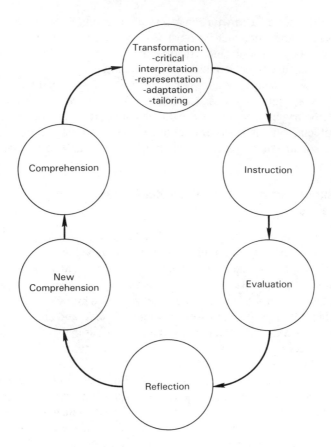

FIGURE 6-1 Model of Pedagogical Reasoning. (From Wilson, S. M., and Shulman, L. S.(1987), "150 Different Ways" of Knowing: Representations of Knowledge in Teaching. In J. Calderhead (Ed.), *Exploring Teacher Thinking.* London: Cassell PLC.)

reflection). Their model is less helpful, I believe, in answering the "what" question. What is the nature of the disciplinary knowledge that teachers need to successfully carry out this transformation process? This question is addressed in the following section.

THE NATURE OF DISCIPLINARY KNOWLEDGE NEEDED FOR GOOD TEACHING

Anyone who has ever tried to teach knows that transforming disciplinary knowledge into a form that students can understand is a difficult process, a process that demands a great deal of subject matter knowledge. How many times have we all said that we "never really understood" some topic until we had to teach it? But what is this "real understanding" that we need in order to teach a topic? Such understanding clearly includes certain facts, concepts, and procedures, but it is something more as well. The purpose of this section is to describe and illustrate the nature of that "something more."

Teaching demands that prospective teachers focus not only on individual facts, concepts, or procedures, but also on relationships. The *structure* of knowledge in a discipline refers to relationships among the facts, concepts, and procedures of a discipline. What are the important themes and how do they tie the details together? How are ideas from one branch of a discipline (or one chapter of a textbook) related to ideas from another? The *functions* or purposes of knowledge in a discipline are the activities that knowledge of the discipline prepares people to accomplish (see Table 6-1). What can we do with our disciplinary knowledge that is personally satisfying or socially useful? The third aspect of understanding, the *development* of knowledge in a discipline, can be analyzed either historically or as it occurs in individual learners. How did we build the growing, changing systems of knowledge that now exist in our academic disciplines? What simpler forms of understanding are available for students who are not ready for mature expertise?

The following passages elaborate these ideas of structure, function, and development, using vignettes from my experiences as a teacher educator to illustrate how difficult it is for beginning teachers to master these aspects of the disciplines that they will teach. All of the vignettes involve prospective secondary teachers with academic majors in the discipline that they will teach. Thus their problems are not attributable simply to ignorance of the relevant facts and concepts. The examples are drawn from mathematics and science, the subjects in which I do most of my work. Readers who specialize in other disciplines, however, can probably supply parallel examples of their own.

Structure of Knowledge

Elaine is a junior mathematics major taking a curriculum course during the second term of her teacher education program. She and her classmates have just read the article by Wilson, Shulman, and Richert (1987) and have completed an assignment in which they were to observe a mathematics lesson being taught and discuss how the teachers transformed disciplinary content, using different representations of knowledge in their lessons. (For example, problems involving the area of figures can be represented and solved in a variety of ways, including figures with squares drawn on them, multiplication of numbers representing length and width, graphs, or algebraic formulas.) Elaine writes in her report:

"Wilson and Shulman wrote about representations for subject matter that teachers use to help if their students understand new material. It is difficult in some subjects to have many different representations for the same subject, for instance, in math. Some material in math can basically be explained in only one way."

*   *   *   *   *

Ann has been very successful in her teacher education program, making grades of 4.0 in every course before student teaching. Now Ann, a biology major, is student teaching in a middle school life science class. I visit her for the first time as her university supervisor.

Today Ann is teaching about atoms, molecules, elements, and compounds, and she does not look like a 4.0 student. Her teaching is uninspired and didactic, her way of distinguishing molecules from compounds is not quite right, and some of her examples are fictitious (He_2, Zn_2).

When I talk to Ann after the lesson she acknowledges her disappointment in her performance and talks about how difficult she finds it to come up with good examples. When she asks for help I ask a question back: How are you going to use these concepts later in the year? Ann says that she doesn't know; it's just something that you have to teach. Her mentor teacher, however, quickly names several topics where these concepts play an important role: Photosynthesis, digestion, respiration, ecological matter cycling. As he does this he mentions examples of elements and compounds that the middle school students will need to be familiar with.

Elaine and Ann were both having difficulties that arose from their failure to see structure, or patterns of relationships among the facts, concepts, and procedures of their disciplines. Elaine had difficulty seeing mathematics as a discipline where multiple representations are possible for any given problem or concept. Although she had often been exposed to such alternative representations, she had not seen clearly the relationships among them. Ann was stymied in her search for examples because she had trouble seeing relationships between the lesson she was teaching and the rest of the course. Elaine's and Ann's difficulties are shared by many other beginning teachers. Most find it very hard to see relationships among the ideas they are teaching and to use those relationships in transforming disciplinary knowledge.

As Phillips (1986) points out, the concept of "structure" can be a slippery one. Knowledge in a discipline clearly does not have the kind of static, easily recognizable structure that we see in the parts of an engine or the books in a library. The structure of an academic discipline is better captured by Toulmin's (1972) metaphor of an "intellectual ecology." We understand ecosystems to be highly structured, but not in a single, static way. Instead, we have a multitude of different ways of describing the interrelations among the organisms in an ecosystem (e.g., trophic levels, matter cycles, energy flow, populations, niches, habitats). Each pattern of relationships is constantly changing as the ecosystem itself evolves. An understanding of an ecosystem entails an appreciation of its multiple interwoven structures.

The ecological example can also be used to illustrate another characteristic of an expert's understanding of the structure of a discipline: The expert recognizes the existence of a variety of different kinds of entities within the ecosystem. To the expert the energy and matter that flow through the organisms of an ecosystem, the habitats that they live in, and the niches that they occupy are as "real" as the organisms themselves. Each of these entities provides its own way of organizing the ecosystem, and an expert can choose the organizing principle that best suits the needs of a particular problem. In contrast, a novice may see an ecosystem as simply a collection of individual organisms. Thus the novice's understanding lacks the concepts or entities that enable the expert to see the structural relationships.

Neither Elaine nor Ann had achieved expertise of the type described above. Elaine saw mathematics primarily as a large collection of algorithms for solving particular types of problems. She had few resources for seeing the relationships among problems or algorithms that she had initially encountered separately. Although Ann could organize her biological knowledge in a variety of ways, she had trouble seeing relationships based on the chemical substances that organisms are made of and that are passed from one organism to another.

The academic disciplines are systems of knowledge so rich and complex that no one could ever fully understand all the structural relationships within them. The transformation of disciplinary knowledge for teaching, however, can be accomplished well only by people who are aware of a rich array of structural relationships within a discipline and who can use those relationships to reorganize their knowledge and make it accessible to students.

Functions of Knowledge

When I evaluate a prospective teacher's plans to teach a unit, I often ask, "Why do want to teach *that*? Why should your students learn it?" I would like to hear justifications that mention activities like those in Table 6–1, arguments that the knowledge will be used for activities that are somehow personally, economically, or socially worthwhile. My students have a great deal of difficulty developing such justifications, however. What comes to them much more easily is some version of "They will need this for the next course."

*　*　*　*　*

A group of elementary student teachers is meeting to discuss mathematics teaching. The discussion is led by Deborah Ball, who challenges them to develop a word problem that can be solved with the expression, "1 3/4 divided by 1/2." Only one student suggests an appropriate example: "How many half cakes are in 1 3/4 cakes?" Most students suggest problems that go through a variety of contortions to arrive at 3 1/2, which they all know to be the correct answer. The following is typical: "I buy 1 3/4 pizzas that are split into four slices each and divide them equally with my friend. How many slices does each of us get?" (Note that this problem actually involves division by two rather than division by 1/2. The logic of the problem is: 1 3/4 = 7/4 divided by 2 = 3 1/2 fourths.)

Ball has also included this question in a series of interviews with secondary mathematics majors. Only two of eight students interviewed have been able to suggest appropriate story problems without considerable difficulty.

The students in the vignettes above were having difficulty relating disciplinary knowledge to activities that students might engage in for purposes other than passing tests, difficulties that I describe as having to do with the purposes or *functions* of disciplinary knowledge. As Table 6–1 indicates, knowledge that we acquire in school does (or at least should) have uses: Academic knowledge helps us to engage in a variety of worthwhile activities. Some of those activities are "practical applications" that have utilitarian value. Other activities we consider personally worthwhile even though they have little practical importance. Most of us consider our lives richer if we can find the Pleiades in the nighttime sky, if we can see echoes of Shakespeare in contemporary literature, or if we understand how the patterns of our lives and our institutions are rooted in the historical past.

Whereas an understanding of the structure of disciplinary knowledge involves seeing patterns of relationships *within* a discipline, understanding function involves seeing relationships *between* the discipline and the rest of the world. Teachers must see how their disciplinary knowledge is related to the events of daily life, to issues they confront as workers and as citizens, and to knowledge in other disciplines. Furthermore, they must help their students become aware of those relationships.

Good teachers need to understand the functions of knowledge in the subjects that they teach for both curricular and instructional reasons. They are constantly faced with curricular decisions, deciding what knowledge is worthwhile and what is not. They must also decide what their students will *do*—what activities they will engage in—during classroom instruction. A good understanding of the functions of disciplinary knowledge is necessary to do either task well.

Development of Knowledge

Betty is a prospective teacher who is a science major and a good student. She is preparing to teach a unit on heat to her fifth grade class. She is puzzled, though, about where to start. She reasons as follows: Heat is a form of energy, so in order to understand heat, the students should understand energy. But I have already tried to teach them about the scientific conception of energy, and they just don't get it. The concept is too difficult and abstract for them. What can I do?

* * * * *

Several secondary biology majors are discussing their plans for teaching one-week units. Most of the unit plans share a common problem: They include far too much content for the time available. One student, for example, plans to cover the following topics in five-day units on fishes: Evolution of fishes, classes of fishes (named in Latin) and their characteristics, adaptation of fishes to their environment, structure, and function of fish body systems (down to the level of parts of the brain). The methods course instructors immediately begin suggesting ways to reduce and simplify the content that she plans to teach. She demurs, "But it's all interconnected!"

The prospective teachers described above are showing awareness of important patterns of relationships: the structure and functions of their disciplines. They clearly understand something of the intricate web of meaning that interconnects the concepts of the discipline. However, they cannot figure out how to communicate with students for whom the concepts are too numerous and web of meaning too intricate to master in the time available. These prospective teachers can see no alternative except to "rip apart" the web of meaning and give their students lists of isolated concepts to practice and memorize. How can they simplify disciplinary knowledge without stripping it of meaning and vitality? To put the issue another way, if understanding requires mastering a set of structural relationships too complex for students to master, then how is it possible to teach for understanding?

There is a way out of the dilemma, a way that involves recognizing and searching for alternate forms of understanding. The knowledge in a discipline can be simplified not by dissecting it into its component parts, but by considering the patterns of its *development*, both in individual learners and in the history of the discipline. David Hawkins (1973) writes eloquently about this kind of teaching with regard to mathematics:

> If a teacher's grasp of subject-matter must extend beyond the conventional image of mathematics, we must then face the question of definition in a new form—what is at stake is not the nature of the end-product usually *called* mathematics, but of that whole domain in which mathematical ideas and procedures germinate, sprout, and take root, *and* in the end produce the visible upper branching, leafing, and flowering which all we here so value, and which wither when uprooted (p. 119).

Toulmin (1972) also uses organic metaphors in discussing the historical development of knowledge in the sciences. He compares the development of scientific concepts to organic evolution, or alternatively to the development of our social and economic institutions. Like the organisms of an ecosystem, Toulmin portrays the concepts of a discipline as drawing their full meaning and vitality only from the network of interrelationships that tie them together. But like an ecosystem, the discipline is always changing. Old concepts evolve into new ones, or new concepts, sometimes imported from other disciplines, compete with the concepts that were there before and alter patterns of relationships. Many people (e.g., Posner, Strike, Hewson, & Gertzog, 1982) have suggested that the development of disciplinary knowledge in individuals follows a similar pattern.

Both Hawkins and Toulmin make a philosophical point that is of practical importance to teachers. Learners cannot assemble disciplinary knowledge from its component parts as we do a machine or a building; instead they must construct meaningful knowledge through a complex process that more closely resembles organic growth or evolution. The task of a teacher, then, is to help learners through this complex developmental process. To do the job well obviously requires substantial understanding of learners, but it places great demands on teachers' subject matter knowledge as well. Teachers must somehow relate their own understanding to the alternate forms or levels of understanding that their pupils bring with them to class. They must deal with multitudes of wrong answers and half-right answers, somehow sorting out what is legitimate and what is problematical about each.

Many teachers manage to avoid these issues, implicitly or explicitly telling their students to "just memorize this," and thus settling for a low literacy curriculum. In order for nonelite students to achieve an attainable form of high literacy, however, teachers must see the relationships between their own disciplinary knowledge and students' alternate views of the world, and they must help students to develop forms of understanding that are incomplete, but still functional.

Summary: Disciplinary Knowledge Needed for Good Teaching

This section has examined *what* teachers need to know about their disciplines in order to teach well, with special attention to that aspect of teaching that Wilson, Shulman, and Richert (1987) describe as the transformation of knowledge. Prospective teachers must know some basic facts, definitions, and procedures in the subjects that they teach; prospective elementary teachers, in particular, often lack knowledge at this level. As the vignettes in this section illustrate, however, even prospective secondary teachers who are familiar with the facts, definitions, and procedures that they are teaching are often poorly prepared to transform their disciplinary knowledge into a form that is meaningful to learners. Their difficulties often involve understanding patterns of relationships. In order to help their students achieve an attainable form of high literacy, teachers must comprehend the *structure* of knowledge, or relationships among facts, concepts, and procedures in their disciplines, *functions* of knowledge, or how disciplinary knowledge is used for personally or socially significant activities, and the *development* of knowledge in the disciplines, or relationships between that disciplinary knowledge and alternate forms or levels of understanding. Successful teaching of a school subject demands an understanding of structure, function, and development of knowledge in the discipline like that described in the "high literacy" column of Table 6-2.

However, as the vignettes above illustrate, I would not characterize most of the students I encounter in teacher education programs as having attained high literacy in their disciplines. The best students have what I might describe as "latent high literacy": tacit understanding of structure, function, and development that they can activate and make explicit with the help of teaching experience and a good teacher education program. Even prospective teachers with majors in their disciplines, however, often enter teacher education programs with what I would characterize as "highly developed low literacy." They know *lots* of facts, definitions, and algorithms, but not very much about the relationships that they will need to master in order to teach well.

We could do better. Academic departments could educate undergraduates about the structure, function, and development of their disciplines. Teacher education programs, graduate or undergraduate, could help prospective teachers improve and use their disciplinary knowledge. I believe that there are deep-seated beliefs and habits of thought on both sides, however, that will serve as barriers to improvement, or even to substantive dialogue about the problem. The next section explores some of those barriers.

TABLE 6-2   Low *versus* High Literacy

CHARACTERISTIC OF KNOWLEDGE	LOW LITERACY	HIGH LITERACY
Structure : What does knowledge consist of?	Facts, algorithms, definitions	Dynamic, changing, richly interconnected conceptual structures
How is it organized?	Lists, outlines	
Function : How is knowledge used?	Work and diversions of lower and lower middle classes: short-term, repetitive activities with prescribed outcomes	Work and diversions of affluent professionals and executive elite: sustained creative or analytical efforts, development of new knowledge
Development : How does knowledge develop in individuals and in society?	Acquisition of facts, algorithms, definitions followed by application	Process of conceptual change similar to organic evolution or ecological succession

BARRIERS TO IMPROVEMENT

The education of prospective teachers begins with academic coursework. If graduate programs of teacher preparation become more common, then academic coursework will constitute most if not all of the baccalaureate education of teachers. This academic coursework perhaps ought to give students a good understanding of the structure, function, and development of knowledge in their disciplines, but sometimes does not. Similarly, teacher education coursework perhaps ought to help students learn to transform their disciplinary knowledge for the purposes of teaching, but sometimes does not. This section explores the question of why professors in both academic and education departments often fail to do a better job.

Barriers to Improvement Among Academic Professors

First, a disclaimer: This section draws on a much less extensive base of personal experience than the section on the nature of students' knowledge. Three of the four vignettes below (and many of my personal convictions) come from discussions with three science professors who worked with me on a project to develop instructional materials for nonmajors' biological and physical science courses (Anderson, 1986). It is perhaps an indication of the general absence of dialogue between educators and academic professors that those are the only academic professors with whom I have had sustained discussions of college teaching, though I have had shorter discussions with many other academic professors.

Academic professors' beliefs about structure and functions of knowledge.

I am discussing a nonmajors' biology course that we all teach with two natural science professors. I suggest that we depart from the order of topics in the textbook, which follows the standard practice of starting with the smallest biological systems, molecules, discussing how they are combined into cells, which are combined into tissues, then organs, multicellular organisms, and so forth up to the largest systems, ecosystems, and the biosphere (Schwab's [1964] "dogmatic order"). I advocate that instead we start with multicellular organisms, the level of organization most familiar to students, then work down to cells and molecules, which are much less familiar to our students (Schwab's "order of inquiry"). The natural science professors see little merit in my argument. The molecules and cells are the building blocks, they say. They should come first.

*   *   *   *   *

I am discussing their academic coursework with a pair of senior biology majors. How many biology tests have you taken at Michigan State, I ask, that were *not* multiple choice (or other short-answer forms such as true-false or fill in the blank)? They shake their heads: Not one. Later, when I direct the same question to another pair of students, they can recall only one biology course whose tests included essay questions.

I argued above that a rich understanding of the structure of a discipline can help teachers be more flexible in their teaching, seeing a variety of ways of organizing and presenting content. Yet the professors in the first vignette, who clearly had a deep understanding of the structure of biology, seemed notably inflexible in their thinking about biology curriculum. They were aware of alternate patterns of relationships, yet they would not use those alternate patterns to organize course content. I attribute our disagreement primarily to differing priorities in the teaching of science. The science professors were concerned primarily with developing a logical presentation of science content; my first priority was the development of student thinking. It is not clear who was "right" in this discussion; it is clear that an understanding of alternative disciplinary structure does not automatically lead professors to think flexibly about curriculum and instruction.

It is also clear that although professors may use their own disciplinary knowledge for the high literacy functions described in Table 6–1, they do not necessarily help their students to do the same. When the primary function for which prospective teachers have used their knowledge is passing multiple choice tests, is it surprising that they sometimes have trouble constructing meaningful, coherent explanations for a roomful of students? Many academic professors seem to define their teaching as a process of explaining a body of content to their students, then testing to see whether the students have learned it. Although this view of teaching seems reasonable, it produces students with a very limited understanding of the functions of disciplinary knowledge and with little skill in using their own knowledge for purposes other than passing tests.

Academic professors' beliefs about the development of knowledge.

In another discussion of the nonmajors' biology course we are talking about whether to include coverage of the Hardy-Weinberg law in teaching about evolution by natural selection. (The Hardy-Weinberg law is used to calculate gene frequencies in populations and to study change due to natural selection.) I point out that most students' explanations of how giraffes came to have long necks or cheetahs became fast runners reveal incorrect understanding of genetics and natural selection. I suggest that improving the students' explanations should be our first priority, and that we don't have time for an adequate treatment of both the explanations and the Hardy-Weinberg law. They disagree, growing frustrated with my arguments about what the students can meaningfully understand in the time available. Finally, one of the professors exclaims, "Look, it's *our* job to teach this stuff and *their* job to learn it, and if they don't understand then they ought to study harder!"

*   *   *   *   *

In a related effort to develop improvements in a nonmajors' physical science course I give the professor a sample of student pretests from his class. The pretests ask the students a series of short essay questions that seem to me to reveal clearly the kinds of misconceptions that the students are bringing with them to the course. A few weeks later he gives me back the tests, unread. "I didn't know how you wanted them interpreted," he says.

The science professors with whom I have worked generally have well-developed ideas about the structure and function of their disciplines (though not always the same as mine). Some are also interested in the historical development of their disciplines (though not necessarily as a source of ideas for their teaching). Many believe quite emphatically, though, that it is the students' job to understand them, and not the other way around. They are often unreceptive to the idea of adapting courses to the developmental needs of their students, regarding such adaptations as attempts to make things easier for students by compromising course standards and the integrity of the discipline.

There is a sense in which their perception is correct. In the first vignette above, for example, I *was* arguing for a less complete and integrated presentation of scientific theory than the one the professors wanted. There are other ways in which standards and integrity can be compromised, however. By covering extensive amounts of content, then relying on multiple choice tests to evaluate student learning, the professors, highly literate in the disciplines themselves, settle for a low literacy curriculum for their undergraduate students.

My perception of the professors with whom I worked is that they found themselves in a curricular dilemma not unlike that of the prospective teacher (described above) who wanted to include so much in her unit on fishes. They were very aware of the network of structural and functional relationships that tie together the concepts of their disciplines, and, lacking a developmental perspective, they saw no way to remove concepts without destroying the network. As a consequence, when they taught they often satisfied their own need to tell their students about as many of those concepts and relationships as possible, rather than satisfying the students' need to develop their own networks of structural and functional relationships.

Thus, prospective teachers are likely to enter teacher education programs sharing their professors' ignorance of how knowledge develops in themselves and other learners. Unfortunately, they probably will *not* share their professors' appreciation of the complex, dynamic structure and functions of the discipline that they have studied, in part because academic professors tend not to think very deeply about how they might help undergraduate students achieve an attainable—though necessarily incomplete—form of high literacy in their disciplines. This clearly puts a considerable burden on teacher education programs to help prospective teachers improve and use their disciplinary knowledge. Unfortunately, most teacher education programs are not up to the challenge.

Barriers to Improvement among Professors of Education

In their book for prospective teachers, *Approaches to Teaching*, Gary Fenstermacher and Jonas Soltis (1986) present, as more or less equally defensible alternatives, three philosophical orientations to teaching, which they label executive, therapist, and liberationist. One of these approaches, the liberationist, advocates a classical high literacy curriculum; it is clearly compatible with Wilson, Shulman, and Richert's model and with most of the discussion above (with the important exception of Bereiter and Scardamalia's concern for nonelite students). Another approach, the executive, is built around the process of specifying objectives, teaching to those objectives, and testing for mastery of those objectives, a technology that seems best suited to a fragmented, low literacy curriculum. The third approach, the therapist, focuses primarily on students' social and emotional growth.

I think I know many professors of education who advocate and use approaches to teaching that resemble the executive therapist orientations in their lack of attention to the comprehension and transformation of disciplinary knowledge. Are these legitimate approaches to teaching? At best, courses based on such approaches do little to help prospective teachers understand what they know about the disciplines that they will teach and how they will use that knowledge in teaching. At worst, such approaches encourage prospective teachers to believe that academic knowledge doesn't really play a particularly important role in good teaching.

As the teaching performance of many university professors indicates, even people who are very highly literate in a discipline are not completely prepared to teach. At the very least, they need a "bridging language" that helps them link their disciplinary knowledge to the job of teaching a roomful of children, and they need practice and help in transforming their disciplinary knowledge for teaching. Most teacher education programs, however, do little to help their students deal with these problems because most teacher educators do not recognize them as curricular priorities.

IMPLICATIONS FOR THE GRADUATE EDUCATION OF TEACHERS

Early in this chapter I suggested that our goal in teacher education should be to prepare teachers who could help all of their students (not just an elite few) achieve an attainable form of high literacy. That is, we should be preparing teachers who can help their students acquire disciplinary knowledge and use it in flexible, creative, productive ways (see Table 6-1), even though they may not fully master the traditional discipline and classics-based curriculum.

I have tried to show in this chapter how teaching in this way demands a great deal of subject matter knowledge. Even if the content being taught is "simple" from a disciplinary point of view, a successful teacher must think deeply and flexibly about the relationships among facts, concepts, and procedures that constitute the structure of knowledge in the discipline, about the many functions that the content to be taught might have in the classroom and outside, and about the many different forms or levels of understanding that students exhibit as they develop disciplinary knowledge.

I have also argued that neither academic courses nor professional education courses are currently doing a particularly good job of helping prospective teachers develop the knowledge that they need. This chapter concludes with some suggestions about how teacher educators can think about and try to meet the challenge of improving prospective teachers' subject matter understanding.

Two kinds of improvements are needed. First, teacher educators need to engage professors of the academic disciplines in dialogue about improvements in teaching of academic courses. Second, courses in teacher education programs themselves need to be improved.

Dialogue with Academic Professors

As I suggested above, dialogue about academic courses between professors of education and professors in the academic disciplines has been limited, partly due to institutional factors, and partly because professors on both sides have held views of their fields that failed to recognize the other's problems and concerns. I am encouraged by developments that now seem to favor such a dialogue, especially in Colleges of Education. The "cognitive revolution" in educational psychology is substantially changing that field, shifting interest from general issues of individual development and instructional design toward the learning of school subjects. Similar developments in content education fields are shifting methods professors and their courses toward greater attention to meaningful understanding of academic content (cf. Anderson & Smith, 1987; Resnick, 1987; Schoenfeld, 1987).

I would like to participate in a dialogue about teaching of academic courses that focuses on two issues. The first is the effectiveness of instruction. Cognitive research on content teaching and learning (cited above) suggests, like the vignettes earlier in this chapter, that students in academic courses are often learning far less than their professors would like to believe. In particular, many students are acquiring large amounts of declarative knowledge without understanding structural and functional relationships well enough to use that knowledge productively. Dialogue that would help academic professors to recognize and to address this problem would benefit not only prospective teachers, but all undergraduate students.

The second issue on which a dialogue could focus is one of curricular priorities. Professors in the academic disciplines tend to teach courses that are designed primarily to socialize students into those disciplines. That is, students are taught the specialized vocabulary, theories, and methods of problem solving that will enable them to communicate and work productively with specialists in the disciplines. Prospective teachers, however, are preparing for careers in which they will communicate primarily with children rather than with specialists.

There are important differences between the two types of communication. Communication with children requires a far less extensive specialized vocabulary, for example, than communication with specialists, but a deeper understanding of how the specialized vocabulary of a field is related to the normal language of the children.

It is obviously unrealistic to expect academic professors to tailor their courses exclusively to the needs of future teachers. It might be helpful, though, if dialogue with educators could help professors in the disciplines consider how important it is for most professionals to communicate effectively with nonspecialists, and to consider what their students need to understand about the discipline in order to communicate effectively. In other words, an attainable form of high literacy for prospective teachers (and for other college students) may involve less acquisition of specialized knowledge and vocabulary and more attention to the structure, function, and development of that knowledge than most academic specialists in the academic disciplines currently believe.

Improving Graduate Teacher Education Programs

Although dialogue with academic departments is desirable and worthwhile, there is a great deal of room for improvement within professional education programs. Graduate programs in teacher education can expect for the foreseeable future that most of their students will enter with a substantial amount of disciplinary knowledge, more than elementary education majors in current undergraduate programs. Like the students in the vignettes above, however, most will find it very difficult to use that knowledge effectively as teachers.

In order to develop expertise in teaching, students in graduate programs of teacher education will have to restructure their academic knowledge and integrate it with the many other kinds of knowledge that they need for teaching. In other words, they will have to develop a form of expertise that encompasses but is not limited to disciplinary knowledge (see Chapters 4 and 8). This has rarely been a curricular priority in teacher education programs, but it should be.

I have been working for the last eight years on a teacher education program that has emphasized restructuring and integration of disciplinary knowledge as a curricular priority (the Academic Learning program at Michigan State University). My work on the program, which was the source of the vignettes in this chapter, convinces me that teacher education programs can do a lot to help their students develop expertise in subject matter teaching.

Some of the activities we have developed for the program are designed to help students restructure and improve their disciplinary knowledge. Activities such as concept mapping (Novak & Gowin, 1984) or solving problems involving relations among subdisciplines can help students improve their understanding of structural relationships. Students can work on understanding functions of disciplinary knowledge by developing examples and analogies to explain subject matter content or by working backwards from the disciplinary knowledge given in textbooks to the problems that that knowledge helps to solve (e.g., "What was the question that scientists were asking when they came up with photosynthesis as an answer?" or Deborah Ball's "1 3/4 divided by 1/2" problem). Prospective teachers can acquire knowledge of students' developmental forms or levels of understanding by interviewing students at different grade levels about specific subject matter topics.

Other activities are possible that help prospective teachers integrate their disciplinary knowledge with their developing knowledge and expertise in other aspects of teaching. Examples of such activities include observation of expert teachers and analysis of how they integrate subject matter and other concerns, interviews with expert teachers about their planning and teaching, and development and teaching of content-focused units (with special emphasis on the use and transformation of disciplinary knowledge).

The list of activities that could be included in graduate teacher education programs is long and varied. The primary issue that such programs must face, however, is one of curricular priorities rather than the development of specific activities. Teacher educators must be aware of the important role that disciplinary knowledge plays in the teaching of all subject matter, and they must be prepared to help their students through the long process of restructuring and integration of disciplinary knowledge that is a necessary part of learning to teach.

REFERENCES

ANDERSON, C. W. (1986, March). *Improving college science teaching: Problems of conceptual change and instructors' knowledge.* Paper presented at the annual meeting of the National Association for Research in Science Teaching, San Francisco.

ANDERSON, C. W. (1987, January). *Incorporating recent research on learning onto the process of science curriculum development.* Commissioned paper for the Biological Sciences Curriculum Study, Michigan State University.

ANDERSON, C. W., & SMITH, E. L. (1987). Teaching science. In V. Richardson-Keohler (Ed.), *The educator's handbook: A research perspective* (pp. 84–111). New York: Longman.

ANYON, J. (1981). Social class and school knowledge. *Curriculum Inquiry, 11*(1), 3–42.

BEREITER, C., & SCARDAMALIA, M. (1987). An attainable version of high literacy: Approaches to teaching higher-order skills in reading and writing. *Curriculum Inquiry, 17*(1), 9–30.

BROWN, A. L., & PALINCSAR, A. S. (1986). *Guided, cooperative learning and individual knowledge acquisition.* (Technical Report No. 372). Center for the Study of Reading, University of Illinois at Urbana-Champaign.

EISEMON, T. O. (undated). *Benefiting from basic education: A review of research on the educational antecedents of school effects.* McGill University. Center for Cognitive and Ethnographic Studies.

ERICKSON, F. (1984). School literacy, reasoning, and civility: An anthropologist's perspective. *Review of Educational Research, 54*(4), 525–46.

FENSTERMACHER, G. D., & SOLTIS, J. F. (1986). *Approaches to teaching.* New York: Teachers College Press.

FLORIO-RUANE, S., & DUNN, S. (1985). *Teaching writing: Some perennial questions and some possible answers.* (Occasional Paper No. 85). East Lansing, MI: Michigan State University, Institute for Research on Teaching.

HAWKINS, D. (1973). Nature, man and mathematics. In A. G. Howson (Ed.), *Developments in mathematical education.* New York: Cambridge University Press.

HIEBERT, J. (1984). Children's mathematics learning: The struggle to link form and understanding. *The Elementary School Journal, 84*(5), 497–513.

HOLLON, R. E., & ANDERSON, C. W. (1987, April). *Teachers' beliefs about students' learning processes in science: Self-reinforcing belief systems.* Paper presented at the annual meeting of the American Educational Research Association, Washington, DC.

NOVAK, J. D., & GOWIN, D. B. (1984). *Learning how to learn,* (2nd ed.). New York: Cambridge University Press.

OLSON, J. (1983, April). *Mr. Swift and the clock: Teacher influence in the classroom.* Paper presented at the annual meeting of the American Educational Research Association, Montreal.

PALINCSAR, A. S., & BROWN, A. L. (1984). Reciprocal teaching of comprehension-fostering and comprehension-monitoring activities. *Cognition and Instruction, 1*(2), 117–175.

PHILLIPS, D. C. (1986, April). *The conceptual minefield of "structure".* Paper presented at the annual meeting of the American Educational Research Association, San Francisco, CA.

POSNER, G. J., STRIKE, K. A., HEWSON, P. W., & GERTZOG, W. A. (1982). Accommodation of a scientific conception: Toward a theory of conceptual change. *Scientific Education, 66*(2), 211–228.

RESNICK, L. B., (1987). Learning in school and out. *Educational Researcher, 16*(9), 13–20.

ROMBERG, T. A. (1983). A common curriculum for mathematics. In G. D. Fenstermacher & J. E. Goodlad (Eds.), *Individual differences and the common curriculum* (82nd yearbook of the National Society for the Study of Education, pp. 121–159). Chicago, IL: University of Chicago Press.

SCHOENFELD, A. H. (1985). *Mathematical problem solving.* New York: Academic Press.

SCHOENFELD, A. H., (Ed.). (1987). *Cognitive science and mathematics education.* Hillsdale, NJ: Lawrence Erlbaum Associates.

SCHWAB, J. (1964). Problems, topics, and issues. In Stanley Elam (Ed.), *Education and the structure of knowledge* (Fifth annual Phi Delta Kappa Symposium on Educational Research). Chicago: Rand McNally.

SHULMAN, L. S. (1986). Those who understand: Knowledge growth in teaching. *Educational Researcher, 19*(2), 4–14.

SKEMP, R. (1978). Relational understanding and instrumental understanding. *Arithmetic Teacher, 26*(3), 9–15.

SMITH, E. L., & SENDELBACH, N. B. (1982). The program, the plans and the activities of the classroom: The demands of activity-based science. In John Olson (Ed.), *Innovation in the science curriculum: Classroom knowledge and curriculum change.* London: Croon-Helm.

TOULMIN, S. (1972). *Human understanding.* Princeton, NJ: Princeton University Press.

WILSON, S. M., SHULMAN, L. S., & RICHERT, A. R. (1987). "150 different ways" of knowing: Representations of knowledge in teaching. In Calderhead, J. (Ed.), *Exploring teacher thinking* (pp. 104–124). London: Cassell PLC.

7

SUPERVISING
STUDENT TEACHERS

Wayne K. Hoy and Anita E. Woolfolk

Student teaching experiences should provide laboratories for critical analysis of practice and active experimentation with a variety of teaching techniques. In schools of education there is growing agreement with John Dewey's assertion that the main purpose of experiential learning must be to make the student teacher a true student of teaching rather than an apprentice seeking to imitate the master (Cruickshank & Armaline, 1986; Holmes Group, 1986; Stones, 1987; Zimpher, 1987). Even though many teacher education programs affirm Dewey's ideal, reality is often not congruent with intent. In fact, most field experiences still reflect the apprenticeship model (Goodman, 1985; Zeichner, 1987).

We begin our analysis with a discussion of the proper balance between the mastery of technique and the development of analytic, reflective habits and attitudes in teaching. Next we turn to the research on student teaching to see just what we know. Then we propose and discuss the basic elements of an effective supervisory program. Using these elements as a guiding framework, we then consider two models of supervision that have as their goals the development of technically competent and reflective teachers. Finally, we conclude with a summary of assumptions about the nature of supervision and improvement of teaching, a review of the current problems in the supervision of preservice teachers, and a set of specific recommendations for improving the supervision of student teachers.

TECHNIQUE AND REFLECTION

Much has been written lately about the teacher as a reflective, inquiring professional and the need to design preparation programs that will develop such individuals. An assumption underlying some of this discussion is that teacher educators must choose between helping their students master technical skills or helping them become analytical and critical. A second assumption is that the development of reflective habits and attitudes is the superior goal. Several scholars of teaching have noted, however, that the two goals are not mutually exclusive choices (Tom, 1985; Van Manen, 1977) and may be difficult to separate in practice (Zeichner, 1987). An emphasis on inquiry does not automatically eliminate a concern with technical skills. Students of teaching can be encouraged to inquire about and reflect on a wide variety of topics: moral, political, or ethical issues; the value of various educational goals; the implicit power relationships found in the classroom or school; the role of the school in society; or alternative instructional strategies for attaining given ends (Tom, 1985). This last emphasis on teaching strategies is likely to create an emphasis on technique. Thus, the distinction between reflection and technique is misleading. Student teachers can be guided by their supervisors to reflect about a range of issues, from how to best teach subtraction to the role of education in a just society.

In spite of this range of issues that, in theory, could be discussed by student teachers and their supervisors, results of research suggest that the actual conversations during supervisory conferences are concerned almost exclusively with technique and classroom management. Usually, there is little talk of larger theoretical or empirical frames that might be used to analyze practice—even in programs where inquiry and reflection about moral and political issues are the avowed goals (Goodman, 1983, 1985; Griffin, et al., 1983; Zeichner & Liston, 1985). Thus, attempts to move away from a concern with technical skills are often unsuccessful. The focus on technique and management is prevalent because these are pressing concerns for all new teachers (Veenman, 1984). To raise questions about alternative goals, power relationships, or moral or ethical concerns is not only seen by harried student teachers as impractical and unrealistic, but such behavior can threaten cooperating teachers and administrators, making life inordinately difficult and dissatisfying for the student teacher. Student dissatisfaction may in turn press university faculty to return to the issues of method and management.

Given these complexities, what should be the goals of student teaching and supervision? Student teachers should learn to be technically competent as well as reflective and self-critical. Without the technical skills required to give clear explanations, plan a lesson, organize and manage classroom rules and procedures, lead a discussion, frame a question, assess student learning, to mention only a few, beginning teachers would be hopelessly ineffective. The research on expert teachers suggests that these very able individuals have at their disposal a range of teaching and management routines. These routines have become automatic and require little deliberation so the teacher is freed to think about the content of the current lesson and students' reaction to it (Brandt, 1986; Leinhardt & Greeno, 1986). Students learn more when their teachers have effective management routines and procedures (Evertson & Emmer, 1982; Evertson, Emmer, Sanford, & Clements, 1983). Experimentally tested models for teaching mathematics (Good, Grouws, & Ebmeier, 1983; Slavin, Madden, & Leavy, 1984) and basic skills (Rosenshine & Stevens, 1986) are available. In brief, the research can provide a good foundation for the beginning teacher.

If preparation stops with the mastery of teaching skills, however, we have done little to accomplish the goal of developing reflective, self-educating professionals. Beginning teachers must be able to select or invent strategies to reach the educational goals of their school's curriculum, but they should also see the value in questioning those goals. Teaching "is an intellectual and an imaginative process, not merely a behavioral one" (Shulman, 1987, p. 41).

Paradoxically, however, too great an emphasis on the development of reflection may undermine its achievement. If the immediate concerns of beginning teachers are ignored and they are given insufficient preparation in the technical aspects of teaching, if they come to their first assignments unable to navigate the daily tasks and activities of classroom life, then these novices are likely to spend a great deal of time and energy developing routines. They may decide that teaching *is* organization and management. These managerial and procedural techniques assume tremendous importance because their absence has caused such difficulties. Students are more likely to discredit their preparation if they feel unprepared to teach.

Evidence for the importance of both technical and reflective goals is found in a recent study of a teacher education program in the Netherlands that strongly emphasizes the development of reflection. Over 50 percent of the graduates responding to a survey said that they had been insufficiently prepared for handling problems of management and motivation. Many teachers found they had to abandon their attempts at analysis and inquiry during the initial years of teaching as they dealt with these problems. One teacher said, "I had the experience that the capacity for reflection is pushed away when you meet a cumulation of conflicts. You feel empty . . . but the ability to face problems returns. I am growing again. I just stood still for a while" (Korthagen, 1985, p. 14).

Thus, it may be that a grounding in technical skills is necessary to free teachers for more analytic thinking and to protect them from the conclusion that such reflection is impractical and unhelpful in teaching. When time, physical and mental energy, and attention can be turned from routine matters of management and instruction to critical analysis of goals, procedures, and outcomes, then improvisation, creativity, flexibility, and thoughtful consideration of alternatives become more likely. This idea is similar to Zahorik's (1986) notion of a hierarchy of teaching skills, moving from technical mastery of research-based practices to the orchestration of practices into a consistent and considered model of teaching and finally to a reflective, inventive teaching style.

The way the initial technical skills are presented to teachers may encourage or discourage the development of reflection. Should students of teaching study educational theory and research in order to identify specific behaviors to emulate (Berliner, 1985b; Gage, 1978) or should the purpose be to gain an understanding of the scientific ethos and the process of systematic inquiry (Buchmann, 1984)? We believe that research and theory provide structures for analyzing experience. As Carter and Doyle (Chapter 4) suggest, teachers can use this kind of information "to activate their own deliberations about events in their classrooms and to modify their own practical reasoning about teaching." If research results are presented as time- and context-sensitive generalizations (Cronbach, 1975) and if preservice teachers are encouraged to be critical consumers of research, then both the development of a core of technical skills and the creation of analytic abilities can be encouraged.

Thus, research and theory should be seen as providing alternatives, suggesting images, opening up new ways of thinking about specific teaching problems and the school as a context for learning (Griffin, 1984). The results of research on teacher effects can be characterized not as prescriptions for practice but as indicative of more general principles that may be artfully adapted in any given situation (Borko, Wildman, & Lalik, 1984). Field experiences designed and supervised by the university can be especially well suited to the task of providing teachers with multiple empirical and theoretical perspectives for analyzing classroom experience (Clift & Warner, 1986). But here again, ideal and reality are not always congruent.

RESEARCH ON STUDENT TEACHING

It is widely held among educators (Campbell & Williamson, 1983; Funk, Hoffman, Keithley, & Long, 1982; Gallemore, 1981) and laypeople alike that field-based experiences in general and student teaching in particular are essential components of effective teacher education. Conant (1963, p. 142) asserts that student teaching is ". . . the one indisputably essential element in professional education." Both college students and practicing teachers consider student teaching the critical element of teacher preparation, often more important than the student's academic or professional course work (Lortie, 1975; Peck & Tucker, 1973). Thus, it should not be surprising that prospective teachers enter into the student teaching experience with some trepidation (Iannaccone & Button, 1964; Tabachnick, Popkewitz, & Zeichner, 1979-1980). The student teaching experience is the capstone of their preparation program.

Contrary to the commonly held view that student teaching is an essential and positive element in the preparation of teachers, the research demonstrates that there is a great deal of confusion surrounding the actual outcomes of the experience. Critics of student teaching point to a body of research that demonstrates that the primary outcome of clinical experience is to make prospective teachers more authoritarian, rigid, impersonal, bureaucratic, and custodial (Emans, 1983; Glassberg & Sprinthall, 1980). Likewise, Koehler (1985), Lanier and Little (1985), and Feiman-Nemser (1983) all paint a bleak picture of the impact of student teaching and its supervision. After reviewing the research, Salzillo and Van Fleet (1977) maintain that "the only function of student teaching which has been identified by the research studies is one of socialization into the profession and into existing arrangements of the school bureaucracy" (p. 28). Although there is a large body of research on preservice field experiences, most of the comprehensive reviews of that literature conclude we still know very little about what actually happens to the student teacher (Davies & Amershek, 1969; Fuller & Bown, 1975; Griffin, Hughes, Defino, & Barnes, 1981; Howey, 1977; Peck & Tucker, 1973; Zimpher, deVoss, & Nott, 1980). Zeichner (1980) suggests that field-based experiences are neither as beneficial as their advocates claim nor as negative as the critics argue; field-based experiences have both positive and negative consequences, many of which are subtle and impossible to identify using traditional quantitative research methods. He argues that quantitative and qualitative methods need to be used in combination to study field-based experiences.

Griffin and his colleagues (1983) completed such a major multisite, multimethod study of student teaching. Their findings are not encouraging. Contemporary research on teaching and schooling had little impact upon the policies and practices of student teaching for either the individuals or institutions in their study. There was no model or conceptualized "point of view" driving the field experiences. Although cooperating teachers and university supervisors in the program were dedicated, wellmeaning, and caring individuals, their awareness of policies, expectations, purposes, and desirable practice was not widespread, and there was little connection between supervisors' feedback and research-validated knowledge. Moreover, the student teachers in this study were encouraged to learn situation-specific teaching strategies rather than more general guidelines for deciding about methods. Finally, the student teaching experience did not appear to function as a gatekeeping mechanism. There were few enforced standards of performance; hence, virtually everyone was passed. No one was denied teaching certification based on his or her performance in student teaching.

Most universities and colleges have little control over either the schools in which they place their student teachers or the selection of cooperating teachers with whom the student will work (Howey, 1977; Lipke, 1979; McCaleb, 1979). Colleges desperately need schools and teachers for their placements; hence, once schools are identified, only the most minimal criteria are used to select cooperating teachers. Griffin and his colleagues (1983) found that probably the most important qualification for the job of cooperating teacher was "availability of time and the willingness to use that time to work with a student teacher" (p. 157). Furthermore, few cooperating teachers receive any training related to their supervising role (Griffin et al., 1983; Thies-Sprinthall, 1984, 1986). The low degree of selectivity and the lack of training for the job almost guarantees, at best, great diversity among the cooperating teachers, and at worst, a cadre of weak and untrained cooperating teachers.

The selection and preparation of university supervisors is not much better. Colleges usually assign their own personnel as supervisors. Some are regular faculty, some are graduate teaching assistants, and others are adjunct faculty. Few colleges have invested in extensive training programs for college supervisors of student teachers. Training in supervision typically ranges from none to experience as a classroom teacher to graduate level preparation in supervision (Griffin et al., 1983). It seems safe to say that in most universities the supervision of student teachers is not a coveted role for professors, either within or outside the school of education.

Given the haphazard selection and training procedures for both university supervisors and cooperating teachers, it should not be surprising that the roles for these positions are confused and often in conflict (Applegate & Lashley, 1984; Bowman, 1979; Boydell, 1986; Emans, 1983). There is little evidence that the university supervisor and cooperating teacher work closely together to foster appropriate teaching behavior in the student teacher. In fact, Grimmett and Ratzlaff (1986, p. 41) conclude from their extensive review of the research in both Canada and the United States that "clear and differentiated supervision roles are conspicuously absent leading in some cases to duplication of function, in others to omission."

The picture that emerges from the research on student teaching is disastrous. Although student teaching is seen as a critical aspect of teacher preparation, its influence on the novice teacher ranges from limited to negative. Neither cooperating teachers nor university supervisors are selected carefully; typically neither is educated for the role of supervisor; and the two roles are often ambiguous, confused, and in conflict. Consequently, more often than not, there is no discussion with student teachers of their classroom performance in light of contemporary theory and research; there is no conceptual perspective driving the field experience; there is no model of supervision guiding attempts to improve instruction; there are no optional teaching strategies considered by the student and cooperating teachers; and there are few enforced standards of performance. Reflective and critical analysis of the teaching-learning process evolving from the student teaching experience is a rare occurrence. Berliner (1985b) goes even further; he argues that student teaching retards the development of analytic skills and "in its present form, militates against the development of the profession" (p. 3). Similarly, the Holmes group concluded that in the typical student teaching experience, "the emphasis is upon imitation of and subservience to the supervising teacher, not upon investigation, reflection, and solving novel problems" (Holmes Group, 1986, p. 62). There is little doubt why teacher education is under attack and why some teacher educators themselves are calling for the reform and restructuring of preservice field experiences.

ELEMENTS OF A PROGRAM OF SUPERVISION

The purpose of this section is to consider how the supervision of graduate preservice teachers might be part of an overall effort to create a "profession equal to the task—a profession of well-educated teachers prepared to assume new powers and redesign schools for the future" (Carnegie Task Force, 1986, p. 2).

Effective supervision is a fascinating yet elusive activity. Indeed, much confusion and misapprehension surround the word itself. Unfortunately, supervision has its roots in the industrial literature of bureaucracy. Close supervision was a classic response to production problems; it was management's attempt to control subordinates. "Evaluation," "rating," "assessment," and "appraisal" are all used to describe supervision of instruction. They are terms consistent with the industrial notion of overseeing, directing, and controlling workers. They are also terms that are inimical to a view of supervision as a process of collaborative effort to improve the teaching-learning process. It should not be surprising, then, that a good many teachers and administrators—rhetoric notwithstanding—view supervision as an administrative tool to observe, rate, and control teachers.

Supervision of student teaching ideally focuses on improvement of the student teacher's classroom instruction. The basic purpose of student teaching is to provide the novice teacher with an opportunity to practice the scientific basis of the art of teaching in an environment where support, aid, and learning are forthcoming. The student teacher, however, is confronted with at least two supervisors, one from the college and another from the school, who often have different perspectives on teaching and supervision. Such a situation frequently produces tension and conflict for the student teacher. Thus, we turn to the organization of student teaching. How might the supervised internship be structured? What elements should be present?

First, all participants in the supervisory process must agree that a main goal of their interactions is for the student teacher to become both technically competent and a more reflective teacher. Second, the student teacher needs a reasonable and powerful set of analytic tools, that is, theoretical, empirical, and practical lenses to magnify experience so that subtle and fleeting relationships between teaching and learning can be examined. Third, the student needs to be involved in a supportive process that stimulates analysis and reflection, suggests avenues for exploration, while gradually encouraging the student teacher to assume more and more independence in this process. Finally, the student teacher needs a social, intellectual, and physical environment that supports experimentation and critical examination. Each of these elements requires a closer look.

Goals and Roles

The first element, an agreement on the goals of supervision, might seem an unnecessary inclusion, but such agreement is far from guaranteed. Research indicates that student teacher, cooperating teacher, and university supervisor may be unclear or in disagreement about the aims of their interactions (Boydell, 1986; Griffin, 1983), and often cooperating teachers simply expect student teachers to emulate their teaching styles. In the absence of the explicit goal to develop reflective and analytic skills, supervision generally is guided by the implicit and unquestioned goal of helping the student teacher cope with the daily dilemmas of classroom life. Thus, discussions with student teachers are most likely to center on finding solutions to immediate and specific problems rather than developing skills of reflection and analysis or even refining a repertoire of techniques (Blumberg, 1976, 1977). Based on their extensive study of student teaching, Griffin and his colleagues concluded that "the conversation of the supervision conferences dealt with events in a particular classroom at a particular point in time. Very rarely did the talk between cooperating teacher and student teacher focus upon what might be called alternate means of understanding and treating classroom events" (Griffin et al., 1983, p. 325).

Assuming that all participants in the supervisory process are clear about the goals, it may still be possible and even advisable for each member to make different and distinctive contributions. The role of the cooperating teacher(s) might focus more on helping the student teacher solve specific and immediate problems, if all parties are aware that the solving of these problems does not constitute the whole of teaching. The immediate situation provides the raw material for analysis. As Dewey (1929) suggests, "Concrete educational experience is the primary source of all inquiry and reflection because it sets the problems, and tests, modifies, confirms or refutes the conclusion of intellectual investigation" (p. 29). Specific problems can be used to examine more general and enduring issues. The theoretical and research knowledge of the university supervisor should complement the practical experience of the cooperating teacher. In the process of critical inquiry, university supervisor, cooperating teacher, and student teacher may each bring different perspectives to bear, which brings us to the next element necessary for effective supervision.

Perspectives for Reflection

In order to become reflective, teachers must have knowledge about teaching that allows them to think critically and creatively. Leinhardt and Greeno (1986) suggest that the cognitive skill of teaching "rest on two fundamental systems of knowledge, *lesson structure* and *subject matter*" (p. 75). The first system, knowledge of how to plan and conduct lessons, is both supported and constrained by the second, knowledge of the subject. Lesson structure is supported by content because without content there would be no lesson. Lesson structure is constrained by content because certain kinds of subject matter may require one type of lesson structure while other subject matter is best taught within a different structure. Other constraints on planning and conducting lessons include the unique circumstances of the class and the particular students involved (Leinhardt & Smith, 1985).

Thus, to make sense of the complexities of the classroom, teachers must have a framework that relates knowledge about *teaching process*, *subject matter*, *situation*, and *students*. Such a framework might actually be a theory of teaching that identifies relevant variables, suggests likely relationships among variables, and poses possible explanations for particular outcomes. This framework might begin with, but need not be limited to, the recent findings in research on teaching, broadly construed. In analyzing *teaching process*, for example, reflective teachers might look to the recent research on direct instruction (Rosenshine & Stevens, 1986), active teaching (Good, 1979), cooperative learning (Slavin, 1983), teacher effects (Brophy & Good, 1986), the activity structures of lessons (Berliner, 1983; Mehan, 1979), academic tasks (Doyle, 1983), classroom participation structures (Erickson & Schultz, 1977), and classroom management (Doyle, 1986; Evertson & Emmer, 1982).

Teachers' thinking about *subject matter* could be enriched by considering the research on children's conceptions and misconceptions about the material being taught (see Chapter 6) as well as teachers' understanding of their subject (Leinhardt & Smith, 1985). To better appreciate the unique *situation* of the class, we might look to research on school effects (Good & Brophy, 1986), class climate (Moos, 1978), and the ecology of the classroom (Doyle, 1981; Gump, 1982). To ensure that the teaching fits the needs and abilities of the *students*, we could look to research on aptitude-treatment interactions (Corno & Snow, 1986), students' thinking (Wittrock, 1986), student motivation to learn (Brophy, 1986), and students' communicative competence (Hymes, 1974). Since the teacher is an active participant in the classroom, not just a passive transmitter of information, we might also encourage teachers to examine their own motivations, concerns, and needs by studying the research on teacher concerns (Fuller & Bown, 1975; Veenman, 1984), expectations (Cooper & Good, 1983), efficacy (Ashton, 1985), and motivation (Silver, 1982). These areas of research, while not telling the teacher exactly how to behave in every situation, do provide tools for analyzing teaching, suggest questions to ask, and highlight relationships to note in examining the day-to-day life of the classroom.

Each teacher preparation program should have its own conception of appropriate and useful perspectives for analyzing and relating teaching process, subject matter, situation, and students. Whatever the particulars of the framework, it seems essential that both the student teacher and the teacher's supervisors operate from the same perspectives. In other words, there should be continuity between what the student teacher learned in prior coursework and the analytic process applied in supervision. Each participant may have special areas of expertise or favorite perspectives, but student teachers and supervisors should share a common vocabulary and grammar of teaching, even if such slight differences in dialect are present. This means not only that supervisors must be knowledgeable about the ideas presented in the student teacher's preservice program, but also that those ideas must make sense to and be accepted by the supervisors, including the cooperating teacher. As Bolster (1983) reminds us, the match between the knowledge of the researcher (usually the basis for preservice courses) and the world of the practicing teacher is not always a good one. We know that supervisors are seldom aware of, much less committed to the academic content of the preservice program. If student teachers are to use the lenses provided in their preservice education to become reflective, deliberate teachers, then those lenses must also be consistently and willingly used by their supervisors.

Supervisory Process and Training

Assuming that student teacher, cooperating teacher, and university supervisor share a common set of goals, understand their roles, and bring a range of perspectives to bear in analyzing classroom experiences, then a supervisory process should be chosen that fits those goals, roles, and perspectives. Whatever the process selected, all participants should be trained to implement it. Here the university supervisor might take the lead, helping both cooperating teacher and student teacher to master the supervision methods.

The recommendation that supervisors should be trained (perhaps even supervised) in their role is not new. Many informal evaluations of student teaching experiences at particular universities as well as formal studies of supervision decry the lack of training and coordination in field experiences. There is some evidence suggesting that an important but seldom recognized element is missing from these recommendations. It is possible that supervision may be more effective if the student teachers themselves are trained in the process. Zeichner & Liston (1985), in study of actual dialogue during supervisory conferences, found that the conceptual level of the student teachers but not of their supervisors predicted the complexity of reasoning and quality of critical discourse during the conference. Thus, the student teachers set the tone and probably the limits of critical thinking for the conference. Given the press for the practical so often mentioned in descriptions of beginning teaching experiences, it may be expecting too much of the supervisor to develop flexible, reflective capabilities in student teachers who have no prior experience with or affinity for this process.

One solution to this problem is to ensure that the preparation leading to student teaching has helped prospective teachers to appreciate the value of critical analysis, gain some practice in reflective thinking, and become more cognitively flexible (Korthagen, 1985). A second approach might be to train the student teachers themselves in clinical supervision and provide practice in both giving and receiving such support (Copeland & Jamgochian, 1985). In this way the prospective teachers may understand the rationale for clinical supervision, learn what to expect, and appreciate some of the benefits of effective supervision. These students may enter their final field experience more accepting of time devoted to analysis and reflection and less focused on survival skills. They may have learned how to benefit from supervision and might initiate productive discussions themselves, not relying solely on the supervisor for direction. This could spark and sustain more enthusiastic critical analysis.

Whatever the form of supervision employed, during student teaching there should be a gradual transition from dependence on the supervisor to self-direction in teaching. It appears that student teachers generally prefer a more directive style of supervision at the beginning of their experiences but shift to preferences for a more nondirective style by the end of student teaching (Copeland, 1982). This makes sense, considering the reality shock (Veenman, 1984) so often described by beginning teachers. The first order of business for shocked student teachers is to get help and direction. These teachers should "receive intensive, supervisory assistance while they gradually learn to function as self-directed teachers" (Locke, 1979, p. 13). Such a move from mediated learning or guided practice to independent performance is in keeping with recent research in such diverse areas as cognitive development (Vygotsky, 1978), participant modeling (Bandura, 1986), and reading instruction (Palincsar & Brown, 1984).

There is evidence that the move to independent teaching does not occur spontaneously for all student teachers. As already noted, the actual content of supervisory dialogue tends to involve advice from supervisors about how to solve specific management, instructional, or interpersonal problems. There is no evidence that this advice changes to nondirective support by the end of student teaching. Furthermore, based on one study of mentoring in teaching, nursing, and law enforcement (Fagan & Walter, 1982), it appears that mentoring relationships between teachers are less likely to develop independence in the protégé than are similar relationships in the other two occupations. Thus, if a gradual transition to independence is not a conscious element of the supervisory process, there is little hope for developing reflective, critical teachers. Two sources of ideas about how to navigate the voyage to independence are developmental models of instruction (Sprinthall & Thies-Sprinthall, 1983; Thies-Sprinthall & Sprinthall, 1987) and Gray and Gray's (1985) mentor/protégé helping relationship model.

The final aspect of a supportive process is the separation of evaluation and supervision. As long as the supervisor is evaluating the performance of the student teacher to determine a grade, then experimentation is likely to be discouraged. Beginning teachers seldom discuss their problems or seek help from colleagues who will be evaluating their performance (Fox & Singletary, 1986). When the evaluative threat is removed, experienced teachers designated as mentors or support teachers often become the source of constructive criticism for new teachers (Huffman & Leak, 1986). The experiences of educators involved with staff development and coaching also bear testimony to the importance of keeping supervision free of evaluative requirements:

> ... the evaluative component of supervision prevents the very climate essential for learning, that of experimentation and permission to fail, revision and trying again while continuously practicing new but still awkward procedures . . . . In divorcing itself from evaluation, coaching provides a safe environment in which to learn and perfect new teaching behaviors, experiment with variations of strategies, teach students new skills and expectations inherent in new strategies, and thoroughly examine the results. (p. 47)

Context for Supervision

Supervision does not happen in a vacuum—it occurs in an institutional context, one that is not typically supportive of critical analysis and experimentation. As we have already seen, usually neither schools nor cooperating teachers are carefully selected. Most public schools do not actively promote inquiry and reflection, and once cooperating teachers are selected, there is little in the way of recognition, rewards, time, or reduction in teaching load that would encourage development of such activity (Zeichner & Liston, 1987). In addition, universities tend to be structurally loose; even in programs designed to prepare reflective teachers, the programs are marked by ideological eclecticism and structural fragmentation (Zeichner, 1985). Consequently, it should not be surprising that student teachers become more custodial, bureaucratic, impersonal, and authoritarian rather than more reflective, critical, professional, and collaborative as a result of student teaching.

The model and practice of student teaching that we are proposing requires a supportive teaching environment, one conducive to critical analysis and reflective practice. Principals need to demonstrate their respect for the professional competence of teachers, and teachers need to exhibit such behavior. Intellectual stimulation for student teachers should come not only from skillful supervisors and cooperating teachers but also from experienced teachers who enjoy working with each other, who are committed to each other, and who are concerned with the intellectual and social development of their students. The significant others for beginning teachers are their experienced colleagues. Student teachers are influenced by the teacher subculture in which they practice. Informal teacher conversations in the halls, cafeteria, and faculty lounge as well as formal discussions in faculty meetings and conferences play no small part in the socialization and education of student teachers. As Waller (1932) observed in his classic analysis of the teacher subculture, "The significant people for a school teacher are other teachers, and by comparison with good standing in that fraternity, the good opinion of students is a small thing and of little price. A landmark in one's assimilation to the profession is that moment when he decides that only teachers are important" (p. 389).

Ideally, the organizational climate of a school in which student teachers practice should be marked by open and authentic interactions among the professional staff. Formal and informal school norms should support the professional autonomy of teachers, high performance and achievement standards, participative management, colleague control, trust, and supervision strategies that stress collaboration and improvement, not inspection and rating. We suspect that the climate of the school may be as important in nurturing teachers who are reflective, critical, and self-directed as skillful cooperating teachers and supervisors. Student teachers need trusted friends, good colleagues, and support as well as intellectual stimulation. They need experienced colleagues who value the role of teacher as professional decision maker. Universities and colleges are severely limited in strategies that they can use to alter the context of public schools; thus, careful selection of cooperating schools is as important as the choice of cooperating teachers and university supervisors.

Although we have discussed the climate of public schools in general terms, there are specific instruments that can be used to measure the work environments of schools. Most of these instruments tap many of the school characteristics identified in the so-called school effectiveness literature as well as organizational conditions that would be conducive to a program of supervision dedicated to improvement of instruction and critical inquiry. Such properties as a press for academic achievement, orderly learning environments, dynamic and supportive leadership, trust, professionalism, faculty involvement in decision making, teacher enthusiasm and pride, agreement of educational purposes of the school, classroom management, and involvement in curriculum development are important aspects of schools. These properties as well as the more general features of openness, health, custodialism, and authenticity of schools can be measured using such instruments as the Organizational Climate Descriptive Questionnaire (Hoy & Clover, 1986; Hoy & Miskel, 1987), Organizational Health Inventory (Hoy & Feldman, 1987), The Pupil Control Ideology Form (Willower, Eidell, & Hoy, 1967), and the School Organizational Dimension Assessment (Wilson, Firestone, & Herriott, 1983). The point is that there are some reasonable instruments that determine the nature of the school's climate and organizational processes. As universities select public schools for internship sites, selection need not be random or impressionistic.

With the four general elements of a program of supervision as guides, we turn our attention to two models of supervision that have as their goal the development of technically competent, reflective teachers.

CLINICAL SUPERVISION

In education, professional practice designed to improve instruction rather than to rate the performance of teachers has been described as clinical supervision (Reavis, 1978). The clinical process includes a preconference, observation, analysis and strategy, and a postconference. The birth of clinical supervision came in the early 1950s when Morris Cogan and his colleagues at Harvard found that supervision of student teachers was not succeeding. Their students' testimonies clearly demonstrated that university supervisors did too little or too much, and in either case, did not help them in becoming beginning teachers (Cogan, 1973, p. 6). Similarly, cooperating teachers were either indifferent or well meaning but unskilled or hell-bent on delivering their own personal ideas about how to teach regardless of the views of the student teacher. From this dissatisfaction and the need to develop a more effective way of supervising interns at Harvard grew a model of supervision that stressed studying classroom behavior in an atmosphere of colleagueship and mutual respect. A central objective of the process is the development of self-directed, analytic teachers who are open to help from other colleagues (Cogan, 1973). The major way in which clinical supervision differs from the earlier, traditional approaches is its emphasis on analysis and cooperation rather than inspection and rating. Although the clinical approach was developed in response to a specific problem in the preparation of preservice teachers, it became a dominant model in the literature on supervision of instruction.

Studies of instructional supervision, however, are not well developed. After a review of research on supervision, Reavis (1978) concluded that teachers are distrustful of supervision as traditionally practiced; they prefer a clinical approach over more traditional practices; and the effects of supervision on teacher behavior and teacher performance are not clear. Although both teachers and student teachers like a clinical approach, does it make a difference? How does the clinical approach affect teacher attitudes and behavior? Does it produce more open, flexible, critical, and analytic teachers? Does clinical supervision improve teaching and student learning? Many scholars (Denham, 1977; Krajewski, 1976; Reavis, 1978; Sullivan, 1980) have lamented the lack of data-based answers to such questions, and although there is some support for the model (Reavis, 1978; Sullivan, 1980), the questions remain.

Despite its popularity with student teachers, teachers, and professors, the clinical model has not been widely implemented in either the supervision of teachers (Sullivan, 1980) or student teachers. In addition to the lack of hard data demonstrating its effectiveness, the process conflicts with the bureaucratic norms of school organizations. School bureaucracies stress standardization, impersonality, conformity, and hierarchical arrangements, all of which run counter to the assumptions and practices of clinical supervision. Bureaucratic norms require that the supervisor initiates and the teacher responds; hence, the responsibility for instructional improvement rests with the officers of the school, creating no need for teachers to develop norms of professional responsibility. Since student teaching typically occurs within the bureaucratic context of public schools, it should not be surprising that such a bureaucratic perspective hampers the development of clinical and professional practices in student teaching.

Even if the limitations imposed by the bureaucracy of the school could be overcome, it is not clear that the clinical supervision model would be the best choice for work with student teachers. Unfortunately, this model is flawed by the lack of a specific definition of improvement of instruction. Typically, the teacher and supervisor supply such definitions without benefit of conceptual guidance. Moreover, teacher behaviors that are appropriate and effective in one setting are not necessarily desirable in another. In contrast to the specificity of other elements of clinical supervision, the expected outcomes are ambiguous (Hoy & Forsyth, 1986; Sullivan, 1980). If improvement of instruction is to become more than a rallying cry, supervisors and teachers must identify the specific aspects of teaching practice to be analyzed, at which levels the analysis should take place, and the ends to which clinical analysis should be directed. That is, the substance of supervision, the criteria for analysis, and the meaning of instructional improvement all need to be defined as the clinical process is applied (Zeichner & Liston, 1985).

A CLASSROOM PERFORMANCE MODEL

If supervision of student teaching is to become more meaningful, then a model of supervision must be used that will (1) clearly define improvement of instruction and guide action toward that end; (2) confront the organizational constraints and opportunities in each school; (3) foster cooperation among the student teacher, cooperating teacher, and university supervisor; and (4) encourage teacher professionalism by developing and reinforcing norms of critical analysis, responsibility, and self-direction. Clinical supervision is a step in the right direction, but the process needs a stronger theoretical focus.

One such approach is the diagnostic model of classroom performance developed by Hoy and Forsyth (1986). The model is based on open-systems theory and focuses on fundamental elements that affect teacher and student behavior in the classroom. These elements exist in states of relative balance, consistency, or congruence with each other. When the basic elements of the classroom system fit together well, the system functions effectively. But if the components conflict, performance problems result. In its simplest form, the model addresses three questions. What are the critical constraints on the classroom system? What are the major elements of the classroom system and the nature of their interactions? What is the nature of the performance of the system?

The classroom performance model answers these three questions first by placing the classroom in a context that describes the opportunity and constraints of the

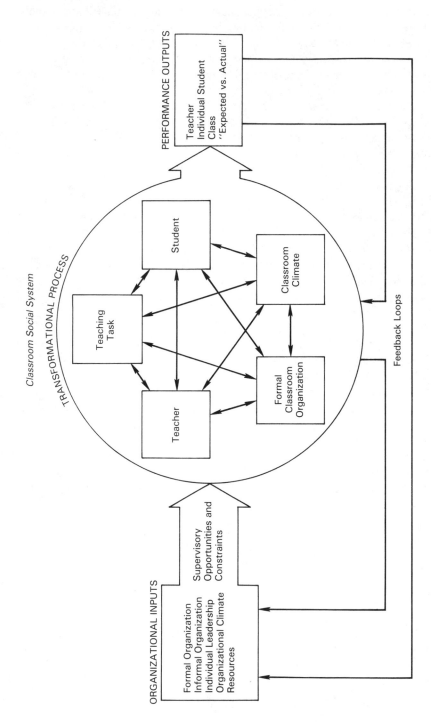

FIGURE 7-1 The Classroom Performance Model. (Taken from Hoy, W. K., & Forsyth, P. B. (1986). *Effective Supervision: Theory Into Practice.* New York: Random House, p. 43.)

school; then, by analyzing the key elements of the classroom system and their inter-actions; and, finally, by assessing the difference between what the teacher wanted to happen in the classroom and what actually did happen. As pictured in Figure 7-1, for-mal structure, informal organization, leadership, organizational climate, and resour-ces are important features of the school that are likely to influence classroom interactions. The teacher, the student, the teaching task, the formal classroom arran-gement, and the informal classroom climate are the five basic elements that, along with their interactions, define the classroom system. Teacher, class, and individual student performances are the three sets of classroom outcomes that provide the basis for diagnosing the effectiveness of classroom performance. Discrepancies between the desired and actual performance levels are supervisory problems—areas to be im-proved. The model postulates that performance is a function of the congruence among the classroom elements—the better the fit between the pairs of elements, the greater the effectiveness of the system.

As in any social system, the vital issue is not what the elements are, but rather the nature of their relationships. The five elements of the classroom produce 10 pos-sible pairs of congruence relationships. For example, to what degree is the formal classroom structure consistent with the informal classroom climate? Are the formal teacher expectations compatible with the informal student norms? Does the classroom climate facilitate the teaching task? It should be clear that incongruence in pairs of elements produces difficulties in the classroom. Using a reading example, congruen-cy in the classroom performance model would require a *task* that is appropriate to the ability of the *students*, suited to the skill of the *teacher*, supported by the *classroom climate*, and sustained by the *formal arrangement* of the classroom activities. If the actual reading achievement of the students did not meet the expectations of the teacher, then one would look to the lack of congruence between elements of the model. Per-haps the sixth grade teacher did not match the reading level of the students with the material, creating a discrepancy between student characteristics and the task; or did not follow a systematic way of calling on readers, creating a discrepancy between the task and the formal arrangement of the classroom; or neglected an informal norm against reading activities before lunch, that is, created a mismatch between task and classroom climate. The specific cause in this example is not important; understanding the model and the necessity of congruence between elements is the point of the ex-ample.

The diagnostic model provides a framework for teachers and supervisors to deal reflectively, analytically, and critically with the analysis and improvement of teach-ing. Although it is not possible to discuss the elements and interactions of the model in detail in this discussion (see Hoy & Forsyth, 1986), the formulation can accom-modate most of the components of effective supervision that have been identified. The elements of the classroom, for example, provide a framework for synthesizing and then using the contemporary theory and research on classroom management and organization, effective instruction, student perceptions, teacher and student motiva-tion, the teaching task, and the ecology of the classroom. Within this system, knowledge about teaching process, subject matter, situation, and student should be considered. Clearly, any teacher or supervisor who attempts to use this diagnostic model for analysis of classroom behavior needs to become familiar with the relevant body of theory and research. Moreover, the formulation demonstrates the importance of the context of the school in any attempt to work with teachers to improve instruction. Finally, the model suggests the aspects of teaching practice to be analyzed and defines instructional improvement in terms of reducing discrepancies between desired and expected outcomes of teachers, students, and classes.

In sum, the implication of the model is that student teachers, cooperating teachers, and university supervisors can use a clinical process to diagnose problems in the classroom by determining the nature and location of incongruent relationships and then planning action to improve them without jeopardizing other well-functioning aspects of the classroom. The model also implies that a variety of configurations of key elements can lead to effective teaching behavior. Consequently, the question is not to find the "one best way" of teaching but to determine effective combinations of classroom and school elements that will lead to desired outcomes. The process of diagnosing incongruencies and developing congruent relationships is not simply an intuitive process but rather a deliberative and systematic one based on theory and research.

CONCLUSIONS

Our general approach to supervision is based on the assumption that the improvement of instruction ultimately rests with teachers themselves. Teachers need the freedom to develop their own unique styles. They need to develop repertoires and learn to vary their approaches according to the situation. Improvement of instruction implies change, and change in teaching behavior requires professional and intellectual stimulation as well as social support. The primary goal of supervision is not simply to help teachers solve immediate problems but to engage with teachers in the joint study of classroom activities through reflective analysis. Successful teacher-supervisor relationships are based on colleagueship, trust, and professionalism.

The supervision of preservice teachers during internship experiences could be part of an overall program to professionalize teaching. But supervision alone cannot accomplish this end. If the research on student teaching and supervision has told us anything, it is that the powers of tradition and context are great. Many factors, working alone and together, pull the preservice preparation of teachers toward an apprenticeship model. Unfortunately, students receive contradictory messages throughout their coursework and field placements. They often enter the schools unprepared for the predictable managerial and organizational demands of teaching. They cope by adopting the behaviors and finally the beliefs that seem to work. We can expect little change in the present situation without a coherent, integrated, and powerful preservice program, without shared vision of the goals of both didactic learning and field experiences within that program, without carefully selected and trained university supervisors and cooperating teachers, without a curriculum (explicit and implicit) for the field experiences that gradually encourages self-direction, reflection, and analysis while developing technical competence, without a university context that rewards high-quality supervision, without a school placement that supports the goals and procedures of the preservice program, and without the constant monitoring of the entire process to determine what is really happening in the educational life of the preservice teacher.

The above list of requirements is staggering, perhaps unrealistic. Even the most thoughtful and well-integrated programs (e.g., Korthagen, 1985; Zeichner, 1987) have had only limited success. While it would be a major step forward to transform the schools so that they are better learning environments for all participants, students, student teachers, and practicing teachers, this is not likely to happen in the near future. More immediate improvement in the preparation of teachers could be expected if the following steps were taken:

1. Place student teachers only in schools that support the development of reflective professionals. Establish genuine collaborative relationships between school and university with practicing teachers serving as clinical professors of education, partners on research teams, and participants in the training of supervisors. Provide real incentives and rewards for all participants.

2. Establish shared goals for the student teaching experience. Seek the commitment of all participants to these goals. Ensure a balance of technical skill and reflective analysis.

3. Select a method of supervision that fits the goals and train all participants, including the student teachers themselves in that method. If possible, conduct some of the training with all participants together.

4. Keep the supervision and evaluation separate. Evaluation is not supervision. Formative evaluation may be a useful supervisory tool, but summative evaluation is likely to conflict with constructive attempts to improve instruction and promote critical inquiry. Remove traditional grading from the student teaching experience.

5. Monitor the supervisory process. Clear goals for the supervisory program and training for participants alone do not guarantee that the intended methods will be practiced. In order to determine the actual "process-in-use," develop a system for reviewing records of supervisory conferences. In addition to providing information about what is actually happening during supervision, these data could be part of ongoing research or evaluation projects.

If we fail to take these steps, it is likely that supervision of student teaching will retain its present form—a form that hinders the development of technically competent, reflective teachers and militates against the development of the profession.

REFERENCES

ANDERSON, C. (1987, May). *The role of education in the academic disciplines in teacher preparation.* Paper presented at the Rutgers Invitational Symposium on Education: The Graduate Preparation of Teachers, Rutgers, The State University of New Jersey, New Brunswick, NJ.

APPLEGATE, J. H., & LASHLEY, T. J. (1984). What cooperating teachers expect from preservice field experience students. *Teacher Education, 24*, 70–82.

ASHTON, P. (1985). Motivation and the teacher's sense of efficacy. In C. Ames & R. Ames (Eds.), *Research on motivation in education: Vol. 2. The classroom milieu* (pp. 141–174). Orlando, FL: Academic Press.

BANDURA, A. (1986). *Social foundations of thought and action.* Englewood Cliffs, NJ: Prentice-Hall.

BERLINER, D. (1983). Developing concepts of classroom environments: Some light on the T in classroom studies of ATI. *Educational Psychologist, 18*, 1–13.

BERLINER, D. (1985a). Laboratory settings and the study of teacher education. *Journal of Teacher Education, 36*(6), 2–8.

BERLINER, D. (1985b). *Reform in teacher education: The case for pedagogy.* Tucson: The University of Arizona.

BLUMBERG, A. (1976). Supervision: What is and what might be? *Theory Into Practice, 15*, 284–292.

BLUMBERG, A. (1977). Supervision as interpersonal intervention. *Journal of Classroom Interaction, 13*, 23–32.

BOLSTER, A. (1983). Toward a more effective model of research on teaching. *Harvard Educational Review, 53*, 294–308.

BORKO, H., WILDMAN, T., & LALIK, R. (1984, April). *Designing a classroom observation system: Accountability for principles rather than behaviors.* Paper presented at the annual meeting of the American Educational Research Association, New Orleans.

BOWMAN, N. (1979). College supervision of student teaching: A time to reconsider. *Journal of Teacher Education, 30*(3), 29–30.

BOYDELL, D. (1986). Issues in teaching practice supervision research: A review of the literature. *Teaching and Teacher Education, 2*, 115–125.

BRANDT, R. S. (1986). On expert teaching: A conversation with David Berliner. *Educational Leadership, 44*(2), 4–9.

BROPHY, J. (1986, October). *Student motivation to learn.* Invited address, annual meeting of the Northeastern Educational Research Association, Kerhonken, New York.

BROPHY, J., & GOOD, T. (1986). Teacher behavior and student achievement. In M. Wittrock (Ed.), *Handbook of research on teaching* (3rd ed., pp. 328–375). New York: Macmillan.

BUCHMANN, M. (1984). The use of research knowledge in teacher education and teaching. *American Journal of Education, 92*, 421–439.

CAMPBELL, L., & WILLIAMSON, J. (1983). Supervising the student teacher: What is really involved? *NAASP Bulletin, 67*(465), 77–79.

CARNEGIE FORUM ON EDUCATION AND THE ECONOMY. (1986). *A nation prepared: Teachers for the 21st century.* The Report of the Task Force on Teaching as a Profession. New York: Carnegie Corporation.

CLIFT, R. T., & WARNER, A. R. (1986). University contributions to the education of teachers. *Journal of Teacher Education, 37*(2), 32–36.

COGAN, M. (1973). *Clinical supervision.* Boston: Houghton Mifflin.

CONANT, J. (1963). *The education of American teachers.* New York: McGraw-Hill.

COOPER, H., & GOOD, T. (1983). *Pygmalion grows up: Studies in the expectation communication process.* New York: Longman.

COPELAND, W. (1982). Student teachers' preference for a supervisory approach. *Journal of Teacher Education, 33*(2), 32–36.

COPELAND, W., & JAMGOCHIAN, R. (1985). Colleague training and peer review. *Journal of Teacher Education, 36*(2), 18–21.

CORNO, L., & SNOW, R. E. (1986). Adapting teaching to individual differences among learners. In M. Wittrock (Ed.), *Handbook of research on teaching* (3rd ed., pp. 605–629). New York: Macmillan.

CRONBACH, L. J. (1975). Beyond the two disciplines of scientific psychology. *American Psychologist, 30*, 116–127.

CRUICKSHANK, D. R., & ARMALINE, W. D. (1986). Field experiences in teacher education: Considerations and recommendations. *Journal of Teacher Education, 37*(3), 34–40.

DAVIES, D., & AMERSHEK, K. (1969). Student teaching. In R. Ebel (Ed.), *The encyclopedia of educational research.* New York: Macmillan.

DENHAM, A. (1977). Clinical supervision: What we need to know about its potential for improving instruction. *Contemporary Education, 49*(1), 33–37.

DEWEY, J. (1929). *The sources of a science of education.* New York: Liverright.

DOYLE, W. (1983). Academic work. *Review of Research in Education, 53*, 287–312.

DOYLE, W. (1986). Classroom organization and management. In M. Wittrock (Ed.), *Handbook of research on teaching* (3rd ed., pp. 392–431). New York: Macmillan.

DOYLE, W. (1981). Research on classroom contexts. *Journal of Teacher Education, 32*, 3–6.

EATON, J. F., ANDERSON, C., & SMITH, E. L. (1984). Students' misconceptions interfere with science learning: Case studies of fifth-graders. *Elementary School Journal, 84*, 365–379.

EMANS, R. (1983). Implementing the knowledge base: Redesigning the function of cooperating teachers and college supervisors. *Journal of Teacher Education, 34*, 14–18.

ERICKSON, F., & SHULTZ, J. (1977). When is a context? Some issues and methods in the analysis of social competence. *Quarterly Newsletter of the Institute for Comparative Human Development, 1*(2), 5–10.

EVERTSON, C. M., & EMMER, E. T. (1982). Effective management at the beginning of the year in junior high classes. *Journal of Educational Psychology, 74*, 485–498.

EVERTSON, C. M., EMMER, E. T., SANFORD, J. P., & CLEMENTS, B. S. (1983). Improving classroom management: An experiment in elementary classrooms. *Elementary School Journal, 84*, 173–188.

EVERTSON, C., HAWLEY, W., & ZLOTNIK, M. (1985). Making a difference in educational quality through teacher education. *Journal of Teacher Education, 36*(3), 2–12.

FAGAN, M. M., & WALTER, G. (1982). Mentoring among teachers. *Journal of Educational Research, 76*(2), 113–118.

FEIMAN-NEMSER, S. (1983). Learning to teach. In L. Shulman & G. Sykes (Eds.), *Handbook of teaching and policy* (pp. 150–170). New York: Longman.

FOX, S. M., & SINGLETARY, T. J. (1986). Deductions about supportive induction. *Journal of Teacher Education, 37*(1), 12–15.

FULLER, F., & BOWN, O. (1975). Becoming a teacher. In K. Ryan (Ed.), *The 74th yearbook of the National Society for the Study of Education,* (Part 2). Chicago: The University of Chicago Press.

FUNK, E. F., HOFFMAN, J. L., KEITHLEY, A. M., & LONG, B. E. (1982). Student teaching program: Feedback from supervising teachers. *Clearing House, 55*, 319–321.

GAGE, N. L. (1978). *The scientific basis of the art of teaching.* New York: Teachers College Press.

GALLEMORE, S. L. (1981). Perceptions about the objectives of student teaching. *Research Quarterly for Exercise and Sport, 52*(2), 180–190.

GALVEZ-HJORNEVIK, C. (1986). Mentoring among teachers: A review of the literature. *Journal of Teacher Education, 37*(1), 6–11.

GLASSBERG, S., & SPRINTHALL, N. (1980). Student teaching: A developmental approach. *Journal of Teacher Education, 31*(2), 31–38.

GOOD, T. (1979). Teacher effectiveness in the elementary school: What we know about it now. *Journal of Teacher Education, 30*, 52–64.

GOOD, T., & BROPHY, J. (1986). School effects. In M. Wittrock (Ed.), *Handbook of research on teaching* (3rd ed., pp. 570–602). New York: Macmillan.

GOOD, T., GROUWS, D., & EBMEIER, M. (1983). *Active mathematics teaching.* New York: Longman.

GOODMAN, J. (1983). The seminar's role in the education of student teachers: A case study. *Journal of Teacher Education, 36*(6), 42–48.

GOODMAN, J. (1985). What students learn from early field experiences: A case study. *Journal of Teacher Education, 36*(6), 42–48.

GRAY, W. A., & GRAY, M. M. (1985). Synthesis of research on mentoring teachers. *Educational Leadership, 43*(3), 37–43.

GRIFFIN, G. (1986). Thinking about teaching. In K. Zumwalt (Ed.), *Improving teaching: 1986 ASCD yearbook.* Alexandria, VA: Association for Supervision and Curriculum Development.

GRIFFIN, G. (1984). Why use research in preservice teacher education: A proposal. *Journal of Teacher Education, 35*(4), 36–40.

GRIFFIN, G., BARNES, S., HUGHES, R., O'NEAL, S., DEFINO, M., EDWARDS, S., HUKILL, H. (1983). *Clinical preservice teacher education: Final report of a descriptive study*, Austin, TX: Research in Teacher Education Program, R & D Center for Teacher Education, The University of Texas at Austin.

GRIFFIN, G., HUGHES, R., DEFINO, M., & BARNES, S. (1981). *Student teaching: A review.* Austin, TX: Research in Teacher Education Program, R & D Center for Teacher Education, The University of Texas at Austin.

GRIMMITT, P. P., et al. (1983). *The challenge of the distributed practicum.* Paper presented at the annual meeting of the Canadian Society for the Study of Education, Vancouver.

GRIMMITT, P. P., & RATZLAFF, H. C. (1986). Expectations for the cooperating teacher role. *Journal of Teacher Education, 37*(6), 41–50.

GUMP, P. (1982). School settings and their keeping. In D. Duke (Ed.), Helping teachers manage classrooms (pp. 98–114). Alexandria, VA: Association for Supervision and Curriculum Development.

HOWEY, K. R. (1977). Preservice teacher education: Lost in the shuffle? *Journal of Teacher Education, 28*, 26–28.

THE HOLMES GROUP. (1986). *Tomorrow's teachers: A report of the Holmes Group*, East Lansing, MI: The Holmes Group.

HOY, W. K., & CLOVER, S. I. R. (1986). Elementary school climate: A revision of the OCDQ. *Educational Administration Quarterly, 22*, 93–110.

HOY, W. K., & FELDMAN, J. (1987). Organizational health: A concept and its measure. *Journal of Research and Development in Education, 20*(4), 30–37.

HOY, W. K., & FORSYTH, P. B. (1986). *Effective supervision: Theory into practice.* New York: Random House.

HOY, W. K., & MISKEL, C. G. (1987). *Educational administration: Theory, research, and practice.* New York: Random House.

HUFFMAN, G., & LEAK, S. (1986). Beginning teachers' perceptions of mentors. *Journal of Teacher Education, 37*(1), 22–25.

HYMES, D. (1974). *Foundations of sociolinguistics*. Philadelphia: University of Pennsylvania Press.

IANNACCONE, L., & BUTTON, W. (1964). *Functions of student teaching: Attitude formation and initiation in elementary student teaching*. Washington, DC: U.S. Office of Education.

KOEHLER, V. (1985). Research on preservice teacher education. *Journal of Teacher Education, 36*(1), 23–30.

KORTHAGEN, F. A. J. (1985). Reflective teaching and preservice teacher education in the Netherlands. *Journal of Teacher Education, 36*(5), 11–15.

KRAJEWSKI, R. J. (1976). Clinical supervision: To facilitate teacher self-improvement. *Journal of Research and Development in Education, 9*, 58–66.

LANIER, J., & LITTLE, J. W. (1985). Research on teacher education. In M. Wittrock (Ed.), *Handbook of research on teaching* (3rd ed., pp. 527–569). New York: Macmillan.

LIENHARDT, G., & GREENO, J. G. (1986). The cognitive skill of teaching. *Journal of Educational Psychology, 78*, 75–95.

LIENHARDT, G., & SMITH, D. (1985). Expertise in mathematics instruction: Subject matter knowledge. *Journal of Educational Psychology, 77*, 247–271.

LIPKE, W. (1979). Give your (student) teachers a break. *Journal of Teacher Education, 30*, 31–34.

LOCKE, E. E. (1979). The supervisor as "motivator": His influence on employee performance and satisfaction. In R. Steere & L. Porter (Eds.), *Motivation and work behavior* (pp. 386–416). New York: McGraw- Hill.

LORTIE, D. (1975). *School teacher: A sociological study*. Chicago: University of Chicago Press.

McCALEB, J. L. (1979). On reconciling dissonance between preparation and practice. *Journal of Teacher Education, 30*, 50–53.

MEHAN, H. (1979). *Learning lessons*, Cambridge, MA: Harvard University Press.

MOOS, R. (1978). A topology of junior high and high school classrooms. *American Educational Resource Journal, 15*, 53–66.

PALINCSAR, A., & BROWN, A. (1984). Reciprocal teaching of comprehension-fostering and monitoring activities. *Cognition and Instruction, 1*, 171–175.

PECK, R. F., & TUCKER, J. A. (1973). Research on teacher education. In R. M. Travers (Ed.), *Second handbook of research on teaching*. Chicago: Rand-McNally.

REAVIS, C. A. (1978). Clinical supervision: A review of the research. *Educational Leadership, 35*, 580–584.

ROSENSHINE, B., & STEVENS, R. (1986). Teaching functions. In M. Wittrock (Ed.), *Handbook of research on teaching* (3rd ed., pp. 376–391). New York: Macmillan.

SALZILLO, F., & VAN FLEET, A. (1977). Student teaching and teacher education: A sociological model for change. *Journal of Teacher Education, 28*(1), 27–31.

SHULMAN, L. S. (1987). Assessment for teaching: An initiative for the profession. *Phi Delta Kappan, 69*(1), 38–44.

SILVER, P. (1982). Synthesis of research on teacher motivation. *Educational Leadership, 39*(7), 551–553.

SLAVIN, R. (1983). *Cooperative learning*. New York: Longman.

SLAVIN, R., MADDEN, N. A., & LEAVEY, M. (1984). Effects of team-assisted individualization on the mathematics achievement of academically handicapped and non-handicapped students. *Journal of Educational Psychology, 76*, 813–819.

SPRINTHALL, N., & THIES-SPRINTHALL, L. (1983). The teacher as an adult learner: A cognitive-developmental view. In G. Griffin (Ed.), *Staff development. The 82nd Yearbook of the National Society for the Study of Education, Part II*. Chicago: The University of Chicago Press.

STONES, E. (1987). Student (practice) teaching. In M. Dunkin (Ed.), *The International Encyclopedia of Teaching and Teacher Education* (pp. 681–685). Oxford: Pergamon.

SULLIVAN, C. G. (1980). *Clinical supervision: A state of the art review*, Alexandria, VA: Association for Supervision and Curriculum Development.

TABACHNICK, B. R., POPKEWITZ, T., & ZEICHNER, K. (1979-1980). Teacher education and the professional perspectives of student teachers. *Interchange, 10*, 12–29.

THIES-SPRINTHALL, L. (1984). Promoting the developmental growth of supervising teachers: Theory, research programs, and implication. *Journal of Teacher Education, 35*(3), 53–60.

THIES-SPRINTHALL, L. (1986). A collaborative approach for mentor training: A working model. *Journal of Teacher Education, 37*,(2), 13–20.

THIES-SPRINTHALL, L., & SPRINTHALL, N. (1987). Preservice teachers as adult learners: A new framework for teacher education. In M. Haberman & J. Backus (Eds.), *Advances in Teacher Education* (Vol. 3, pp. 35–56). Norwood, NJ: Ablex.

TOM, A. R. (1985). Inquiring into inquiry-oriented teacher education. *Journal of Teacher Education, 36*(5), 35–44.

TOREN, N. (1969). Semi-professionalism and social work: A theoretical perspective. In A. Etzioni (Ed.), *The semi-professions and their organization*. New York: Free Press.

VAN MANEN, M. (1977). Linking ways of knowing with ways of being practical. *Curriculum Inquiry, 6*, 205–228.

VARAH, L. J., THEUNE, W. S., & PARKER, L. (1986). Beginning teachers: Sink or swim? *Journal of Teacher Education, 37*(1), 30–34.

VEENMAN, S. (1984). Perceived problems of beginning teachers. *Review of Education Research, 54*, 143–178.

VYGOTSKY, L. S. (1978). *Mind in society: The development of higher mental processes*. Cambridge, MA: Harvard University Press.

WALLER, W. (1932). *The sociology of education*. New York: Wiley.

WILLOWER, D. J., EIDELL, T., & HOY, W. K. (1967). *The school and pupil control idealogy*. University Park, PA: Pennsylvania State University Studies Monograph No. 24.

WILSON, B. L., FIRESTONE, W. A., & HERRIOTT, R. E. (1983). *School Organization Dimension Assessment: An introductory guide*. Philadelphia: Research for Better Schools.

WISE, A. (1986). Graduate teacher education and teacher professionalism. *Journal of Teacher Education, 37*(5), 36–40.

WITTROCK, M. (1986). Students' thought processes. In M. Wittrock (Ed.), *Handbook of research on teaching* (3rd ed., pp. 297–314). New York: Macmillan.

ZAHORIK, J. A. (1986). Acquiring teaching skills. *Journal of Teacher Education, 37*(2), 21–25.

ZEICHNER, K. (1983). Alternative paradigms for teacher education. *Journal of Teacher Education, 31*(6), 45–55.

ZEICHNER, K. (1980). Myths & realities: Field-based experiences in preservice teacher education. *Journal of Teacher Education, 31*(6), 45–55.

ZEICHNER, K. (1985). Preparation for elementary school teaching. In P. Burke & R. Heideman (Eds.), *Teacher competence: Issues in career-long teacher education* (pp. 62–97). Springfield, IL: Thomas.

ZEICHNER, K., & LISTON, D. (1987). Teaching student teachers to reflect. *Harvard Educational Review, 57*, 23–48.

ZEICHNER, K. M., & LISTON, D. (1985). Varieties of discourse in supervisory conferences. *Teaching and Teacher Education, 1*, 155–174.

ZIMPHER, N. (1987). Current trends in research on university supervision of student teaching. In M. Haberman & J. Backus (Eds.), *Advances in teacher education* (Vol. 3, pp. 118–150). Norwood, NJ: Ablex.

ZIMPHER, N., DEVOSS, G., & NOTT, D. (1980). A closer look at university student teacher supervision. *Journal of Teacher Education, 31*(4), 11–15.

8

ASSESSING THE TEACHER AS A REFLECTIVE PROFESSIONAL: NEW PERSPECTIVES ON TEACHER EVALUATION

Penelope L. Peterson and Michelle A. Comeaux

INTRODUCTION

In their recent recommendations for reform of teacher education and the teaching profession, both the Holmes Group and the Carnegie Commission Task Force have proposed a new model of the teacher. Through new graduate programs in teacher education, the Holmes Group (1986) has proposed to develop "competent teachers empowered to make principled judgments and decisions on their students' behalf," who "possess broad and deep understandings of children, the subjects they teach, the nature of learning and schooling, and the world around them," and who "exemplify the critical thinking they strive to develop in students" (p. 28). The Carnegie Commission (1986) echoed these assertions and added that teachers "must be able to learn all the time. . . . Teachers will not come to school knowing all they have to know, but knowing how to figure out what they need to know, where to get it, and how to help others make meaning out of it" (p. 25).

Paper presented at the Rutgers Invitational Symposium on Education on "The Graduate Preparation of Teachers," the Graduate School of Education, Rutgers, The State University of New Jersey, New Brunswick, New Jersey, May 7, 1987. Work on this paper was supported in part by the Center for Policy Research in Education which is funded by a grant from the U.S. Department of Education, Office of Educational Research and Improvement (Grant No. OERI-6-86-0011). The views expressed in this paper are those of the individual authors and are not necessarily shared by the U.S. Department of Education, the Rand Corporation, Rutgers University, or the University of Wisconsin-Madison.

Both the Carnegie Commission Task Force and the Holmes Group seem to suggest that an appropriate image of the teacher is one of the teacher as a "reflective" or "thoughtful" professional. Moreover, they highlight several important qualities of the "reflective" professional. First, the reflective professional is engaged continuously in the process of learning. Not only is the reflective professional engaged in "learning to learn" and in "higher-order learning," but she also inspires and facilitates this kind of higher-order learning in her students. Second, the above image of the reflective professional defines the teacher in terms of the kind and quality of the decision making, thinking, and judgment in which the teacher engages, not just in terms of her behavioral competencies. Teachers' cognitions, judgment, and learning processes become important dimensions for evaluating the teacher. Finally, the above image of a teacher suggests that teachers' thoughts, knowledge, judgments, and decisions will have a profound effect on the way teachers teach as well as on students' learning and achievement in their classrooms. Thus, evaluation of teachers' thinking, decision making, and judgment becomes an important part of determining quality in teaching.

Unfortunately, most teacher evaluation procedures currently in use are insufficient to evaluate the important qualities of the teacher described above (Peterson, 1987; Shulman, 1986a, 1987). Current procedures are narrow in scope and tend to be based on a model of the teacher as a technician who must possess certain skills or behaviors to teach, as well as certain basic skills in cognitive areas such as language and mathematics. These approaches emphasize the use of observational data and content-area examinations in order to assess the teacher's behavioral and basic skills, but fail to assess adequately the teachers' ability for reflective practice or the quality of her reflection. Thus, new assessment approaches are needed to evaluate this new kind of teacher who will be prepared in graduate programs. In addition, to become truly professional, members of the teaching profession must "create relevant and defensible standards of entry to the profession of teaching" (Holmes Group, 1986, p. 65).

OVERVIEW

In this chapter we present several new approaches to evaluating the beginning teacher. These approaches are based on a model of the teacher as a reflective professional and are compatible with the curriculum that will form the basis for the graduate preparation of teachers in many institutions, particularly those adopting the Holmes Group recommendations. These approaches may be useful in evaluating the novice teacher prior to a clinical internship and during the internship year (e.g., Holmes Group, p. 65). In addition, these approaches might serve as models to be used by the recently created National Board for Professional Teaching Standards to develop standards and procedures for professional licensure. This board has been endorsed by the American Federation of Teachers, the National Education Association, the Carnegie Task Force (1986), and the Holmes Group (1986).

To develop these new approaches to teacher evaluation, we draw on theory and research from several scholarly literatures. We begin by discussing research on teacher thinking and decision making. We show how the literature supports a developmental model of the teacher as a reflective professional. We then discuss expert-novice studies related to teaching. From these literatures, we argue that the reflective teacher might be distinguished from others by the quality of her professional knowledge, and we define this professional knowledge. Thus, teachers' professional knowledge needs to be a focus of new evaluation procedures. We provide a framework for conceptualizing teachers' professional knowledge. Finally, we examine the scholarly literature on evaluation in the medical profession to determine to what extent the medical profession might serve as a model for evaluation in the teaching profession. From the above literatures, we derive several techniques that may be useful in evaluation, including paper-and-pencil simulations, video and computer case study simulations, and "stimulated-recall" interviews following actual teaching. We discuss pros and cons of these techniques including issues of reliability and predictive validity. We also discuss what steps must be taken before any of these new teacher evaluation procedures might be implemented.

RESEARCH ON THE TEACHER AS REFLECTIVE PROFESSIONAL

In the past decade, researchers on teaching have moved from a conceptualization of the effective teacher as a technician who must possess certain technical skills or behaviors to a broadened conceptualization of the effective teacher as a "reflective professional" (Shulman, 1975, 1986a). These researchers have been engaged in studying teachers' thinking, planning, decision making, knowledge, and understanding as determinants of effective teaching.

A Developmental Model of the Teacher as Reflective Professional

In their recent chapter in the *Handbook of Research on Teaching*, Clark and Peterson (1986) reviewed the research to date on teachers' thinking and decision making. From their review of a decade of research, they concluded that the image of the teacher as a reflective professional is "not far-fetched." As thoughtful professionals, teachers have more in common with physicians and lawyers than they have with technicians. From the research to date they sketched out the following picture of the teacher as a reflective, thoughtful professional:

> The emerging picture of the teacher as a reflective professional is a developmental one that begins during undergraduate teacher education (or even earlier) and continues to grow and change with professional experience. The teacher education majors who would become professionals in this sense are firmly grounded in the disciplines and subject matters that they will teach. Their study of subject matters focuses on both content and on the cognitive organization of that content in ways useful to themselves and to their future students. They have had both supervised practice in using their behavioral skills and strategies of teaching and have also been initiated into the less visible aspects of teach-

ing, including the full variety of types of planning and interactive decision making. The maturing professional teacher is one who has taken some steps toward making explicit his or her implicit theories and beliefs about learners, curriculum, subject matter, and the teacher's role. This teacher has developed a style of planning for instruction that includes several interrelated types of planning and that has become more streamlined and automatic with experience. Much of this teacher's interactive teaching consists of routines familiar to the students, thus decreasing the collective information processing load. During teaching, the teacher attends to and intently processes academic and non-academic sociocognitive events and cues. These experienced teachers have developed the confidence to depart from a planned course of action when they judge that to be appropriate. They reflect on and analyze the apparent effects of their own teaching and apply the results of these reflections to their future plans and actions. In short, they have become researchers on their own teaching effectiveness. (Clark & Peterson, 1986, pp. 292-293)

Recent scholarly research on teaching has provided support for the image of the teacher as a reflective professional. The research has documented that teaching is a complex and cognitively demanding process that requires professional knowledge in a wide variety of areas, including pedagogy and the content to be taught, as well as skills in planning, evaluating, and making decisions interactively during teaching. This professional knowledge develops over time with education and experience. Furthermore, the kinds of thinking, reflecting, and decision making that make a developing teacher professional may be considered as separate and distinct from the technical skills or competencies necessary for teaching—the teaching methods, teaching strategies, and teaching behaviors that the teacher has in his or her repertoire of teaching techniques. A repertoire of these behavioral skills and technical competencies for a teacher's classroom performance may be necessary but insufficient to make a teacher a truly reflective professional. Thus, teachers' professional knowledge, judgment, understanding, and ability to reflect on their own teaching are important determinants of quality teaching. Recent research on experts and novices provides some insights on the development of professional knowledge, understanding, and reflection.

The Development of Expertise in Teaching

Researchers in cognitive psychology studying learning and development of expertise have provided some insights into the development of teaching skills. Rumelhart and Norman (1979), for example, proposed a schema-based view of learning that involves accretion, restructuring, and turning. Evidence for a schema-based view of teaching can be found in the work of Carter, Cushing, Sabers, Pinnegar, & Berliner (1987), Peterson and Comeaux (1987), Leinhardt (1983), and Calderhead (1983).

Similarly, in his ACT* theory of learning, Anderson (1983) also described learning as a three stage process in which the learner first acquires declarative knowledge, represented as propositions or "knowing that"; then proceduralizes the knowledge (i.e., "knowing how"); and, finally, "fine tunes" the procedures, represented as productions. Research on differences in the performances of experts and novices in various domains has supported Anderson's theory (see, for example, Chi, Glaser, and Rees, 1982; Larkin, McDermott, Simon, and Simon, 1980; Voss, Greene, Post, and Penner, 1983). Carter and Doyle (Chapter 4) provide an excellent discussion of both the research on expertise and the research on expertise in teaching.

The Development of Expertise Through Teacher Education

The research on the development of expertise in teaching has implications for how teacher educators might conceptualize teachers' professional knowledge as well as for how teacher educators might think about the growth of teachers' professional knowledge at each stage in the teacher's development from student, to intern, to novice, and finally to career professional teacher. For example, teachers may need to acquire a base of content knowledge in the subject fields through general liberal study and a base of professional knowledge through professional education courses before they can be expected to act on that declarative knowledge. Acquisition of procedures may come primarily from a variety of experiences in a variety of settings—laboratory, college classrooms, and school classrooms.

Some researchers have begun to examine whether novices can be furthered along the developmental path through instructional mediation. Although the studies are few to date, preliminary results are encouraging. Schoenfeld and Herrmann (1982) found, for example, that at the end of 18 months of instruction on mathematical problem solving, college freshmen's and sophomores' perceptions of mathematics problems were more like those of experts than those of "novice" students in the control group. Neely (1986) conducted a study aimed at facilitating cognitive monitoring—a metacognitive skill that has been found to characterize "expert" teachers (Housner & Griffey, 1985; Leinhardt & Greeno, 1986). Neely instructed novices or preservice teachers in the cognitive monitoring of lesson planning and implementation. Teachers in the treatment group received examples of self-questions useful for the planning phase of teaching (e.g., Is this going to be too easy or difficult for this group? How will I check on student understanding?), had the examples modeled for them, and were given the opportunity to rehearse the strategy as they planned and taught a 30-minute lesson in creative writing during their final week of field experience. Preservice teachers who received the instruction showed significant improvement in their lesson plans and lesson implementation compared to a control group who did not receive the instruction. Such results are encouraging because they suggest that a metacognitive skill that is characteristic of "expert" teachers can be facilitated or taught to "novice" teachers through teacher education.

One aspect of metacognition is that of *reflecting* on one's own thoughts, for example, weighing consequences, predicting outcomes, planning alternatives, and examining one's beliefs, theories, and assumptions. Indeed, the metacognitive knowledge and skill underlying the ability to reflect on one's own thoughts and actions may be *the* characteristic that distinguishes the reflective professional teacher from others. Several researchers are investigating means for promoting reflection in preservice teachers and ways to measure reflective thought (Korthagen, 1985; Zeichner & Liston, 1987; Zeichner, Liston, Mahlios, & Gomez, 1987). This research may offer insights into this important stage of development and may provide some information on the roles of teachers' declarative and procedural knowledge in the development of reflection in teachers.

CONCEPTUALIZING THE PROFESSIONAL KNOWLEDGE OF THE REFLECTIVE TEACHER

The research suggests that experts can be distinguished from novices, and reflective teachers, in general, can be distinguished from all others by their degree of professional knowledge and understanding, as well as by their ability to be aware of their own thinking. In his work developing new teacher evaluation procedures for the Carnegie Task Force's National Board of Professional Standards, Shulman (1986a,b) argued cogently for the importance of evaluating teachers' knowledge. In particular, Shulman (1987) defined seven domains of teachers' knowledge as follows:

content knowledge or understanding of the subject matter

general pedagogical knowledge, with special reference to those broad principles and strategies of classroom management and organization that appear to transcend subject matter

curriculum knowledge, with particular grasp of the materials and programs that serve as "tools of the trade" for teachers

pedagogical content knowledge, that special amalgam of content and pedagogy that is uniquely the province of teachers, their own special form of professional understanding

knowledge of learners and their characteristics

knowledge of educational contexts, ranging from the workings of the group or classroom, the governance and financing of school districts, to the character of communities and cultures

knowledge of educational ends, purposes, and values, and their philosophical and historical grounds (Shulman, 1987, p. 8)

In conceptualizing the professional knowledge of the reflective teacher, we have taken Shulman's (1987) seven domains to represent one dimension of a two-dimensional matrix. The second important dimension is the *type* of knowledge as identified by recent cognitive theorists discussed above. Thus, we propose that each of Shulman's domains may be crossed with three kinds of knowledge—declarative knowledge, procedural knowledge, and metacognitive knowledge. The result is a 7 x 3 matrix representing the 21 categories of professional knowledge required of the reflective teacher. Table 8-1 presents this matrix.

We return to this framework in our later discussion as we consider how and when these categories of teacher knowledge might be best evaluated. We turn now to the scholarly literature on evaluation in the medical profession to determine to what extent the medical profession might serve as a model for evaluation in the teaching profession.

TABLE 8-1   A Conceptualization of Teachers' Professional Knowledge and Points of Assessment During Teacher Education

Types of Knowledge	Categories of Teachers' Professional Knowledge*						
	Content Knowledge	General Pedagogical Knowledge	Content-Specific Pedagogical Knowledge	Curriculum Knowledge	Knowledge of Learners	Knowledge of Educational Contexts	Knowledge of Educational Ends
Declarative Knowledge	I	II	II	II	II	II	II
Procedural Knowledge	I	III	III	III	II	II	II
Metacognitive Knowledge	III	III	III	III	III	III	III

Note: Roman numerals indicate time points of assessment during teacher education as follows:
I = After completion of general-liberal studies and prior to beginning professional education courses and pedagogical coursework or clinical training.
II = Any time after completion of Assessment I and after completion of professional education courses and pedagogical coursework; may be prior to or concurrently with the clinical internship.
III = After completion of an approved internship and completion of approved graduate coursework in teacher education.

* From Shulman, 1987.

THE MEDICAL PROFESSION AS A MODEL FOR EVALUATION

Both the Holmes Group and the Carnegie Task Force have used the medical profession as a prototype for evaluation in the teaching profession. The medical profession may be analogous to the teaching profession because it emphasizes the evaluation of professional knowledge and because the medical profession assumes that professional knowledge develops over time as the student moves through medical education, internship, residency, and professional practice.

To obtain state licensure as a physician, most states require candidates to pass either the National Board of Medical Examiners (NBME) exam or the Federal Licensing Examination (FLEX). The NBME examination seems to be based on a developmental model of the growth of professional knowledge in medicine because it is divided into three parts; these parts may be taken by candidates at varying times in their schooling. The medical student may take Part 1 during any year of medical education without having taken any prerequisite or specified medical courses. Similarly, the only requirement for the student to take Part 2 is passage of Part 1. Finally, the candidate may elect to take Part 3 after passing both Parts 1 and 2, having received the M.D. degree from an approved medical school in the United States or Canada, and having served as a hospital intern or resident for at least six months. Alternatively, the candidate may take the FLEX given by the Federation of State Medical Boards. The FLEX is a three-day examination which candidates may not take until after they have completed medical school and an internship or residency, depending on state requirements.

Format of the National Board of Medical Examiners (NBME) Examination

The NBME exam is composed of three parts. Part 1 tests knowledge of the basic medical sciences, including anatomy, microbiology, and pathology, and is given over a two-day period. The exam consists of six booklets, each containing 150-175 items that present the problem in a narrative, tabular, or graphic format followed by multiple-choice questions on the problem. Items test not only medical knowledge, but also discrimination, judgment, and reasoning. However, when medical knowledge is the focus of the item, the knowledge tested is typically declarative knowledge and is less frequently procedural knowledge.

Part 2 is also given over a two-day period and consists of six booklets of approximately 150 items each. Part 2 tests knowledge of the clinical sciences such as internal medicine, pediatrics, and preventive medicine. In addition to traditional multiple-choice questions, Part 2 includes "clinical problems presented in the form of case histories, charts, roentgenograms, photographs of growths and microscopic pathologic specimens, laboratory data, and the like, and the candidate must answer questions concerning the interpretation of the data presented and the relation to clinical problems" (Frohlich, 1985, p. 5).

Part 3 assesses general clinical competence. The first three booklets consist of multiple-choice questions that require the candidate to interpret clinical data presented primarily in pictorial form such as pictures of patients, charts, or electrocardiograms. The fourth booklet consists of written simulation items called Patient Management Problems (PMPs) that are designed to measure the candidate's clinical judgment (see Frohlich, 1985).

The PMPs differ from the case history multiple-choice type questions because they provide immediate feedback to the examinee, through the use of specially designed pens that the examinees use to highlight or uncover information for each option that they select. For example, if the examinee asks for data on a patient's vital signs following a recommendation to begin the patient on adrenalin, the examinee's chosen highlighted answer reveals the patient's blood pressure, pulse, and respiratory rate. Examinees receive data based on their responses to earlier choices and may use that information as a basis for making further decisions about data gathering, or for intervention as the patient simulation continues. Thus, the PMP can be scored both for errors of commission as the examinee highlights an inappropriate response or errors of omission if the examinee fails to uncover a necessary response.

Scoring and Validity of the National Board of Medical Examiners Exam

In setting standards for scoring and passing the NBME exam, the Board has chosen to establish relative standards rather than absolute ones. Because of the difficulty in setting an absolute standard for a group of medical students who vary in experience and coursework taken, the NBME has set different standards for different reference groups consisting, for example, of students who take Parts 1 and 2 earlier or later in their education, students who take the exam for the first time, and students who are candidates for National Board certification. Most medical schools permit students to make only three attempts at passing the NBME exam (Cleghorn, 1986).

A major weakness of the NBME exam is that researchers have found little evidence for predictive validity of the exam. For example, Williamson (1976) concluded that studies showed little correlation between performance on medical board examinations and performance in medical practice. A major reason for lack of demonstrated predictive validity of the medical exam to actual medical performance may be because "there is no generally accepted measure for measuring physician performance and consequently, the criteria against which the earlier test scores may be matched are lacking" (Schumacher, 1978, p. 66).

Because of these predictive validity problems, medical educators have begun investigating alternative methods of assessment of clinical skills in medicine. We turn now to an analysis of three of these methods.

Alternative Methods of Assessment of Clinical Skills in Medicine

Medical educators are currently developing and studying three methods as alternatives to assess clinical skills in medicine: computer-based simulations; interactive videodisc simulations; and "confederate" patient simulations.

Computer-based simulations. Because of the unique capabilities of the computer, a Computer Based Examination (CBX) is able to provide a more sophisticated simulation of a clinical experience than are the paper-and-pencil PMPs. Aburto and Haertel (1986) have described the CBX as follows:

> (The CBX) is an open-ended, uncued branching simulation with no predetermined paths to follow. The candidate may implement medical and surgical interventions as desired, may transfer the patient among home, emergency room, hospital, intensive care, and office setting, may order x-rays which will appear on the video display terminal and may otherwise simulate almost any medically relevant action that could be taken with a real patient. The computer keeps a detailed log of candidate actions, and automatically scores the candidate on critical actions (decision logic), overall quality of care (acceptable or not acceptable), and cost-effectiveness. Each problem is based upon a script which tells how the case will progress. (p. 24)

The CBX makes use of the computer's ability to keep track of time and thus can monitor the time it takes a candidate to gather data or make a decision as well as serve as a simulation in real time. Moreover, preliminary research has shown that the CBX measures elements of physician competence that are different from those assessed by multiple-choice tests and by paper-and-pencil PMPs and that physicians' scores on the CBX correlate positively with their actual performance records in practice (Aburto & Haertel, 1986). However, Diserens, Schwartz, Guenin, and Taylor (1986) indicated that at least nine cases were needed to achieve a reliability level of above .7 for a candidate's score on the CBX.

Interactive videodisc simulations. Interactive videodisc simulations combine the capabilities of a microcomputer with those of video technology and thus have all the advantages of CBX, including an internal time clock, elaborate branching capabilities, recordkeeping of responses, and ease in scoring plus the additional feature of being able to incorporate and use "live" sequences of action as shown on the video screen. A concrete example is a simulation of a case in emergency medicine produced by Intelligent Imaging Corporation, San Diego, California. The simulation begins in a hospital emergency room with a doctor and nurse standing around chatting, when suddenly information is called in regarding an incoming patient, Eugene Wilson, who is suffering from chest trauma due to a motorcycle accident. As the emergency medical technician on the ambulance gives the staff vital information, the emergency room staff begins to get ready for the arrival of Mr. Wilson. Mr. Wilson is wheeled in on a stretcher moaning and bleeding most realistically, and the doctor turns to the screen and says, "What would you like to do first?" From that point on in the simulation, the examinee is in charge of what happens. He or she orders tests, examines the patient, administers drugs, or takes other clinical actions as desired. The examinee makes choices through a system of menus on the computer screen. The results of the examinee's choices are shown as "live" action video sequences or as written comments on the computer screen. At the end of the simulation, examinees are provided with a breakdown of their performance in terms of cost effectiveness and errors of commission and omission. In addition, examinees are given information on how their performance compared to that of an expert. The expert also explains how she would have handled the case and her reasoning on certain decisions. Thus, the "emergency room program" might be an effective technique for use in formative evaluation or for teaching clinical skills during medical education.

"Confederate" patient simulation. A third method of assessment currently under study by the American Board of Internal Medicine is the use of "confederate" patients in a live simulation to assess clinical skills in medicine (Stillman et al., 1986). The "confederate" patient is trained to display certain symptoms to the medical candidate so that the candidate must interact with the standardized "confederate" as though he or she were a real patient. At the end of the patient examination, the "confederate" patient becomes the evaluator, records the candidate's responses, and rates communication skills of the candidate. A testing committee analyzes the ratings and the candidate's exam worksheet and then provides feedback to the candidate. Stillman et al., (1986) found that they could obtain a reliable assessment of the clinical skills of 336 resident physicians with approximately 6 to 10 simulated "confederate" patients per resident in one day's testing time at a cost of approximately $200 per resident.

IMPLICATIONS FOR TEACHER EVALUATION

In the following discussion of teacher evaluation procedures, we draw extensively on the research, theory, and evaluation practice from the medical profession. Although the evaluation procedures used in medical education have several distinct advantages such as the solid research base, well-developed assessment of a variety of skills and knowledge, and widespread acceptability by the medical profession and others, these procedures may not be particularly appropriate for evaluation of teaching. However, the overall segmentation of the NBME exam as well as the timing of the examination seems to provide a useful model for teacher evaluation.

Segmentation and Timing of the Examination

Following the three-part model of the NBME exam, we suggest that the reflective professional teacher might be evaluated at three different points in his or her graduate program in teacher education. Table 8–1 presents the points of evaluation as well as summarizes the type of professional knowledge that would be evaluated at each point. Although this proposed model of assessment might be used to drive the order and progression of the teacher education curriculum, this does not necessarily have to be the case. For example, reflection and other complex meaningful tasks can be taught early in a student's education. In fact, if not taught early and continuously, these complex abilities may not develop at all (Anderson, 1987).

The student in teacher education would be allowed to take Part I of the Teacher Examination after completion of general-liberal studies and prior to beginning professional education courses, pedagogical coursework, and clinical training. Part I of the examination would test the teacher education students' knowledge, both declarative knowledge and procedural knowledge in the content domains. The teacher education candidate would be allowed to take Part II of the Examination any time after passing Part I. The teacher education candidate might be advised to complete Part II prior to or concurrently with the clinical internship. Part II would assess candidates' general pedagogical knowledge, curriculum knowledge, and content-specific pedagogical knowledge, as well as their knowledge of learners, contexts, and ends. As in Part I, Part II would consist primarily of written multiple-choice items or essay items that might also make substantial use of case studies of students, teaching, and classrooms to assess declarative knowledge of general pedagogy and content-specific pedagogy.

To be eligible to take Part III of the exam, candidates would first have to pass Parts I and II. Moreover, they would have to have completed an approved internship and approved graduate coursework in a teacher education institution. Part III would assess primarily the candidate's procedural knowledge in the domains of general pedagogy, curriculum knowledge, and content-specific pedagogy although the test might also include a few items to test declarative knowledge in these domains as well. In addition, Part III of the exam would test candidates' metacognitive knowledge in all seven domains. Peterson (1988) provided some examples of teachers' metacognitive knowledge of general pedagogy and content-specific pedagogy and ways of assessing this knowledge. To assess adequately candidates' procedural and metacognitive knowledge of general pedagogy, curriculum, and content-specific pedagogy, Part III would probably have to include some innovative assessment procedures, such as classroom simulations or interviews. Similarly, new assessment techniques might be needed to assess metacognitive knowledge of content, learners, contexts, and ends. We discuss several of these new assessment methods below.

In addition to a three-part examination as described above, we recommend the possibility of providing an option for teacher education candidates to take the entire examination at one point in time. This would follow a format and timing procedure similar to that of the FLEX. Such a procedure might be particularly appropriate for teacher education candidates in nonstandard graduate programs of teacher education who want to achieve certification in teaching.

The three-part teacher examination described above might be used not only for summative evaluation or certification purposes, but also for formative evaluation. Medical schools may receive a student's scores on the subtests of each examination if requested, and some schools provide remedial courses and assistance to students who fail (Cleghorn, 1986). Similarly, results of each subtest in the teacher examination might be shared with teacher candidates, and teacher education programs might provide remedial help in the form of tutoring, seminars, classes, or guided independent study. Students who fail should be allowed to take the examination again.

Format of Items to Be Used in Teacher Evaluation

To assess adequately the teachers' professional knowledge in the categories in Table 8–1, evaluators will need to use a variety of formats of assessment items. These include the more traditional multiple-choice format items as well as some more innovative items using simulations.

Multiple-choice format.   The variety and type of multiple-choice questions used in the NBME exam seem to be far superior to many of the multiple-choice items used in current teaching examinations of teachers' professional knowledge. Thus, some of these items in the National Board might serve as models for the development of items to test teachers' professional knowledge. The multiple-choice format is perhaps best used to test declarative or propositional knowledge.

The use of case histories on the NBME exam is particularly intriguing and may provide an example that is worth emulating in teacher evaluation. For example, to test declarative knowledge of general pedagogy, educators might construct an item such as the following sample case history, which describes a recalcitrant student who is continually demanding the teacher's attention:

Ms. Smith teaches ninth grade English. Ms. Smith is attempting to involve the class in a discussion of Edgar Allen Poe's "The Telltale Heart." As she is listening to one of the students comment on the old man in the story, she notices that a student named Brian is carrying on a whispered conversation with another student. Brian has been a constant source of distraction in the classroom since the first day of class. He often talks out of turn, walks in late, volunteers to answer a question, and then when called upon, replies with a silly answer. Ms. Smith thinks that Brian's behavior is often aimed at attempting to get her attention. Based on her pedagogical philosophy, she has decided to ignore Brian's conversation rather than to reprimand him. She continues to focus her attention on the student leading the discussion and when that student is done talking, she praises that student for his insightful comments.

Question: Ms. Smith's reaction to Brian's actions is most likely based on which of the following pedagogical philosophies?

A. Humanistic
B. Cognitive
C. Behavioral
D. Constructivist

While the above case study might be adequate to assess declarative knowledge, more elaborate simulations might be needed to assess teachers' procedural knowledge or metacognitive knowledge. We turn now to an analysis of these simulations.

Written simulations.   The medical profession has been successful in using written simulations—Patient Management Problems (PMPs) to assess a physician's problem-solving skills, as well as their content knowledge. PMPs are designed to simulate a physician's encounter with a patient and the procedures that the doctor uses to gather data, generate a hypothesis as to the cause of the symptoms, diagnose the illness, and recommend treatment. Use of PMPs on a teaching examination assumes that the task of a teacher is analogous to the task of the physician—the teacher's task is to diagnose and treat a student who has a "problem."

While such a view of the task of a teacher and the relationship of the teacher to a student might be accurate to describe the task of a learning disabilities teacher or a special needs teacher, this view does not describe accurately the task of a teacher in a regular classroom for several reasons. First, classroom teachers generally do not interact one-on-one as a doctor does with a patient. In contrast, the teacher typically deals with many individuals and problems simultaneously as she interacts with all students in her class. Second, the data-gathering procedures of a doctor and a teacher are not necessarily analogous. In obtaining information, the physician reads a chart, orders laboratory tests, and examines the patient for symptoms. On the other hand, the teacher often gathers much of her information from observing the child's interactions with materials, classmates, and the teacher herself over an extended period of time. Often teachers may obtain additional information from a call to the family, from guidance counselors, or from other teachers. Thus, the important information in a "case" for a teacher cannot often be reduced to a written description on paper, but is gathered by the teacher over an extensive period of time with a significant amount of interaction with the child or children. Thus, the teacher's familiarity with the child and with her class is extremely important in determining both how she gathers information and how she reacts or makes decisions about the child or the class. Third, a physician is primarily in a position of reacting to a problem presented by a patient, while most teachers adopt a proactive stance of "business as usual" until a problem presents itself (Peterson & Clark, 1978).

Lastly, in teaching, the correctness of a "diagnosis" is often not known to the teacher for weeks or months. Moreover, there is typically more than one way to treat a problem based on alternative pedagogical knowledge and philosophies. The correct procedure that the teacher selects for diagnosis and for acting on the problem undoubtedly may depend both on the nature of the problem and the child involved. In medicine, a patient either gets better, dies, or decides to see another doctor. In teaching, a student often does not get "better" for some time, rarely dies although he or she may get "sicker," and does not usually have the option of transferring to another teacher.

Given these tremendous differences between the clinical setting in medicine and in teaching, the format of the PMPs does not seem to be applicable directly to evaluation in teaching. Written simulations would obviously need to be much more complex and to include, for example, descriptions of entire classrooms rather than descriptions of a single child. Given these limitations, other types of simulations rather than written simulations might be more appropriate.

Computer-administered simulations. While some educational researchers have explored the use of the computer for teaching classroom skills and for assessment of teachers (Copeland, 1987; Strang, Badt, & Kauffman, 1987), these computer simulations suffer from many of the same limitations as written simulations. Such computer simulations seem to be low in ecological validity. For example, in no way is the candidate's interacting with written or graphic material presented on a computer screen comparable to the teacher's complex verbal and nonverbal interactions in a classroom of students. Further, even those researchers who have developed computer simulations have provided no data to show that how a teacher behaves or thinks when presented with a computer-administered simulation is similar to how the same teacher thinks when presented with the reality of the classroom situation in which teachers' thoughts and actions are affected by the pressures of time, simultaneous demands, district and building policies, limited materials, interruptions, and a host of other constraints and opportunities. Although with advances in technology, computers have increasing power and capabilities for branching and manipulation of information, they still can not simulate the complexity of a real classroom situation.

Simulated classes or "confederate" students. The medical profession has begun to make use of "confederate" patients or simulated patients to assess medical professionals. Similarly, Shulman and Sykes (1986) suggested the use of a simulated class to assess teachers. They described such an assessment as follows:

> The in-basket simulated class can also serve as the setting for the actual planning and delivery of instruction during the Presentation Phase of the examination. Here the candidate plans a lesson for this class based upon an analysis of the text he has completed earlier. The planned lesson is then presented to either a group of experienced teacher-examiners playing the roles of students, or to an actual group of students who are hired to portray a class. The presentation is videotaped to make later analysis possible. (pp. 17-18)

Such an approach is similar to the use of simulated patients for assessment of clinical skills in medicine. However, the use of "confederate" patients or simulated patients may be more appropriate for medicine than for teaching. Physicians often deal with patients who are strangers. Thus, a simulated patient who is a stranger is an ecologically valid situation for a physician. On the other hand, teachers typically deal with students that they have known for an extended period of time. Teachers' effectiveness depends on the knowledge that they have developed of their students and their classes. Thus, requiring a teacher candidate to present a lesson to a group of "confederate" students might be a task that is completely unlike the task that teachers face in presenting the lesson to their actual classes with whom they are familiar. Assessing teachers' professional knowledge using this strange task may not be in any way predictive of the teacher's knowledge and behavior in an actual classroom situation.

A second problem with the use of simulated classes is the problem of obtaining a reliable estimate of a teacher's score across simulated situations. Medical educators have documented that at least nine simulated cases may be needed to achieve a reliability of above .7 for medical candidates. Given the documented intraindividual variability of teachers in their behavior across teaching situations (Shavelson & Dempsey-Atwood, 1976; Shavelson, Webb, & Burstein, 1986), a similarly large number of simulated situations may be necessary to estimate a stable score for teacher candidates across simulated situations.

A more useful procedure might be to videotape interns teaching in their own classes over several situations and use these for the purposes of teaching evaluation. Use of the teacher's own class would make the testing situation ecologically valid and would provide the number of situations needed for more reliable and stable assessments. However, use of the teachers' own class as the "stimulus" for testing items makes the stimulus nonstandard across teachers. Thus, it may be more difficult to construct items that would be the same and could be asked of all teachers. On the other hand, one might adapt "stimulated-recall" interview procedures that have been used successfully to assess teachers' reflection and thinking abilities during classroom teaching (Clark & Peterson, 1986; Peterson & Clark, 1978). In this procedure, the researcher videotapes the teacher teaching, plays back segments of the videotape to the teacher, and then interviews the teacher about her knowledge, thinking, and reflections. We discuss some possible interview questions that might be asked in such a situation in our discussion of video simulations that follows.

Video simulations or interactive videodisc simulations. Of the existing and new simulation methods being used in medical evaluation, perhaps the most promising for teacher evaluation is the interactive videodisc simulation. The interactive videodisc has the capability of presenting the simulation of teaching in the classroom in a far more real-life and complex manner than does any of the other media discussed above. Alternatively, in the absence of a computer, a video simulation might be used with a live interviewer presenting the questions.

It is easy to imagine a videodisc that presents the teacher with a "live" scene from a classroom including close-up shots of individual students or the teacher as well as broad views of the entire classroom. Teacher candidates might be asked to consider the unfolding actions from the point of view of the simulated teacher and to choose responses based on a particular educational philosophy, as described in the sample case history above. Alternatively, they might be given a goal and asked how they would achieve it, given the information available to them from the scene. On the other hand, they might be asked what information they would need in order to analyze effectively what is happening in the classroom. Finally, teachers might be asked questions to determine their metacognitive knowledge or ability to reflect in the areas of content knowledge, general pedagogical knowledge, and content-specific pedagogical knowledge.

Recently, researchers have begun to use video vignettes of classroom scenes coupled with interview questions to assess teachers' reflection. For example, Peterson & Comeaux (1987) found that experienced high school social studies teachers differed significantly from inexperienced teachers (preservice social studies teachers) in their metacognitive knowledge of general pedagogy. In other words, the experienced teachers were significantly more reflective in their analyses of classroom teaching and learning situations and their interpretations of the teaching "problem" were significantly more elaborate and complex than were inexperienced teachers'. All teachers were shown videotapes of three classroom scenes enacted for the study by an actual secondary social studies class.

Each teacher first viewed the videotaped scene, and then was asked by the interviewer to remember as many of the events in the scene as he or she could. The interviewer also asked the teacher to describe a specific point at which a different decision could have been made by the teacher, and to explain what alternative he or she would have chosen, and why. Finally, the teacher was asked whether he or she could think of any other points at which a different decision could have been made by the teacher and to describe the decision.

Results indicated that experienced teachers recalled more of the classroom events than did novice teachers. More importantly, however, experienced teachers' analyses of the classroom teaching and learning situations appeared to reflect an underlying knowledge structure that relied heavily on procedural knowledge of classroom events, as well as on higher-order principles of effective classroom teaching. Thus, in their approach to problems that occurred during interactive classroom teaching, experienced teachers more often discussed the problems in terms of pedagogical principles, procedures, and higher-level pedagogical principles. In sum, the study by Peterson and Comeaux (1987) might serve as a model for designing assessment procedures using videotaped classroom vignettes and interviews.

Stoiber (1988) has also developed videotaped vignettes of an elementary classroom to be used for assessing teachers' capability for reflection. In Stoiber's assessment procedure, she first showed the beginning part of the videotape up to the point before the teacher intervenes in the classroom management situation. At this point, Stoiber asked "midstream" questions such as, "Describe what is happening in this situation" and "What actions would *you* take (as a teacher)?" Then Stoiber presented the teacher candidate with the rest of the videotape in which the teacher attempts to deal with the management problem and does not succeed. At the end of the videotape, the candidate was asked further questions, including "Would you have acted differently (than this teacher)? How?" Stoiber is developing procedures for scoring preservice teachers' reflective thinking as measured by the audiotaped, transcribed responses to these questions. Stoiber has data comparing preservice elementary teachers who completed a 10-week program on reflective teaching compared to preservice teachers in a control group who did not participate in such a program. In addition, Stoiber has information from experienced elementary teachers who have viewed these videotaped vignettes and responded to the interview questions. Thus, these experts may provide criteria for scoring the responses of the novice in terms of their procedural knowledge as well as their metacognitive knowledge of general pedagogy in the area of classroom management.

Although more realistic than the other types of simulations mentioned above, video simulations and interactive videodisc simulations are not without problems. The video simulations described above still lack ecological validity because they are based on teachers' viewing and thinking about a "strange" class that they do not know. As described above, one possible way of overcoming this problem is to use videotaped examples of the teacher's own class coupled with a standard interview protocol and a standard way of coding or scoring the teacher's responses (see, for example, Clark & Peterson, 1986; Peterson & Clark, 1978). A further limitation is the computer's inability to deal with open-ended responses. Thus, a teacher would be limited to the choices presented by the computer, although the teacher may have valid or creative alternatives if she were allowed to construct her own. A possible way around this problem is the use of a live interviewer. Alternatively, open-ended responses might be allowed at various points in the simulation. These open-ended responses might then be audiotaped and transcribed. Open-ended questions would permit the candidate to write responses to justify and explain her answer. Such a response may better reveal a teacher's thinking process and assessment of the situation. This format has been used on an experimental basis in the California Bar Examination in 1980 (Aburto & Haertel, 1986). Moreover, such audiotape protocols have been scored reliably and analyzed for teachers' reflective thoughts (see, for example, Peterson & Clark, 1978; Peterson & Comeaux, 1987).

CONCLUSION

Recently, one of the authors was reading and discussing an article in the Education Life section of the *New York Times* with a friend of hers, a physician of internal medicine. Included were seven items from the National Teacher Examination test of professional knowledge. The author has over nine years high school teaching experience plus teaching experience at the college level; the physician has no teaching experience. Both decided to complete the seven sample items and compare their scores. The teacher predicted that she would undoubtedly outscore her friend. Much to her surprise, she and her physician friend scored exactly the same—six out of seven answers correct—and in addition, they both missed the same question. The physician inquired of the teacher, "I wonder if we'd score the same if you were asked questions on professional knowledge from the board certifying exam in internal medicine?" Needless to say, the teacher felt she knew the answer to that question: any answers that she would get right on the medical exam would be due to lucky guessing.

The above scenario shows the problems that exist with current evaluation procedures to test teachers' professional knowledge. However, it is difficult to imagine the above scenario occurring if teacher educators were to follow the suggestions that we have made for how to conceptualize teachers' professional knowledge and for how to reliably and validly assess that knowledge. The goal of current reforms in teaching and teacher education should be to create new teacher evaluation procedures that will measure the unique qualities of the reflective teacher and that will consistently discriminate her from others, including nonteachers as well as reflective professionals in other fields.

REFERENCES

ABURTO, S., & HAERTEL, E. (1986). *Executive summary of study group on alternative assessment methods.* Stanford, CA: Teacher Assessment Project, Stanford University.

ANDERSON, C. W. (1987, April). *Three perspectives on cognition and their implications for science teaching.* Paper presented at the annual meeting of the American Educational Research Association, Washington, DC.

ANDERSON, J. R. (1983). *The architecture of cognition.* Cambridge, MA: Harvard University Press.

CALDERHEAD, J. (1983, April). *Research into teachers' and student teachers' cognitions: Exploring the nature of classroom practice.* Paper presented at the annual meeting of the American Educational Research Association, Montreal.

CARNEGIE FORUM ON EDUCATION AND THE ECONOMY. (1986). *A nation prepared: Teachers for the 21st century.* The Report of the Task Force on Teaching as a Profession. New York: Carnegie Corporation.

CARTER, K., SABERS, D., CUSHING, K., PINNEGAR, S. & BERLINER, D. C. (1987). Processing and using information about students: A study of expert, novice, and postulant teachers. *Teaching and Teacher Education, 3,*(2), 147–157.

CHI, M., GLASER, R., & REES, E. (1982). Expertise in problem solving. In R. J. Sternberg (Ed.), *Advances in the psychology of human intelligence.* Hillsdale, NJ: Lawrence Erlbaum.

CLARK, C. M., & PETERSON, P. L. (1986). Teachers' thought processes. In M. C. Wittrock (Ed.), *Handbook of research on teaching* (3rd ed., pp. 255–295). New York: Macmillan.

CLEGHORN, G. D. (1986). Policies of U.S. medical schools on the use of NBME part I and part II examinations. *Journal of Medical Education, 61*(2), 954–957.

COPELAND, W. D. (1987). Classroom management and student teachers' cognitive abilities: A relationship. *American Educational Research Journal, 24*(2), 219–236.

DISERENS, D., SCHWARTZ, M. W., GUENIN, M., & TAYLOR, L. A. (1986). Measuring the problem-solving ability of students and residents by microcomputers. *Journal of Medical Education, 61,* 461–466.

FROHLICH, E. D. (1985). Medical qualifying examinations. In E. D. Frohlich (Ed.), *Rypins' medical licensure examinations: Topical summaries and questions.* Philadelphia, PA: J. B. Lippincott Co.

THE HOLMES GROUP. (1986). *Tomorrow's teachers: A report of the Holmes Group.* East Lansing, MI: The Holmes Group.

HOUSNER, L. D., & GRIFFEY, D. C. (1985). Teacher cognition: Differences in planning and interactive decision making between experienced and unexperienced teachers. *Research Quarterly for Exercise and Sport, 56*(1), 45–53.

KORTHAGEN, F. A. (1985). Reflective teaching and preservice education in the Netherlands. *Journal of Teacher Education, 36*(5), 11–15.

LARKIN, J., MCDERMOTT, J., SIMON, D. P., & SIMON, H. A. (1980). Expert and novice performance in solving physics problems. *Science, 208,* 1335–1342.

LEINHARDT, G. (1983). Novice and expert knowledge of individual students' achievement. *Educational Psychologist, 18*(3), 165–179.

LEINHARDT, G., & GREENO, J. (1986). The cognitive skill of teaching. *Journal of Educational Psychology, 77*(3), 75–95.

NEELY, A. (1986). Planning and problem solving in teacher education. *Journal of Teacher Education, 37,*(3), 29–33.

PETERSON, P. L. (1987, April). *Teaching for educational excellence: The challenge is now.* Invited address given at the Indiana University Annual Education Conference on "Current Perspectives on School-Based Evaluation," Bloomington, Indiana.

PETERSON, P. L. (1988). Teachers' and students' cognitional knowledge for classroom teaching and learning. *Educational Research, 17* (5).

PETERSON, P. L., & CLARK, C. M. (1978). Teachers' reports of their cognitive processes during teaching. *American Educational Research Journal, 15,* 555–565.

PETERSON, P. L., & COMEAUX, M. A. (1987). Teachers' schemata for teaching and learning: The mental scaffolding of teachers' thoughts during classroom instruction. *Teaching and Teacher Education, 3*(4), 319–331.

RUMELHART, D. E., & NORMAN, D. A. (1978). Accretion, tuning, and restructuring: Three modes of learning. In J. W. Cotton & R. Klatzsky (Eds.), *Semantic factors in cognition.* Hillsdale, NJ: Erlbaum.

SCHOENFELD, A. H., & HERRMANN, D. J. (1982). Problem perception and knowledge structure in expert and novice mathematical problem solvers. *Journal of Experimental Psychology, 8*(3), 484–494.

SCHUMACHER, C. F. (1978). Reliability, validity, and standard setting. In J. P. Hubbard (Ed.), *Measuring medical education* (2nd ed.). Philadelphia, PA: Lea & Febiger.

SHANKER, A. (1985). *The making of a profession.* Washington, DC: American Federation of Teachers, AFL-CIO.

SHAVELSON, R. J., & DEMPSEY-ATWOOD, N. (1976). Generalizability of measures of teaching behavior. *Review of Educational Research, 51,* 455–498.

SHAVELSON, R. J., WEBB, N. M., & BURSTEIN, L. (1986). Measurement of teaching. In M. C. Wittrock, *Handbook of research on teaching* (3rd ed., pp. 50–91). New York: Macmillan.

SHULMAN, L. S. (1975). *Teaching as clinical information processing* (Report of Panel Six, National Conference on Studies in Teaching). Washington, DC: National Institute of Education.

SHULMAN, L. S. (1986a). Paradigms and research programs in the study of teaching: A contemporary perspective. In M. Wittrock (Ed.), *Handbook of research on teaching* (3rd ed., pp. 3–36). New York: MacMillan.

SHULMAN, L. S. (1986b). Those who understand: Knowledge growth in teaching. *Educational Researcher, 15*(2), 4–14.

SHULMAN, L. S. (1987). Knowledge and teaching: Foundations of the new reform. *Harvard Educational Review, 57*(1), 1–22.

SHULMAN, L. S., & SYKES, G. (1986, May). A national board for teaching: *In search of a bold standard.* Paper prepared for the Task Force on Teaching as a Profession, Carnegie Forum on Education and the Economy. Stanford, CA: Stanford University.

STILLMAN, P. L. et al. (1986). Assessing clinical skills of residents with standardized patterns. *Annals of Internal Medicine, 105,* 762–771.

STOIBER, K. C. (1988). *The effects of technical principle, reflective decision making, and integrated strategy skills training on preservice teachers' classroom management competence.* Unpublished doctoral dissertation, University of Wisconsin-Madison.

STRANG, H. R., BADT, K. S., & KAUFFMAN, J. M. (1987). Microcomputer-based simulations for training fundamental teaching skills. *Journal of Teacher Education, 38*(1), 20–25.

VOSS, J. F., GREENE, T. F., POST, T. A., & PENNER, B. C. (1983). Problem solving skills in the social sciences. In G. H. Bower (Ed.), *The psychology of learning and motivation* (Vol. 17). New York: Academic Press.

WILLIAMSON, J. W. (1976, March). Validation for performance measures. In *Conference on extending the validity of certification.* Evanston, IL: American Board of Medical Specialties.

ZEICHNER, K., & LISTON, D. (1987). Teaching student teachers to reflect. *Harvard Educational Review, 57*(1), 23–48.

ZEICHNER, K., LISTON, D., & MAHLIOS, M. (1987, April). *The structure and goals of a student teacher program and the character of supervisory discourse.* Paper presented at the annual meeting of the American Educational Research Association, Washington, D.C.

9

GRADUATE PROGRAMS OF TEACHER EDUCATION AND THE PROFESSIONALIZATION OF TEACHING

Virginia Richardson-Koehler

and Gary D. Fenstermacher

Some recent education reform proposals call for two essential and interrelated structural changes: changes in the organization of teaching, and a change from undergraduate to graduate degree status for initial teacher preparation (see, for example, "The Phoenix Agenda", Joyce & Clift, 1984; The Council of Chief State School Officer's *Staffing the Nation's Schools*, 1984; Carnegie Task Force, *A Nation Prepared*, 1986; Holmes Group, *Tomorrow's Teachers*, 1986). While much has been written both supporting and criticizing these proposed changes (see, for example, the entire issues of *Teachers College Record*, Spring, 1987, and *Educational Policy*, vol. 1, no. 1, 1987), the goal these reforms are presumably to achieve, the professionalization of teaching, is seldom questioned. This chapter examines the arguments for professionalizing teaching and raises doubts that the laudable goals set forth in the reports would be realized by the form of professionalization proposed therein.

While other chapters in this volume examine aspects of the reform proposals related to the graduate preparation of teaching, this chapter explores what appears to be the *raison d'etre* for the reform proposals: to raise the status of the teaching occupation to a profession. Specifically, we will examine the particular form of professionalization proposed in these reports. What effects might this form have on schools and their students? Are there other ways of helping teachers become experts without the potentially adverse effects of the proposed structural changes in teaching? We answer these questions by examining the key characteristics of the Holmes Group and

Carnegie proposals and the grounds on which they are based. We suggest that the particular form of professionalization proposed in these reports may be neither desirable nor necessary to the restructuring of teacher education programs; there may be alternatives that are more likely to succeed in achieving the larger goals expressed in these reports.

KEY CHARACTERISTICS OF REFORM PROPOSALS

Many of the key proposals in the Holmes and Carnegie reports are aimed at upgrading the status of the profession and of colleges of education. This upgrading will occur, the reformers believe, through structural changes in elementary and secondary schools and new requirements for initial teacher preparation. Both reports stress the interactive nature of the changes—that alterations of the kind proposed for teacher education cannot be accomplished without corresponding alterations in school settings. As Judge (1987) notes, it is "the nature of teaching and the distribution of teaching tasks and rewards that must first be changed. Only then can claims for any form of professional status be realistically sustained" (p. 32).

Both the Carnegie and Holmes reports appear to be motivated by a strong desire to improve the quality of education, but the reasons for improvement are grounded in quite different perspectives. The Carnegie report ties our declining performance in the world economic system to the abysmal state of education and suggests that this problem threatens our democratic roots. The Holmes report is less dramatic and simply suggests that the dissatisfaction with schooling in America is longstanding and increasing; therefore both teaching and efforts aimed at improving teaching need to change. The Carnegie report is rooted more in economic and political arguments, a predictable slant, given the business and commercial membership of the commission. The Holmes report has much of the flavor of the modern academy; given its authorship by deans of education in research universities, this perspective comes as no surprise.

Structural Changes in Schooling and Teacher Education

Both reports propose that teachers should receive their initial teacher preparation in graduate rather than undergraduate programs. In the Carnegie report, this feature is initially introduced as a means of raising the status of teaching such that the public would be willing to pay higher salaries to teachers. Both reports stress the need for a good subject matter and liberal arts undergraduate experience, and a one- or two-year graduate credentialing or Master of Arts in Teaching (M.A.T.) program. The present elementary undergraduate major, they suggest, is weak in subject matter courses, while the secondary undergraduate major is light on professional preparation courses.

The Holmes Group report suggests that professional preparation courses should be improved by focusing on the teaching of specific subjects, based on recent research in these areas. The Carnegie report suggests that the National Standards Board's licensing exams will, in part, determine the curriculum for the preparation programs.

Reform in elementary and secondary schools is an essential element of both reports. This reform includes some means of hierarchically differentiating staff functions, providing more pay to those at higher levels, and permitting more faculty involvement in decision making. The Holmes Group career ladder proposal includes the three levels of instructor, professional teacher, and career professional. Individuals would be selected for these levels on the basis of their initial and later formal preparation. The Instructor would begin teaching after receiving a B.A., the professional teacher would require an M.A. in teaching, and the career professional, a doctoral degree or the equivalent. The levels would be differentiated on the basis of degree of autonomy, salary, and extrainstructional functions. The lead teacher of the Carnegie report is similar to the Holmes Group career professional. Both the lead teacher and the career professional would be involved in staff development, school decision making, and so on. Lead teachers would receive an Advanced Teaching Certificate from the National Board of Standards and would require some advanced graduate work.

Teachers Viewed as Change Agents

In both reports, teachers are viewed as the primary agents for improving the quality of education; and consequently they are the persons most affected by the proposed reforms. Because the reports focus on teachers rather than on teaching, they consider teacher characteristics, supply, demand, and incentives rather than classroom activities. Concern is expressed about the quality of students entering teaching and attention is directed to attracting more intellectually capable teachers. Better entering students are necessary to attain, through teacher preparation, the ideal described by the Holmes Group report: "competent teachers empowered to make principled judgments and decisions on their students' behalf . . . [who are] careful not to bore, confuse, or demean students . . . [and who] are especially critical for these growing numbers of educationally at-risk children" (Holmes Group, 1986, pp. 28–29). For the Carnegie report, these people "have a good grasp of the ways in which all kinds of social systems work, . . . must think for themselves if they are to help others think for themselves, be able to act independently and collaborate with others, and render critical judgment" (p. 25).

Both reports suggest that we can attract such persons with higher pay and a more "professional" work environment. A professional environment is regarded as one that is more autonomous and less bureaucratized than is presently the case. It is one where teachers share in the decision making and participate in non-classroom-focused activities such as inducting new teachers into the system.

The two reports differ on which institution should be the initiator of reform and guardian of standards. For the Holmes Group report, it is the loosely federated research universities that set standards for teacher education and exchange research-based knowledge about teaching practice. In the Carnegie report, it is a newly created

National Board for Professional Teaching Standards, with a majority of members elected by Board-certified teachers.

Assumptions in the Reform Proposals

The two major forms of structural change proposed in the reports, the graduate degree status of initial teacher preparation and the differentiation of the teaching occupation, are designed to meet two interrelated goals: increasing the quality of education for all students and professionalizing the teaching occupation. Arguments showing the relationship between the structural changes and increasing the quality of education are not well articulated in either report. The value of the specific form of professionalization proposed is virtually unexamined. We wonder whether the proposed view of teaching and schooling will indeed improve the quality of education, and whether professionalizing the teaching occupation in the manner suggested is a goal to which we should aspire.

As Judge (1987) points out, the proposal for graduate degree programs in teacher training requires a change in the structure of the teaching occupation. The change proposed is the hierarchical differentiation of staffing. These changes are proposed for both elementary and secondary schools and are designed to provide a higher quality of education by attracting and retaining higher quality teachers. These higher quality teachers will be attracted to and retained in teaching because the sustained work of obtaining higher degrees will be rewarded with higher status positions in the school hierarchy and higher pay. The range of possible effects of such a system on the education of our students is not examined. Indeed, it is simply assumed that advanced graduate preparation and the concomitant hierarchically structured teaching occupation will bring great educational value to students and teachers and presumably to parents and the general citizenry, as well. These contentions and assumptions deserve more careful scrutiny, beginning with the notion of professionalizing teaching.

THE PROFESSIONALIZATION OF TEACHING

All of the recent reform reports argue that teaching can and should be considered a profession and that teachers ought to be regarded as professionals. Indeed this aspiration is accepted as if it were virtually a divine right of teachers. Denied status and credibility for so long, teachers now have the opportunity to gain what is rightfully theirs. Recognition as a professional is presumed to follow the so-called "knowledge base" that has emerged in the field of teaching. This knowledge base, it is argued, places teaching among the highly specialized human service fields and requires that teachers be accorded extensive autonomy and control over their work settings. It is presumed that teaching will achieve its rightful place in the same historically inevitable way as law and medicine achieved theirs. Almost no one asks whether we truly wish teachers to be like lawyers and physicians, or whether they could be like lawyers and physicians and still retain all that we regard as excellent about teaching. A closer look at the parallels yields some interesting insights.

One does not need a scientific study to gain a sense of the typical relationships between physicians and patients. All verbal communication is couched in the title "Doctor_____." One seldom sees a physician's name without the "M.D." following it, unless the physician specifically wishes not to be identified as such (as when an airline passenger). Physicians infrequently discuss their processes and procedures with patients and rarely explain what they are doing (save in the most simple, typically condescending ways). After an encounter with a physician, the patient may have a vague idea what is wrong and some modest procedures for curing oneself (e.g., take three of these pills a day [you may not know what you are taking], check into this hospital, go to that laboratory for these tests).

This behavior has been quite characteristic of those most likely to be regarded as professionals. It is as if they are saying to their patients or clients: "Do what I tell you to do and you will be well again (or safe, or free), but do not try to do what I do, and do not—under any circumstances—try to figure things out for yourself." The occupations we usually think of as professions place considerable distance between the provider and the recipient. This distance is zealously protected, by arcane language, by technical procedures, by licensure, and a number of other devices that mystify and distance the client or patient.

Second Thoughts on Professionalizing Teaching

Given these untoward consequences of professionalization in medicine and law, it seems a propitious time, in the face of calls for professionalizing teaching, to pause and ask whether it might not be advantageous to inquire how the professionalization of teaching will affect the relationship between the teacher and the learner and, almost as important, the relationship between teacher and parent. Many of the indications we have from law and medicine are that the trappings of professionalization will increase the social, communication, and psychological gaps between the provider and recipient, and between provider and the recipient's significant others. Soder (1986) puts the point well:

> Professionalization is a tempting strategy for groups aspiring to higher status. However, the strategy is usually one selected more on the basis of sidelong glances at purportedly successful occupations that have made the grade than on the basis of careful calculation. In the rush to get on with it, the risks of professionalization strategies are often ignored. The strategy, for example, can have the effect of reducing professional stature and authority. . . .(p. 5)

Might there be a better approach to capitalizing on our enhanced knowledge about teaching, while gaining the credibility needed to act effectively as a teacher?

Our concern is that we not ape the known, highly regarded professions merely because there are some historical parallels between their evolution and that of teaching, or because we are frustrated with the perceived lack of status and prestige afforded to the occupation of school teacher. There is enough that strikes us as unsatisfactory about law and medicine *as professions* that we might specifically wish to avoid becoming what they have become. (We wish to take nothing away from the good work of physicians and lawyers, rather only to object to some of the ways these occupations have come to be organized and extended in society.) In place of teaching becoming a profession like law and medicine, we might consider law and medicine becoming a profession like teaching might become (Shulman, 1985).

There may be some merit to this thought, as both law and medicine have recently become more educative in the way their practitioners work. Physicians are more willing to teach patients how to diagnose common maladies and care for themselves. For example, many parents are now trusted by physicians to use an otoscope to examine and diagnose recurring ear infections in their children, and—mirabile dictu—the parents might even be trusted to initiate the taking of an antibiotic (with, of course, the proviso that the child is brought in to the physician's office first thing Monday morning). Lawyers have expressed support for client involvement in law, through such mechanisms as small claims court and the self-preparation of basic legal documents. Thus, there are signs of lawyers and physicians wanting to enable and empower their clients by teaching them how to do the things they do.

This "new look" in law and medicine might lead a skeptic to toss off our concern about teachers becoming like physicians and lawyers with the comment that some professionals have simply developed poor manners in the course of occupational maturation. The skeptic might say that some distancing and mystification are a small price for all the good that has come to humanity. Physicians have made great strides in keeping us well, and lawyers have, despite our always poking fun at them, helped society to uphold and sustain its commitment to the rule of law. Why, then, fret over the relatively mild consequences of professionalization? Furthermore, recognizing these mildly unsavory consequences ahead of time might even permit us to fine-tune the occupational maturation of teaching so that it successfully avoids these minor pitfalls.

This is a tempting rebuttal to our concern, but one unlikely to succeed. The difference in aims between teaching, on the one hand, and law and medicine, on the other, is, by itself, sufficient to lead us to ask whether copying the occupational maturation of law and medicine will diminish or enhance the capacity of teaching to achieve its aims. Furthermore, the context for the professionalization of teaching seems to be very different from that for the other major professions. In the case of teaching, the reformers are proposing altering the character of an occupation that is nested within a highly developed and complex *system* of schooling. Both these points merit further discussion, and we will consider each in some depth. We turn first to the system of schooling, then follow that with a look at the aims of teaching.

Teaching in the Context of School Systems

In his provocative analysis of the emergence of the common school in American society, Katz (1975) argues that during the half-century from 1800 to 1850, Americans had a choice about how the nation might organize education. Katz contends that there were four possible models of organization, and there were systems of schooling in place exemplifying each of the models. As the nation moved into the mid-nineteenth century, one model became increasingly dominant, that of incipient bureaucracy. By the late 1800s, that model dominated nearly all education in the United States. There may be an instructive parallel here, for this present period in our history may be one of choices among competing models for framing the occupation of teaching. We are concerned that the recent reform reports have closed off discussion of possibilities other than professionalization in the manner of medicine and law.

One aspect of professionalizing teaching that is often overlooked in the reform rhetoric is the tight connection between professionalization and bureaucratization. The reform reports argue for professionalization as a means of promoting teacher autonomy in the workplace and control over the occupation itself. Overlooked in this claim that professionalization will bring autonomy and self-governance is an acknowledgment that bureaucratic organization has been the route to such professionalization as presently obtains in teaching. Yet despite the fact that bureaucratization has served as a mechanism for professionalization, bureaucratization is typically regarded as the enemy of autonomy and professional self-governance.

To explain this point, we return to one of the organizational models discussed by Katz (1975), called "democratic localism." Democratic localism is a form of local control, with a high degree of parent and community participation (a kind of "town meeting" governance of schooling). Efficiency and organizational rationality are far less regarded in democratic localisms than responsiveness, public control, and local involvement. It is most interesting to note the reasons Katz gives for the failure of democratic localism to become the dominant form of school organization: "The feature [of democratic localism] that has encouraged the most deviation has been antiprofessionalism. Democratic localists in most places were forced to recognize the appalling quality of teaching and, despite their ideological preference, realized the need to develop professional teaching training" (p. 49).

What is not immediately obvious in the modern reformers' calls for professionalization, but becomes quite clear in historical perspective, is that there is a close relationship between the bureaucratization of schooling and the professionalization of teaching. It is unlikely that teaching could have reached the state of professionalism it has attained were it not for the bureaucratization of schooling. Yet the current reform reports argue for the professionalization of teaching as if this were an antidote to the bureaucratic control of teaching. That view misses, we think, the very intimate connection between the bureaucratic organization of schooling and the professional character of teaching in school settings.[1]

This historical perspective raises a question whether the professionalization of teaching can be sustained outside the bureaucratic structure of schooling. The Holmes Group and Carnegie Commission participants may have been similarly troubled, for their proposals fall squarely into the web of bureaucracy. The proposals argue that the way to professionalize teaching is to structure it hierarchically, with degrees and credentials, different functions and responsibilities, and various levels of power and influence associated with each level of the hierarchy. This structure strikes us as an almost paradigmatic case of bureaucratic organization. Does it lead to higher quality education for students and increased autonomy and self-control for teachers? Part of the answer can be found in a case study recently completed by one of the authors.

A CASE STUDY IN STRUCTURAL CHANGE

The hierarchical structure proposed by the Holmes Group, Carnegie, and many other reports can be examined by describing an elementary school that has restructured itself along the lines proposed in the Holmes Group report and then examining what is happening to teachers and students in that school. While one school obviously does not generalize to the universe of schooling, this case raises questions concerning the consequences of such restructuring.

Desert View is an elementary school that has been examined in depth as a part of a study of at-risk students funded by the Exxon Foundation (Richardson-Koehler, Casanova, Placier, and Guilfoyle, 1987). The focus was on the schooling experiences of six at-risk grade 3 students in each of two schools. An understanding of their experiences was gained by interviewing the students, their parents, teachers and other experts in the school, and the principal. The students were observed in their classrooms, and school features were noted by the enthnographers.

Desert View is a K–6 elementary school in a lower middle class suburb of a medium-sized Southwestern city. Approximately 80 percent of the students are bilingual or Limited English Proficient. For two years preceeding the study, the faculty and administrative staff of Desert View were engaged in a reform process. Together, they read the extensive reform literature, developed a five-year plan, and radically reorganized the delivery of instruction. The new structure involved working in teams of two or three grade levels. Teachers taught to their strengths, and self-contained classrooms were no longer the norm. Students moved from teacher to teacher depending upon the subject matter and individually diagnosed problems.

A career ladder plan in the district allowed the school to promote a number of their teachers to team leaders. These individuals taught for a half a day and worked on leadership activities for the other half. The students went home early one day a week, providing a considerable amount of time for the teams to meet. The teachers actively participated in the governance of the school.

The school was known for its handling of learning-disabled children. A number of experts were associated with the school, and the teachers themselves received training in the various categories of learning disabilities. The teachers participated as peers with the experts in diagnosing problems and providing remediation for these children.

The effects of this system on the *teachers* in Desert View was to shift a considerable amount of their time and attention away from their students and classroom toward the systemics of schooling: collective planning and decision making, and staff development. The team leader, for example, taught in the morning and performed leadership activities in the afternoon. Such activities, in fact, involved a considerable amount of paper work rather than contact with other teachers.

The teachers appeared to be ambivalent about this structure. On the one hand, they liked the idea of common goals and other teachers being responsible, part of the time, for their children. On the other hand, they were uncomfortable with giving up their students for even a part of the day, because they had less of a sense of the whole child when they were not in their home classrooms. The one exception to this was the least effective and least confident teacher who seemed perfectly willing to allow other teachers and the specialists to take over the responsibility for her "problem" students.

The new structure created considerable management problems, with students constantly moving in and out of the classroom. The team leaders gave up their classrooms for one-half of every day, and, at least in the team that was observed, considerable time was devoted to the team leader and her substitute (also an experienced teacher) resolving differences. Further, the newly structured system created considerable stress, particularly at evaluation time. While the teachers agreed upon the general goals, they differed considerably on the means to implement them. Discussions of implementation strategies were extremely stressful for the teachers. Such ambivalence about systemics activities has also been described by Eisenhart, Shrum, Harding, and Cuthbert (in press).

The day seemed very choppy for all students, but particularly for those needing the extra help. Students' completion of assignments and worksheets was important to all teachers, and the at-risk students often missed recess in order to catch up with their fellow students on their assignments. A learning-disabled student could be in contact with five or six experts/teachers in one day, rushing from classroom to classroom. The observed students were exhausted at the end of the day (as was the observer).

Regular students could experience two homeroom teachers and a number of others in one day. The lesson segments were short and there was little coherence among them. The teachers differed considerably in terms of their management systems, classroom communication rules, and behavioral and content learning expectations.

The faculty and principal of the school prided themselves on good contact with the *parents* of their students. They were all bilingual and knew the neighborhood well. Indeed, the climate of the school was warm and caring. However, it was clear from the interviews with teachers and parents that communications were less than perfect. Two of the at-risk students in the sample were described by teachers as foster children. It took one call on the part of the researcher to determine that neither was. One stayed with her aunt after school until the mother could pick her up after work, and the other lived with his mother. The parents who were seen in the school were in the cafeteria, garden, or office rather than in the classrooms.

This school represents just one example of the type of school structure proposed in the recent reports that is required to support graduate level teacher preparation programs in research universities. What was happening to teachers and students in that school may relate to some factors other than the staffing structure in the school.

Further, the problems encountered may be specific to elementary schools. Nonetheless, the case poses some issues that must be considered in the push toward redesigning elementary and secondary schools in the image of higher education. The following themes emerged from the case study, and deserve further exploration:

Teachers spent more time on systemics and less time on instruction.

The systemics include team meetings for collective decision making, meetings with other team teachers and experts concerning individual children, staff development, and evaluation. Since teachers who are involved in these activities are not in classrooms with students, one of four things must happen: the day must be shortened, teachers must stay longer in school, class sizes become larger, or more teachers or other adults be hired. At Desert View, the amount of time students spent in school was shortened, and more teachers were hired. While this may not be a problem for the individual teacher, it places great burdens on schools and causes problems for the children. The system becomes much more complex, creating increased management problems. Interpersonal communications and potential for conflict are increased.

Contact with a number of teachers during the school day created both educational and social problems for individual students.

The teachers in Desert View felt that the team approach taught students to become adaptable as they moved from one teacher to the next. While adaptability may be considered a virtue, such learning may become more important to students than other types of learning such as cognitive skills. Further, such a system may be particularly detrimental to low achieving students. Good (1986, p. 101) pointed out that low achieving students have a particularly difficult time moving from one teacher to another. Further, an excessive amount of time was spent in transitions from classroom to classroom.

A hierarchically differentiated staffing system places higher status on the functions not performed by those at the lowest level: in this case, on systemics activities.

A model for hierarchically differentiated staffing can be found in higher education. In these institutions, teaching is often the least admired and rewarded function. Most of the lower level courses are taken over by graduate students or instructors and assistant professors. This same structure is now being proposed for elementary and secondary schools. The instructors would do the low level teaching; the career professionals would have more autonomy and would be more involved in collective decision making; and the lead teachers would be only partially involved in teaching. The systemics, therefore, become more important than teaching, and those performing them receive greater rewards.

The tensions between teaching and performing systemics will undoubtedly be stressful to many teachers. At the Schenley High School Teacher Center in Pittsburgh, for example, a number of the Clinical Resident Teachers (CRTs) asked to go back to regular teaching after one or two years because of the stress they felt concerning this tension. The CRTs worked with visiting teachers as clinicians, ran seminars, and continued to teach. They felt themselves to be, first and foremost, teachers; the other staff development activities took them away from their primary function, and the stress of balancing both was severe (Bickel & Pine, 1984).

It is perhaps the case that the flat organization of schooling has been highly functional in the performance of its primary activity: teaching. Structures for the differentiation of staffing must be developed so as to maintain the priority of the teaching function while allowing teachers some leeway to perform necessary and interesting functions. As Conley & Bacharach (1987) point out:

> It is not necessary to change the job structure in teaching to promote a model of internship and development. That is, there is nothing inherent in the existing job structure of public education that prevents districts from involving teachers in decision making, providing them with more development support, or creating internships for teachers. (p. 34)

Surely a structure could be developed that would be compatible with the egalitarian norms of the teaching occupation (Lortie, 1978) and would at the same time enhance the conditions of teaching. The consideration of egalitarianism leads quite naturally into a discussion of the democratic ideals of teaching.

TEACHING IN A DEMOCRACY

Earlier in the chapter we stated that the reform proposals did not adequately account for interrelationship of the structural or systemic properties of schooling and the call for professionalizing teaching. We also stated that the proposals did not examine the relationship between the aims of education and the call for restructuring teaching and teacher education. We examined the structural aspects of schooling and professionalization in the prior discussion. We turn now to the matter of the aims of education and the effects on these aims of the call for restructuring teaching and teacher education.

The nexus of democracy and education is so thoroughly a part of academic discussions of education that elaborate justification is not needed here. One need only recall Jefferson's words to be reminded of the essential connection: "That nation which expects to be both ignorant and free—in a state of civilization—expects what never was and never will be" (quoted in Cremin, 1966, p. 5). Nearly every major theorist of democracy has argued that the extension of the franchise to all adults is meaningless if every adult cannot participate, by reason of ignorance, in the civic life of the nation. Put bluntly, democracy is an empty ideal without an educated citizenry.

Of course, as Wringe (1984) points out, there are multiple versions of democracy, not all of them calling for the elaborate education of every adult in the nation. In corporate democracies, a small governing body is empowered to make decisions intended to ensure the welfare of all concerned. In liberal democracies, on the other hand, the people themselves have a voice in shaping what is in their best interest. Pratte (1987, p. 159) states this idea succinctly: "The point of participatory democracy is that those involved, those who will be most affected by the decision to be made or the action to be taken, actually take part in the discussion and take the decision, and the responsibility for the decision, themselves." The United States has, since its founding, sought to be a liberal democracy, with participatory democracy serving as the highest attainment of the liberal theory of democracy.

To achieve this end, schools were founded in order to extend the privilege of democratic participation to the people. This commitment to schools began early in the life of the nation, and has continued through the present. Article III of The Northwest Ordinance of 1787 indicates just how early a fledgling nation pledged itself to education: "Religion, morality, and knowledge being necessary to good government and the happiness of mankind, schools and the means of education shall forever be encouraged." This nation has committed itself to full equality of educational opportunity in a way that no other nation of the past has done, nor has any other nation in these times dedicated itself to this end with both the conviction and the resources that have characterized the United States.

The American dream of full equality for all is a distinctly democratic ideal, deeply dependent on education as its primary means of realization. Given our dependence on education to realize the democratic ideal, it is odd that there has been so little discussion of the impact of teaching reform proposals on the relation between education and democracy. The reform reports do make the customary, now perhaps mandatory, mention of this nation as a democracy dependent on its schools and teachers. The Carnegie report, for example, expresses concern about our status as a world leader and the relative academic showing of our students in comparison with the children of other nations. The Holmes Group advocates a strong teaching force as a contribution to the educational accomplishments of the nation. But neither report examines in much detail the impact of its recommendations on the duties and opportunities for teachers to contribute to the realization of the democratic ideal.

For example, take the quite simple point that Carnegie and Holmes propose hierarchies of teacher attainment, autonomy for teachers, and a strong voice in governing the affairs of the school. What kind of a democracy is being put into place with these proposals? More importantly, how democratically are such teachers likely to behave in their dealings with other school and nonschool personnel? At a minimum, these reform proposals suggest an elite cadre of teachers, whose primary cachet is specialized knowledge and a capacity to perform in ways that are currently regarded as effective.

Given the ethos of teaching built up from the reform proposals, what is the likelihood that the teacher trained according to these reform programs will be committed to democratic ideals in his or her own teaching behavior—much less in creating classroom environments that reflect democratic ideals and principles? We see, instead, in the reform proposals, a kind of political conservatism and epistemological conceit—wherein one's interest is in applying technical expertise to remediate diagnosed deficiencies and produce pupils whose test-taking performance is nearly as good as that of their teachers (all of whom, if the proposals before us succeed, will themselves have taken tests to get into the profession, to become licensed to teach, and to hold advanced professional standing in the teaching hierarchy).

It is not here contended that such reform proposals as Carnegie and Holmes are antidemocratic. Rather, we wish to consider the possibility that teachers of the kind argued for in the Carnegie and Holmes reports may not serve the democratic ideal well, and, if we are correct, what might be done to prevent this consequence. As mentioned above, perhaps there is more to the desire of many teachers for a "flat" organization of teaching than we have previously been willing to consider. Such a structure may permit more equality of consideration and influence than would be the case with the tiered organizations argued for in Carnegie and Holmes. Further, a flat structure of this kind may send a far more democratic message to learners than the hierarchical and bureaucratized structures now under consideration.

Jane Roland Martin (1987) recently criticized the Holmes agenda in something of the way we are inclined to do here. Contending that the Holmes proposals for the liberal education of teachers smacked of the preparation of Platonic guardians, Martin said that the Holmes Group failed to "consider the consequences for the hidden curriculum of schooling of an undergraduate teacher education designed along Platonic lines." Martin then asks whether we should "not expect that those who have been taught to lead a guardian's life will pass on to their pupils the guardian's disdain for manual labor, ambivalence about practical action, and distrust of feeling and emotion?" (p. 408).

Perhaps Martin exaggerates here, as it is unlikely that educating teachers or pupils as Platonic guardians would succeed, no matter how hard we tried. Yet the underlying point should not be lost: New knowledge and skill can as easily serve as a mechanism for gaining status and prestige as for personal freedom and the liberation of the mind. Depending on how the knowledge and skill are articulated systemically, they may be used far more as an occasion for status and control than for freedom and liberation. The consequences of this outcome for the nexus between democracy and education are enormous. The manner and form of professionalizing teaching may diminish the teacher's capacity to establish democratic environments, act on democratic principles, and model democratic behavior, or it may enhance these capacities. We believe that the reform proposals placed before us by the Holmes Group and the Carnegie Commission deserve careful scrutiny from this perspective.

RECONSIDERING PROFESSIONALIZATION

There is much that is good in the Carnegie and Holmes proposals. There is also much that we believe is the occasion for concern. Our concern is that the learner is not drowned in the bath water that the reformers seem to want to use to clean up teaching and teacher education. We believe there is an important and expanding knowledge base about teaching and schooling and that it can and should be used by teachers. (Indeed, one of us is responsible for a rather hefty book that addresses research-based practices for educational practitioners; see Richardson-Koehler, 1987). We believe that teacher education and schooling must be restructured. We believe that teachers deserve more societal praise and support than they are receiving.

We also believe that the system of schooling, as it is now structured and run, may have within it some features that ought to be more fully understood, and perhaps retained. The relatively flat organizational structure for teaching may have great utility for effecting cooperation and collegiality in ways that might be more worthwhile and successful than universities have been able to attain. This same one-dimensional structure may also permit a greater exercise of democratic governance and modeling than would be the case with a more hierarchical structure. With regard to the education of teachers, the short period of professional preparation that currently characterizes initial teacher preparation may, on further scrutiny, be grounded in quite good and proper reasons—though in our haste to make schools look more like universities, we may not be able to see what is worthwhile in what is already there. Perhaps teachers in training are already taught more than they can possibly apply in practice—until such time as they have practical experience to use as a base for acquiring further academic knowledge.

In a provocative essay on the professionalization of teachers, Hoyle (1985) discusses the difficulty of navigating between advanced knowledge and theory and a practical, human orientation to the persons being served. He wonders whether the established professions, were they still in the early stages of their development, might not also be addressing the same questions that now puzzle us about professionalizing teaching. Hoyle concludes:

> It is unlikely that teaching will become the new model profession. However, it is possible that if teaching can improve the ways in which practitioners acquire and utilize practice-relevant knowledge, its clientele will benefit greatly. The paradox is that it is unlikely to enhance its own status in the process. (p. 53)

If we ignore the sociology of knowledge, we could, perhaps, argue that there is no dichotomy between knowledge and expertise on the one hand and contextually wise and personally concerned practice on the other. Indeed, we would then say that persons are better served when those who serve them are steeped in the knowledge of their field and skilled at its practice. This view is certainly the one adopted in the Holmes Group and Carnegie Commission reports. Yet, as far as we can ascertain, there is little in the sociology of knowledge, the sociology of organizations, the history of education, or the political science of democracies that permits us to embrace the professionalization proposals of the reform reports in the form they are presented.

There are, indeed, tensions—sometimes dilemmas—between the individual and the organization, the scholar and the practitioner, the expert and the democrat, and between the medical and legal occupations and the teaching occupation. Our challenge is to come to grips with these tensions and dilemmas in ways that promote education as a means to liberate the mind and enable morally grounded action, in ways that encourage teachers to think and act as they desire their students to think and act, and in ways that sustain and promote the continuous process of inducting new citizens into democratic governance.

Until we have faced these issues in a more probing and illuminative way, there is much to recommend making but minor adjustments that reflect good sense and good practice. As Thomas Green (1984) reminds us, institutions are resistant to change for good reasons and bad. Among the good reasons is that those who argue for change may see the existing imperfections imperfectly, and were our vision clearer, the way things are may be far more sensible than they appear at first. As we gain clearer focus and firmer purchase on the world that is there, perhaps we will think quite differently about the world we want to achieve.

NOTES

[1] The connection between professionalization and bureaucratization is explored in Adler (1985) and Doyle (1976). Doyle notes that many students of education believe that "bureaucratization somehow places an absolute limit on the possibility of professionalizing. More recent scholarship suggests, however, that the distance and conflict between these two processes are not as great as had been assumed" (p. 25).

REFERENCES

ADLER, S. (1985, April). *The irony of professionalism.* A paper presented at the annual meeting of the American Educational Research Association, Chicago, IL.

ATKIN, J.M. (1985). Preparing to go to the head of the class. *The Wingspread Journal (Special Section on Teacher Education),* 1–3.

BICKEL, W., & PINE, C. (1984). *Notes on Center Development: Memo to Board of Visitors.* Pittsburgh, PA: Schenley High School Teacher Center, Pittsburgh School District.

CARNEGIE TASK FORCE ON TEACHING AS A PROFESSION. (1986). *A nation prepared: Teachers for the 21st century.* New York: Carnegie Forum on Education and the Economy, Carnegie Foundation.

CONLEY, S., & BACHARACH, S. (1987). The Holmes Group Report: Standards, hierarchies, and management. In J. Soltis (Ed.), *Reforming teacher education* (pp. 30–37). New York: Teachers College Press.

CREMIN, L. A. (1966). *The genius of American public education.* New York: Vintage Books.

DOYLE, W. (1976). Education for all: The triumph of professionalism. In O. C. Davis, Jr. (Ed.), *Perspectives on curriculum development, 1776–1976.* Washington, DC: Association for Supervision and Curriculum Development.

EISENHART, M., SHRUM, J., HARDING, J., & CUTHBERT, A. (forthcoming). Teacher beliefs: Definitions, findings, and directions. *Educational Policy.*

GOOD, T. (1986). What is learned in elementary schools. In Tomlinson, T. M., & Walberg, H. L. (Eds.), *Academic work and educational excellence* (pp. 87–114). San Francisco: McCutchan.

GREEN, T. F. (1984). *The formation of conscience in an age of technology.* Syracuse, NY: Syracuse University Press.

HAWLEY, W. (1986). A critical analysis of the Holmes Group's proposals for reforming teacher education. *Journal of Teacher Education, 36,* 47–51.

HOLMES GROUP EXECUTIVE BOARD. (1986). *Tomorrow's teachers: A report of the Holmes Group*. East Lansing: MI: Holmes Group.

HOYLE, E. (1985). The professionalization of teachers: A paradox. In *Is teaching a profession?* (2nd ed., pp. 44–54). Bedford Way Papers, No. 15. London: University of London Press.

JOYCE, B., & CLIFT, R. (1984). The Phoenix agenda: Essential reform in teacher education. *Educational Researcher, 13*(4), 5–18.

JUDGE, H. (1987). Reforming teacher education: A view from abroad. *Education Week, 6*(39), 32.

KATZ, M. B. (1975). *Class, bureaucracy, and schools*. New York: Praeger.

KOEHLER, V. (1984). *University supervision of student teaching*. Report No. 9061. Austin, TX: R & D Center for Teacher Education, University of Texas. (ERIC Documentation Reproduction No. ED270439).

LORTIE, D. (1978). *Schoolteacher*. Chicago: University of Chicago Press.

MARTIN, J. R. (1987). Reforming teacher education, rethinking liberal education. *Teachers College Record, 88*, 405–409.

PRATTE, R. (1987). Social heterogeneity, democracy, and democratic pluralism. In K. D. Benne & S. Tozer (Eds.), *Society as educator in an age of transition: Eighty-sixth yearbook of the National Society for the Study of Education* (pp. 148–185). Chicago: University of Chicago Press.

RICHARDSON-KOEHLER, V. (1987). *Educators' handbook: A research perspective*. New York: Longman.

RICHARDSON-KOEHLER, V., CASANOVA, U., PLACIER, P., & GUILFOYLE, K. (1987). *Positioning students for success: A final report to the Exxon Education Foundation*. Tucson, AZ: College of Education, University of Arizona.

SCHLECHTY, P. (1984, April). *Restructuring the teaching occupation: A proposal*. Paper prepared for the American Educational Research Association Project: Research contributions for educational improvement. Washington, DC.

SHULMAN, L. S. (1985, October). *A course of treatment*. Invited address, American Association of Medical Colleges. Washington, DC.

SODER, R. (1986). Tomorrow's teachers for whom and for what? Missing propositions in the Holmes Group Report. *Journal of Teacher Education, 37*(1), 2–5.

Staffing the nation's schools: A national emergency. (1984). Washington, DC: Council of Chief State School Officers.

WRINGE, C. (1984). *Democracy, schooling and political education*. London: George Allen & Unwin.

10

GRADUATE TEACHER EDUCATION AND TEACHER PROFESSIONALISM

Arthur Wise

The professionalization of teaching is a possible solution to the major crisis facing American education over the next decade or so. And graduate education is an essential component in the professionalization of teaching, as it has been in the professionalization of other occupations.

Supply and demand projections suggest a strong upturn in the demand for teachers in the years to come. Of particular importance will be the supply of talented young people willing to commit themselves to teaching. The past decade witnessed a decline in the quality of young people willing to commit themselves to teaching. The causes are not difficult to understand. Teachers' salaries declined over the last decade quite markedly, though they are now beginning to increase. I do not believe that they will increase sufficiently to solve the problem that lies before us unless professionalization occurs. The working conditions of teachers have similarly deteriorated for at least a decade. Surveys of teachers conducted over the years suggest that the level of dissatisfaction with working conditions has increased quite dramatically. The job itself is intrinsically less satisfying than it once was. Most profoundly, though, the last decade experienced two revolutions—revolutions that have meant talented women and talented members of minority groups now have better opportunities available to them. These groups, of course, have constituted in the past a captive labor

Reprinted from the *Journal of Teacher Education*. (1986, September-October), pp. 36–40, with permission.

force for teaching. These groups, which could be exploited at low wages, can no longer be counted upon to staff the nation's schools. We do not yet know the full implications of these revolutions upon the teaching force. The effects on schools have been masked because they occurred during a decade when schools did not hire many teachers. Now we face a decade in which schools will have to do substantial hiring of teachers and will have to contend with the fact that talented young people have other options and may not so easily be drawn to teaching (Darling-Hammond, 1984).

BUREAUCRATIC VS. PROFESSIONAL ACCOUNTABILITY

We are at a major turning point. We will make a decision about what kind of teaching force we will have, or we will make no decisions. In either case, we will determine the kind of teaching force we will have. As education has been thrust into the political arena, the extravagant rhetoric of the education reports—crisis and reform—must now confront the reality of a large upturn in the demand for teachers at a time when talented young women and members of minority groups have other opportunities.

We have to go back three decades to understand where we are. Starting in the 1950s, policymakers, and to a lesser extent, the public, became dissatisfied with the quality of teachers in public schools. At least they were persuaded that there was a tremendous unevenness in the quality of teaching in the public schools. They undertook a number of new policy initiatives that were intended to ensure a certain standard of teaching (Wise, 1979). These initiatives have had the paradoxical effect of making teaching unattractive precisely to the kinds of people whom we would most like to see in teaching. Policymakers introduced standardized curricula, bureaucratic reporting requirements, hierarchical evaluation systems, and standardized testing of students, all in an effort to improve teaching. As teachers have been compelled to comply with bureaucratic requirements, they have found it increasingly difficult to teach their students in ways they find to be academically sound. As they have increasingly had to violate their own standards of good teaching, their frustration has increased and their job satisfaction has declined (Darling-Hammond & Wise, 1985). Equally as important, their students, the next generation of potential teachers, have been observing their teachers' growing disaffection with teaching.

The efforts were to strengthen bureaucratic accountability in education, but there is another form of accountability—professional accountability. Whereas bureaucratic accountability demands conformity to prescribed routines, professional accountability demands performance in accordance with a set of standards. With regard to teaching, professional accountability means that practicing teachers should be held accountable for teaching academic subjects in intellectually honest and practical ways and for making appropriate instructional decisions on behalf of their students and classes.

The public, however, does not have confidence in and has been given no reason for having confidence in the quality of people who are teaching in our schools. That has occurred because teaching lacks rigorous control procedures and rigorous educational standards. Currently, the view is widespread that teacher education is not rigorous and that prospective teachers receive a less adequate general and liberal education than do students bound for nearly all other professions and many occupations. While most prospective secondary school teachers do take majors in their subject fields, they take fewer credits in the majors and fewer of these courses at the upper level (Galambos, 1985). I need not repeat the various views that are held, but if those views are to be changed, schools of education must visibly alter what they do.

Currently, teachers do not receive a well-supervised induction into teaching. Other professions provide a structured transition from the training period to the full performance of the profession's responsibilities. These professions provide an opportunity for the novice to learn to translate theory into practice and to learn about the aspects of the job that cannot be taught in the professional school classroom. Importantly, the novice's induction is accomplished under supervision so that clients are not harmed while the novice is learning.

The teacher certification process is perceived as not working well. Teachers currently may be certified without preparation to become teachers, without passing meaningful formal requirements. In other professions, the "license-to-practice" is awarded only upon completion of most of the following: a full general education, a full college major, a professional education, a supervised induction, a period of practice, a written examination, and a performance test. The combination of knowledge and practical experience qualifies the individual for examination. The profession itself, with state sanction, manages the process by which candidates are judged qualified to enter the profession. In teaching, the state alone, through approval of teacher education programs, seeks to ensure the qualifications of individual candidates. The state approves the program in the school of education. The school of education then reports that a candidate has completed the approved program. The candidate is then entitled to state certification. In effect, the school of education is attesting to the efficacy of its instructional program. It is uncomfortable whenever it must conclude that it has failed a student. Moreover, the budget of the school of education is tied to the number of its students. Thus, the more students admitted, retained, and graduated, the more secure the school's budget and faculty positions. It is not a criticism of schools of education to point out that every other profession has found it desirable to sever the automatic coupling of school graduation and professional licensing. A conflict of interests is otherwise inherent.

In education, the path of duplicity continues. New teachers are hired in a non-tenured status on the assumption that they will be carefully scrutinized during their initial years of teaching. According to state law, a careful assessment of whether or not the teacher should be tenured must be made. Yet few believe that the tenure decision is a discriminating decision. In sum, teachers are not treated as professionals because no quality assurance process exists to convince policymakers that they merit the public confidence to operate professionally. The public must be assured in advance that a professional has been equipped by virtue of education and certification to operate without continuous direction and supervision.

GRADUATE TEACHER EDUCATION
AND A TEACHING PROFESSION

Graduate education is one step in the process of professionalizing teaching. Professions are different from occupations. Professions operate under a different standard of accountability than do occupations. Occupations that have become professions have done so, in part, by reforming their education and certification processes. In order to operate as a profession, a group must convince the public that persons who are designated as members of that profession have the competence to practice it.

Initially, stress must be given to entry-level quality control. The training of teachers is roughly where medicine was early in the century and where law was several decades ago. The problem is not only a problem of substance but also appearance. These professions were moved to strengthen quality control. Of course, every time they moved to strengthen quality control, they opened themselves up to the charge that they were being protectionist. Every move by any profession to strengthen quality control may be interpreted by its antagonists as a protectionist move. Any action to upgrade may be construed one way by friends and another way by enemies. Many of the early moves taken by other professions were steps to control their own processes.

Too much may have been made of the idea that a special knowledge base is prerequisite to create a profession. A knowledge base is necessary, but it may not be the most important ingredient. Most early moves that other professions took could not be substantiated by research. Where were the multiple regression analyses to show the effects of going from no law school to one year, two years, or three? What research supports the idea that students be college graduates before they are allowed to enter law school? Why do you have to graduate from college before you are allowed to study medicine? Why must you study so much basic science before you are allowed to study medicine? Credible arguments could be and were made, but not with the level of empirical evidence that we insist upon in our circles. Why do educators have such high standards of evidence?

The important fact is that other occupations organized to become professions. They recognized that if anyone can "hang a shingle out" (or if anyone can "hang a shingle out" with minimal preparation), then no special status inheres to membership in the profession. If there is no special status, there is no reason for the public to have confidence in the profession—and no reason to pay members of the profession especially well. Indeed, if the demand for the services of the profession increases, while entry requirements remain minimal, large numbers of new entrants will depress pay or at least keep it from increasing.

CONNECTICUT COMMISSION REPORT

These were observations recently taken into account by the Governor's Commission on Equity and Excellence in Connecticut. The primary focus of the Commission was on teaching and teachers, and it came to an important set of conclusions about teacher education, certification, and induction (Governor's Commission on Equity and Excellence in Connecticut, June, 1985). With regard to teacher education, it recommended that a 5-year program be required for all prospective teachers prior to their entry into the classroom. The recommendation was not based upon a belief that it takes a particular amount of time to prepare to become a teacher—teachers can be prepared in two years or three years or four years or six years. (Not so long ago, it was done in two.) Instead, it was based upon the belief that:

> A comprehensive liberal education is at the heart of effective teaching. This means that students preparing to become teachers must achieve not only breadth of learning through exposure to a variety of inquiry and subject matter, but also depth of learning through intense study in a chosen academic field. Since teachers are charged with transmitting our cultural and scientific heritage to their students, it is particularly important that they be at least as liberally educated as members of other professions. (p. 13)

The Commission felt quite strongly that teachers themselves need to be brought into the quality control process. They advanced the idea of establishing a professional standards board comprised of a majority of elementary and secondary school teachers. That professional standards board, which would be analogous to professional standard boards that operate in other professions, would have the following responsibilities:

> Develop, disseminate, and monitor high standards of professional performance; set professional standards for training, licensing and professional development; test teachers' knowledge of subject matter and understanding of pedagogy and performance in the classroom; determine means of support for new teachers; monitor the quality of the profession, its individual members, its preparation programs, and its continuing learning structures. Teachers must be in control of standards of excellence in their profession and they must be held accountable to them.... In virtually every other profession, state boards comprised mainly of members of the profession oversee entry to the profession. It is now time for teachers to assume that responsibility. If teachers play a more substantial role in shaping and implementing the standards of their profession, the Commission believes that more able and committed individuals will be attracted to and retained in teaching. (p. 14-15)

The Commission voted to endorse the idea of a more intensive induction process through the provision of state funds to support a beginning teacher program. It recommended a state-wide minimum salary of $19,500.00 and a redesign of the state aid formula so that it would encourage local school districts to use infusions of state aid in the restructuring of the salary schedule. Teacher professionalization, including graduate education, received a major political push in Connecticut.

ADVANTAGES OF GRADUATE TEACHER EDUCATION

During most of the 20th century, there has been a shortage of teachers. The surplus of the recent past is only the second one of this century. For most of this century, it has been an uphill climb to raise standards, and yet, through most of this century, standards have been elevated. In 1935, 10 percent of all elementary school teachers had a B.A., half of junior high teachers had a B.A., and 85 percent of high school teachers had a B.A. In 1946, only 15 states required teachers to have a B.A. Ten years later, 35 states required that teachers have a B.A. By 1955, a period in which it was very difficult to staff the schools, 70 percent of all elementary school teachers had a B.A., and 97 percent of high school teachers had a B.A. Some might even speculate that schools were better able to meet those shortages by making becoming a teacher more demanding (Sedlak & Schlossman, 1986).

Some years back, the teacher was among the most highly educated members of the local community. Now, particularly in communities where public opinion is shaped, teachers may be among the less educated. It may be simply that teachers have to play catchup since the overall level of educational attainment has become higher. For example, the degree of choice in business is an M.B.A. It was not so many years ago that most people going into business had either no degree or at most a bachelor's degree. We may be watching the escalation of educational credentials. It may also be that knowledge in all fields is becoming more complex and so requires more time to acquire.

A master's degree, which is the next logical step in this process of upgrading credentials, offers several advantages. There are various ways to organize a program. One approach is the 4 + 1 + 1 model—a liberal arts degree followed by a one-year university-based master's degree in education followed by a one-year school-based internship. A 5 + 1 model where bachelor's and master's work is integrated is also possible, but would not offer the greatest advantages. What are the advantages of a master's degree in education?

It will ensure that all teachers are liberal arts graduates. Prospective teachers would not *ipso facto* be less educated than anyone else with a college degree.

It will ensure, especially useful at the high school level, that all teachers are exposed to the subject matter they will teach and that they know as much as any other college graduate who majors in that field.

It will package pedagogical and professional knowledge and provide it to students who have the intellectual tools and maturity to benefit from it.

It will ensure that all teachers are exposed to the pedagogical knowledge base. No one could become a teacher without it.

It will improve the image of teacher education by making it look more like the education of other professionals.

It will provide access to teaching and to teacher education to those who decide to teach after the age of 19.

Presently, students who wish to become teachers must make the commitment by the time they are 19. If a college graduate decides at the age of 25 or 45 to become a teacher, he or she has a more difficult time. A one-year self-contained Master of Education program would make it possible and manageable for a person at any stage or age to consider becoming a teacher. The creation of the 4 + 1 + 1 creates a relatively inexpensive program, of short duration, which can be subsidized, if necessary, when shortages become critical. Policymakers could, with a very short lag time, solve any imbalances that arise. The master's degree program provides an impetus for reconceptualizing teacher education. It is relatively easy to implement and, when coupled with certification reform, prepares teachers in whom the public can have confidence.

THE CHOICE: PROFESSIONAL TEACHERS OR WARM BODIES

The implications for strong graduate teacher education lie beyond the university. The supply of teachers is running out just as the demand is increasing. If rigorous standards are not put in place and enforced, states and school districts will reduce standards to fill classrooms. The practices of the 1950s and 1960s will reappear, and indeed they have begun to reappear, and indeed they have begun to reappear. They are called "labor-day-specials," "the breath test," "warm-body-in-every-classroom," and "any college graduate can teach." Policymakers around the country have begun to attempt to solve the supply problem with the rediscovery of emergency, temporary, and alternate certification procedures. They make the following hastily generalized argument: You know, if Albert Einstein showed up in our local school district, he could not be hired to teach. Therefore, we should alter our procedures so that if Albert Einstein shows up, we can hire him. They then create alternate certification procedures and hang out advertisement—but Albert Einstein does not show up. Instead, those who show up are people who have not figured out what to do with their lives or people who cannot find a job. In fact, this course of action is guaranteed to produce this result. Because supply is not limited under this approach, the wages of teachers will be depressed, and they will remain depressed. There is no incentive for policymakers to raise salaries significantly. If any college graduate can become a teacher, the prestige of the occupation is similarly depressed. If wages and prestige are kept low, then most teachers will be drawn from among those who have few other options. This sequence of events is really quite predictable and simple. The implications, however, are rather disturbing.

PROFESSIONAL TEACHING IN PUBLIC EDUCATION

What will happen is that schools will let in a large number of teachers in whom the public will not have confidence. A decade from now, we can be sure that parents, policymakers, and the public will be even less satisfied with the quality of teachers than they are now. Policymakers will respond to this concern by redoubling their calls for teacher evaluation, the testing of students, standardized curriculum, standardized teaching, and standardized learning. Lacking confidence in teachers, policymakers will design and impose even more refined versions of teacher-proof-curricula. Many qualified young people who try teaching will beat a hasty retreat, but that is not the final result. Education-minded parents who can afford it will respond to this new crisis in confidence by abandoning the public schools. They will seek professional teaching where it can be found—in private schools, in private schools, which now exist or which will be created by those who see a market opportunity. Already in certain cities, middle-class white and minority parents, judging that education quality has fallen to an unacceptable level, have abandoned the public schools. In these places, there is a two-class educational system—one for those who can afford it and one for those who have no choice. That is what will happen if we lumber along as we are now.

For a different result, we must create a process of teacher education and certification that inspires confidence in the quality of teachers. This upgrading has been the practice of other occupations that have become professions. The consequence of enforced standards is the possibility that supply may be restricted. Entry becomes, by definition, selective. The public has, therefore, confidence in those who survive the selection process. This confidence should translate into a greater willingness to pay salaries and provide working conditions that will attract and retain highly qualified teachers. The matter of salaries is always difficult. Current political rhetoric is rich with the suggestion that legislators, governors, and school boards are ready to pay high salaries if only they can be convinced that teachers are sufficiently talented to deserve high salaries. Yet, just desserts are probably not the most powerful determinant of wages in any line of work. Supply and demand is. As the United States faces a growing demand for teachers, the number of persons who are allowed by certification and other policies to be called "teachers" will determine wages. While teachers' salaries may rise some, in a kind of *quid pro quo* exchange for increased standards, they will rise even more as the supply of "teachers" is restricted.

How we provide the right set of working conditions is a more subtle and complex phenomenon. The creation of working conditions appropriate to the professional conception of teaching will be incremental. As the percentage of professional teachers increases, the political and bureaucratic climate of the schools will change. The perceived need for regulatory and bureaucratic oversight will decline. As oversight declines, teaching will be able to attract and retain highly talented practitioners. Teachers who see themselves as professionals will compel a redesign of working conditions. As the perceived need for regulatory and bureaucratic oversight declines, the budget for these functions will become available for the redesign of the teaching environment.

Teachers will then be able to teach in a professional manner. They will have a firm grasp of the subjects they teach, and they will be able to be true to the intellectual demands of their disciplines. They will be able to analyze the needs of the classroom and students for whom they are responsible. They will know the standards of practice of their profession. They will know that they will be held accountable for teaching their courses and for meeting the needs of their students. Teachers will be free from the demand to teach a prescribed curriculum using stylized methods to prepare students for standardized tests. Instead, they will feel compelled to teach with intellectual honesty and practical foresight. They will teach students to read for knowledge and enjoyment, not simply to acquire testable reading skills. They will teach students to think mathematically, not simply to work problems. They will teach students to analyze, not simply seek the right answers. They will foster creative thinking and creative writing. Quite simply, teachers will teach professionally, the way the best teachers have always taught when allowed to do so. Parents concerned about the quality of education will not have to turn to private education to find professional teaching.

We have choices ahead of us. The choices will be difficult, some would say impossible. I think that the problems that lie before us cannot be solved by any one party, including the university community. Partnerships will be necessary.

THE CONSTITUENCY FOR REFORM

Who are the constituents for the reform of teacher education? Everyone wants our teachers to be better and more thoroughly educated. But everyone has many other interests as well. Education deans and graduate deans are probably constituents for the reform of teacher education, but they alone are not powerful enough. We could hope that parents would be constituents for the reform of teacher education for, after all, they profit from efforts to upgrade the quality of teachers. But it is too much to expect them to worry about the reform of teacher education. Those who are the most sophisticated and the most knowledgeable and the most likely to be in a position of influence are also those who have another way out. When the public schools become intolerable to them, they can bail out. The new baby boomlet, which is now in kindergarten and first grade, is stretching the capacity of the private education system. I do not think we can count on parents as the necessary constituency. It could be business, but here, too the interests of business are diffuse and long-term. Besides, business can have it either way. It can find its skilled work force in the private system and its less skilled work force in the public system.

The major constituents for the reform of teacher education are teachers. Teachers can take control of the certification process just as professionals in other fields have. Only teachers have the right incentives to maintain quality in the face of sharp increases in demand. If we leave the decision processes as they are now, lying somewhere between the state department of education and the colleges of education, we will guarantee that standards will be relaxed to whatever level is necessary to ensure a warm body in every classroom. Only the profession itself, in concert with university officials and professors, with the support of other interested citizens, can possibly save public education in this country. Otherwise, all the ingredients are in place for the creation of a two-class education system in the United States. We are moving in that direction. If we do not find a way to attract and retain talented people in public school teaching, we can be pretty sure of a two-class school system. As a component in the professionalization of teaching, graduate teacher education is necessary to help preserve our common public school tradition.

REFERENCES

DARLING-HAMMOND, L. (1984). *Beyond the commission reports: The coming crisis in teaching*. Santa Monica, CA: The Rand Corporation, R-3177- RC.

DARLING-HAMMOND, L., & WISE, A. E. (1985, January). Beyond standardization: State standards and school improvement. *Elementary school journal*.

GALAMBOS, E. C. (1985). *Teacher preparation: The anatomy of a college degree*. Atlanta: Southern Regional Education Board.

SEDLAK, M., & SCHLOSSMAN, S. (1986). *Who will teach? Historical perspectives on the changing appeal of teaching as a profession*. Santa Monica, CA: The Rand Corporation, R-3472-CSTP.

Teachers for today and tomorrow. (1985, June). Hartford, CT: Governor's Commission on Equity and Excellence in Connecticut.

WISE, A. E. (1979). *Legislated learning: The bureaucratization of the American classroom*. Berkeley: University of California Press.

11

UNANSWERED QUESTIONS IN GRADUATE TEACHER PREPARATION

Reneé T. Clift

The authors of the previous chapters and many other thoughtful educators whose work has been cited in those chapters disagree about the placement of initial teacher preparation and about the content and the process of continuing education. It is obvious that there is no consensus that a move away from undergraduate teacher preparation is necessary, desirable, or even possible. Therefore, this chapter will highlight the stated and the implied issues raised by the previous authors rather than taking a stand for or against eliminating undergraduate teacher preparation, and will conclude with a discussion of those factors to be considered if our ultimate concern is the quality of teacher preparation.

For organizational purposes, I have grouped the issues surrounding the initial preparation of teachers into four categories: (a) the bureaucratic nature of teacher education, (b) reflective practice as a goal of teacher education, (c) the curriculum of learning to teach, and (d) definitions of the teacher educator. The first and second categories have received the most attention from national reports arguing for cooperative arrangements between departments, colleges, school districts, and individual schools. It is argued that such arrangements will facilitate the process of learning to teach and will lead to the professionalization of teaching, thus enhancing the status of teacher practitioners. Critics of the reform proposals have tended to focus their arguments on the third category, noting that discussions of content are often neglected during discussions of structure or form. The fourth category raises questions about those who will implement the recommended changes, questions that are only beginning to surface in the current debates.

THE BUREAUCRATIC NATURE OF TEACHER EDUCATION

Teacher education is directly and indirectly controlled by a number of agencies that regulate content, credentials, course offerings, and course sequencing. In Texas, for example, 1987 legislation limited undergraduate preservice teacher preparation to no more than 18 hours of professional coursework, six of which must be student teaching. In addition, the undergraduate degree in education has been abolished, even though more is being demanded of teacher education programs. For example, universities are expected to prepare prospective teachers in a number of specified areas, including multicultural education, reading disabilities, the education of exceptional students, learning theory, and instructional management. Furthermore, the success of preparation programs will be evaluated based on the accomplishments of their graduates on both paper-and-pencil tests and observational assessments of classroom teaching performance. Enforcement of this legislation is the province of the Texas Education Agency, the administrative arm of the State Board of Education.

While certification is channeled through the Texas Education Agency, university course offerings and course changes must pass through a different agency, the Coordinating Board for Higher Education. Should Texas universities decide to abandon undergraduate course offerings entirely and rely only on graduate preparation of teachers, final approval rests with the Coordinating Board. If new courses are necessary, the Coordinating Board must approve each course. This state level approval can come only after recommendations have passed departmental committees, college committees, and university committees charged with overseeing undergraduate and graduate education. Clearly, decisions about the future of teacher preparation in Texas and in other states do not rest solely with schools and departments of education.

Decisions about teacher preparation are also shared with school districts and school boards. The same 1987 Texas legislation described above mandated an induction year for all teachers that is supervised jointly by a school district and a university. Not only must the university system and the school system develop joint programs, they must also agree on how those programs are to be funded. If the legislature will not provide special funds (and no funding was allocated for this legislated induction program), financial resources for such a program must be reassigned from university and/or district budgets.

When resources are not available, the curriculum and the process for training skilled, reflective classroom teachers are not likely to be the major foci of administrative discussions concerning the various facets of the new legislation within school districts or universities. As Haberman reminded us in the *National Society for the Study of Education Yearbook on Teacher Education*, "We live in an era when bureaucratic power rather than ideas are the major issues. The content of teacher education will be relatively neglected in this struggle" (Haberman, 1975, p. 320). One of the first, and the most important, questions facing all universities—and Texas universities in particular—concerns the degree to which universities are free to develop teacher education programs. Will a move to graduate education encourage and enable universities to design and implement teacher education programs that prepare novices to begin a career in teaching? Or will legislators move to restrict graduate degrees as they have undergraduate degrees?

Arthur Wise (Chapter 10) suggests that the increase in legislation and other forms of bureacratic accountability for teachers is the result of decreased respect for university-based teacher education, partially due to the absence of control procedures and quality control standards in the teaching profession. Wise argues that the separation of preparation and licensing procedures, as is the case for physicians, lawyers, and cosmetologists, will enable universities to set rigorous entry level standards and develop relatively autonomous teacher education programs.

It is not clear whether the adoption of Wise's recommendations will resolve the accountability issue while creating serious financial problems for teacher education programs and for other university programs. As Judge (1982) pointed out, many universities are loath to raise standards for admission to teacher education because the ensuing drop in student enrollment would mean a loss of revenue for other colleges and departments that depend on the surplus generated by education majors. Weinstein (see Chapter 3) documents that a move to graduate education in at least one university produced an initial drop in enrollment and increased the financial resources needed to train the prospective teacher. One very practical question that must be answered is economic. Will a move to graduate education be supported by the university and the state, or will it prove to be more expensive than most universities can afford? The answer to this question depends in part on the university's willingness to allocate resources to teacher education programs.

Perhaps, as Berliner (1984) has argued, it is time to lobby for increased resources in teacher education, an area that has been grossly underfunded in many universities. Will teacher educators be able to argue successfully for appropriate resource allocations, and will they use these resources to increase the quality of the teacher education program? Certainly, Weinstein's case studies suggest that both faculty and students perceive increased status for graduate programs. She also documents that at least one university has been successful in arguing for increased university support, while another has had to struggle to meet the increased costs. One point regarding teacher educators and teacher education is clear. Given the complex bureaucratic agencies that can directly affect the content, structure, and financing of professional education, teacher educators must become more adept at working within the system and must become proactive in the political processes that affect teachers and their education.

REFLECTIVE PRACTICE AS A GOAL OF TEACHER EDUCATION

A common vision of the teacher as a thoughtful, reflective professional guides both of the major proposals for the reform of teaching and of teacher education. Mastery of content and pedagogy are essential, but not sufficient.

> Teachers must have a greater command of academic subjects and of the skills to teach them. They also need to become more thoughtful students of teaching, and its improvement. (Holmes Group, 1986, p. 4)

> They [teachers] must be able to learn all the time, as the knowledge required to do their work twists and turns with new challenges and the progress of science and technology. . . . Teachers must think for themselves if they are to help others think for themselves, be able to act independently and collaborate with others, and render critical judgement. (Carnegie Forum, 1986, p. 25)

The education of such teachers presumes that teacher educators are themselves thoughtful students of teaching and its improvement. The University of Florida's Proteach program (Ross, 1987), the University of Houston's RITE program (Clift, Nichols, & Marshall, 1987), and the University of Wisconsin's elementary program (Zeichner & Liston, 1987) are only three examples of teacher education programs at the graduate and the undergraduate levels that encourage novice teachers to become more thoughtful and reflective. Early reports on these programs illustrate the myriad problems that arise when institutions strive to accomplish major changes in program structure and concept. One of those problems relates to faculty commitment. Will education faculties make a strong commitment to allocating their time and energy to working with prospective teachers? Will the university setting encourage and reward such a commitment? These questions must be answered affirmatively before any change is possible, but administrative encouragement and reward are not sufficient.

Fullan (1982) stresses the importance of sharing the meaning of change. Although the impetus to move toward a teacher education program that emphasizes critical analysis and thoughtful practice many come from administrators or from a small group of faculty members, the successful implementation of such a program depends on

> the relationships between these new programs and the thousands of subjective realities embedded in people's individual and organizational contexts and their personal histories. How these subjective realities are addressed or ignored is crucial for whether potential changes become meaningful at the level of individual use and effectiveness. (p. 35)

Faculty members who are accustomed to lecturing to 200 undergraduate teacher education students and who work closely only with select graduate students may find it difficult to adopt changes that require them to work closely with prospective teachers. Organizational contexts that convey status only to the preparation of doctoral students and not to the preparation of teachers will exacerbate the problem.

Weinstein's case studies (see Chapter 3) suggest that a move to graduate teacher preparation may enhance the status of teacher education within schools of education and within the university, thus making a commitment to change more rewarding for university faculty members. But her case studies also document possible problems. Academic turf struggles may arise between advocates of subject methods courses and advocates of generic education courses. In some programs, the tendency to condense coursework following a move to graduate preparation contradicts our knowledge that learning to teach takes time. Transforming an undergraduate teacher preparation program into a graduate program is a simple matter compared to changing faculty instructional patterns. And yet, changes in instruction are mandatory if the goal of teacher education is truly to encourage critical analysis and reflective practice.

Schon (1983, 1987) has written extensively on the relationships between initial professional education and the eventual goal of reflective practice. Using case studies from studio art and the performing arts, he argues that learning involves a necessary but inexplicable interaction between learning by doing and learning from instruction. The professional educator is at once a model and a coach who guides the novice through simulated tasks while encouraging the novice to act, to reflect in action, and to reflect on the outcomes of that action. His vision of a knowledgeable practitioner is similar to those of the Holmes and Carnegie reports; his vision of educating those practitioners implies small, personal, interactive preparation programs. Learning would develop gradually as students begin to "think" like professionals. The transition from student to professional would be accomplished through critical dialogues between the student and the "coaches" as they analyze situations, experiment with solutions to problems, and continuously evaluate practice.

Self-evaluation and evaluation from an expert "coach" are crucial elements in Schon's concept of learning reflective practice. Hoy and Woolfolk (see Chapter 7) suggest that this role is frequently assigned to the student teaching supervisor, but that the term "supervision" has a dualistic connotation that can make both the role and the person in that role suspect. Often supervisors are persons in a bureaucracy who oversee, direct, and control workers. This role conflicts with the concept of encouraging novices to experiment, to make mistakes, and to learn throughout the process. Hoy and Woolfolk argue that supervisors who help student teachers should not be expected to summarily evaluate; rather they should advise, suggest, and encourage a gradual move toward independence from the supervisor. To make supervision workable, universities need control over field placements in settings where goals are shared. More importantly, university-based teacher educators must be committed to working with supervisors and with prospective teachers in field settings.

Each of the teacher education partners must be able to separate supervision from summative evaluation. Peterson and Comeaux (see Chapter 8) address this issue as they point out the gaps between our long-term goals for teachers and the methods we use to evaluate those teachers. If current evaluation procedures are based on the concept of teacher as technician and fail to assess the teachers' developing capacity for reflection and thoughtful decision making, the prospective teacher will learn what is tested. Becker, Geer, Hughes, and Strauss's (1961) pioneering study of medical students documented the students' overriding concern for performing well in those areas that are graded. Our own preliminary studies of prospective teachers' responses to a shift toward reflection and critical analysis in the teacher education program at the University of Houston (Clift, Nichols, & Marshall, 1987) indicate that testing for content mastery works against programmatic goals of reflection and inquiry.

Peterson and Comeaux, likewise, would separate education and summative evaluation. They propose an evaluation matrix based on the National Medical Board's three-part examination that attempts to test more than a prospective physician's knowledge of medicine. Part I tests declarative knowledge, Part II tests problem-solving ability and declarative knowledge, and Part III tests general clinical competence and the interpretation of clinical data. Although this model holds promise for teacher evaluation, the medical boards are not without problems, because they do not reliably predict the quality of medical performance. It is likely that there will be similar problems with national evaluations of teaching.

Perhaps a more serious problem in translating medical evaluation practices into the evaluation of teachers is that teachers deal with classroom groups, not individual cases. As several authors in this volume have noted, teacher-experts have a particular knowledge of their own classes, a knowledge that cannot be readily transferred from class to class or from teacher to teacher. This raises yet another question, one that Shulman and colleagues (Shulman & Sykes, 1986) are attempting to answer as they develop prototypical tests for a national board examination for teachers. Will it be possible to develop sets of standardized tests that can reliably and validly measure those qualities of knowledge organization and implementation possessed by competent teaching professionals? Will states adopt national tests, thereby surrendering some control over the education of teachers? Will the profession's vision of teaching competence be shared by state legislatures and school districts?

Educators themselves disagree about the vision of the professional teacher. Richardson-Koehler and Fenstermacher (see Chapter 9) argue that current reform proposals conceive of teaching as a hierarchically structured profession with the highest level responsible for staff and curriculum development. Teachers become change agents within the school as they make local decisions about curriculum, instruction, and students. While some would question whether teachers, as opposed to school boards, should make those decisions, there is also a question about the intrinsic rewards of such decision making and the hierarchical structure that makes such decisions possible.

Richardson-Koehler and Fenstermacher present a case study of a school that has experimented with one model of differentiated staffing. Experience in this school cautions that a move toward greater involvement with staff and curriculum development may shift teachers' attention away from students. In several instances, students in the school who needed extra help received less attention and assistance. This introduces the question of what we mean by the nature of professionalism. If we mean that to become more professional a teacher must become more distanced from the client, and the "treatment" must become more mysterious, then Richardson-Koehler and Fenstermacher argue that we are working against a basic concept of public education in a democratic society. A hierarchy of teaching, with selected teachers unilaterally deciding curricular and instructional goals, may work against the democratic ideal of community participation in schools. They caution that before we begin massive restructuring of public school organization, we should understand more about the advantages of the current "flat" structure. We must also consider the interactions between selection and evaluation mechanisms and a vision of teachers who represent diverse cultural and ethnic groups.

As Zeichner (Chapter 2) pointedly reminds us, this is not the first time that professors and practitioners have considered the merits of moving to graduate level programs for the preparation of teachers. We have learned that graduate programs can attract academically talented individuals if financial support for program development and for student aid is available and if high-powered recruiting is implemented. We also know that graduates do not leave the teaching profession more quickly than their undergraduate counterparts and that, in many cases, they are perceived as superior first-year teachers. Other than principals' perceptions, however, we do not know very much about the overall quality of the teachers produced by earlier graduate preparation programs.

Zeichner's review noted that programs such as the Ford M.A.T. projects failed to prepare teachers from diverse cultures to work in equally diverse schools. He cautions that "generating another set of elite, academically-oriented programs that primarily serve the interests of the already most advantaged in our society is not a defensible course for the next generation of programs to pursue, by default or otherwise" (p. 25). Although rigorous entry standards and evaluation mechanisms are laudable, it is possible that such standards, coupled with a move to graduate education, will hamper education schools in their attempts to attract, retain, and encourage members of all cultures and ethnicities. Universities will need to assume greater responsibility for preparing teachers to work in ethnically and culturally diverse school settings—a goal that is not strongly emphasized in most proposals for reform.

THE CURRICULUM OF LEARNING TO TEACH

Arguments in favor of graduate teacher preparation suggest that an undergraduate education free of professional education courses can and will enable novice teachers to concentrate on learning subject matter first, then move into professional training. As Joyce and Clift (1984) argued, anyone who is enrolled in a graduate program wherein the sole focus is teacher preparation is able to concentrate attention and effort on learning to teach. The graduate program at the University of Maryland (Mc-Caleb et al., 1987) is perhaps a better illustration of this concept than the case studies Weinstein reports. In this program a cohort group of graduate students works with faculty members and with teachers in selected school sites during a three-semester program. Students who enter this program are aware that they are not allowed to divide their attention between learning to teach and a full-time job, nor are they allowed to work on other degrees while participating in the program. Although this program is too new to evaluate the graduates, enrollment has increased steadily each year and faculty support has also increased.

Another argument favoring graduate preparation holds that graduate students will be better prepared in their content areas. This argument is less persuasive when viewed alongside recent criticisms of liberal arts education (e.g., Bloom, 1987) and thoughtful analyses of academic pedagogy and the teaching of teachers. Anderson (see Chapter 6) raises serious questions about content area professors' abilities and inclinations to articulate their views of disciplinary knowledge. Most of us have heard statements similar to those expressed by Anderson's colleague, a professor of geology: "It's *our* job to teach this stuff and their job to learn it, and if they don't understand then they ought to study harder" (p. 101). Anderson suggests there is little reason to suspect that graduate teacher education programs will be any better than undergraduate ones without a substantial change in the system. He argues that the development of good teaching practice is hindered when academic preparation is provided by content area professors who have thought very little about what disciplinary knowledge is useful for teaching and how it can be mastered, and professional preparation is the responsibility of education professors who are committed to theories of teaching that ignore the acquisition of academic knowledge.

Even if we are convinced that graduate programs will allow greater concentration on learning to teach and at the same time assure better subject matter preparation for prospective teachers, we must still face criticisms by Tom (1986) and others that the teacher education reform reports have generally ignored the curriculum of teacher preparation. Three chapters in this volume have given considerable attention to issues surrounding a beginning teacher preparation curriculum. Carter and Doyle discuss the nature of expertise in teaching, with particular regard to the ways teachers structure and maintain academic work systems in classrooms and the ways that this knowledge might inform teacher preparation curriculum. Borko also discusses the nature of expertise in teaching, but differs from Carter and Doyle's focus on work systems. She argues that once routines are established, teacher experts can focus on the learning environment and on the students' experiences within that environment. Anderson's chapter discusses the nature and the substance of content area (or subject matter) knowledge. Each of these chapters suggests a number of important questions related to the content of teacher preparation and to the time allotment for delivering that content.

Anderson defines content area knowledge as the fusion of three elements: (a) a sophisticated understanding of how the relationships between facts, concepts, and procedures are structured, (b) a detailed awareness of the diverse functions (or purposes) of the different types of knowledge; and (c) an understanding of how knowledge develops within the discipline and how this is recapitulated within individuals. Even when all three elements of this knowledge are present, learners (who are teachers) have a difficult time transforming their knowledge in order to teach other learners. "Learners cannot assemble disciplinary knowledge from its component parts as we do a machine or a building; instead they must construct meaningful knowledge through a complex process that more closely resembles organic growth or evolution" (Anderson, Chapter 6).

Anderson's argument implies that a teacher preparation curriculum should enable the future teacher to examine his or her store of knowledge, to work on gaps, and to begin to develop learning experiences in which that knowledge can be transformed (Wilson, Shulman, & Richert, 1987) so that other learners may acquire it. This suggests that teacher educators would be wise to reexamine changes in programs that emphasize generic teaching skills and the elimination or reduction of requirements in content area pedagogy.

Carter and Doyle directly address the issue of preparation in generic skills. They note that while many researchers and practitioners (and state evaluation systems, see McCaleb, 1987) advocate research on teaching effectiveness as the content base for graduate preparation, we know very little about how novice teachers learn to implement this research because most of the research has been conducted with experienced teachers. Implementing research on teaching effectiveness is mediated by context and by reflection on the implementation process (for a particularly informative account of implementation, see Muir, 1980). Carter and Doyle suggest that research on teaching effectiveness provides students with analytic categories that help to organize information about instructional planning and instructional management. Expertise in teaching is specialized and is specific to the class and the content.

Effective teachers tend to direct and sustain classroom activities by focusing on work systems in classrooms. Carter and Doyle suggest that the teacher education curriculum should be organized around common pedagogical problems that the prospective teachers will have to solve. Much like Schon (1987), they argue for clinical practicum experiences such as case studies, simulations, and interactive videos that will help develop a tacit knowledge (Polanyi, 1967) of classrooms and teaching situations. They add an important caveat with their reminder that *expertise* is not the goal of an initial teacher preparation curriculum. Learning to teach well requires extensive time and experience.

None of these authors argues that graduate preparation is more likely than undergraduate to promote quality in teacher education. Borko's chapter documents that subject matter knowledge is a concern for graduate students and that they have a difficult time making a transition to pedagogical thinking. Often they are not even aware of the problems they have encountered. Borko emphasizes the importance of content preparation as a foundation for learning to teach, but she notes that "one of the most difficult aspects of learning to teach is making the transition from a personal orientation to a discipline to thinking about how to organize and represent the content of that discipline in ways that will facilitate student understanding" (Borko, Chapter 5). Prospective teachers must all learn how to integrate texts with textbook information to design instruction in multiple forms. This does not occur because of one course or one practicum experience. Together, these three chapters highlight the issue of the time needed to prepare novice teachers and the time needed to develop expertise.

Graduate preparation is desirable only to the extent that it will permit the development of a basic curriculum for a beginning teacher. That curriculum should accomplish at least three goals. It should prepare prospective teachers to make a commitment to teaching and the field (or fields) that they plan to teach so that the remainder of the experience can be geared toward this end. Attainment of this goal would mean that prospective teachers are prepared to deal with the inherent ambiguity of learning to teach and to work with mentors toward a personal resolution of that ambiguity. Also, prospective teachers should be prepared to study the content area(s) at the level they plan to teach. Thus if a teacher is preparing to teach third grade, she should be prepared to restudy the content covered in third grade with a view toward mastering all three domains described by Anderson: structure, function, and development. Finally, teachers should be willing to examine the contexts of teaching and the implications for teaching practice in diverse educational contexts.

The second goal of a teacher preparation curriculum is to provide learning experiences that will enable novices to experiment with solutions to problems related to all three phases of teaching: planning, instruction, and postinstructional evaluation and reflection. Such learning experiences could range from written and oral responses to educational problems, to simulated teaching, to controlled teaching of a small number of students, to clinical teaching. The foci of these experiences should be ongoing dialogues between novice and self, novice and mentor, and novice and others who are learning to teach. Attainment of this goal would mean that the prospective teacher has a clear vision of what is known and what remains to be explored. In other words, the student will have begun the transition to pedagogical thinking.

The final goal of a teacher preparation curriculum is to create learning experiences that will permit continued growth and reflection. This could be done through professional development schools, but it could also be handled through a university-based practicum in which teachers from several schools and with varying degrees of experience meet to discuss plans, problems, and progress. Seminars with content area experts, researchers, and teacher educators could provide an ongoing forum for self-examination as new ideas are introduced and options for dealing with immediate problems are discussed.

Our present system for learning to teach places novices in the awkward position of presenting themselves as experts while knowing that "something" is either wrong with the system or with them. It is no wonder that graduates are so often critical of teacher preparation when they begin jobs that expect first-year teachers to perform as well or better than experienced teachers. All of us—teacher educators, prospective teachers, and school practitioners—should openly acknowledge that expertise is a function of experience. We can then begin to talk about those experiences that will assist novices to become experts. This leads us to a set of questions related to the definition of teacher educator that has not been addressed or even fully articulated.

DEFINITIONS OF THE TEACHER EDUCATOR

Who is responsible for teacher education? This question is not asked in a frivolous manner, nor is it a reexamination of the bureaucratic involvement discussed earlier. The answer to this question is, in my opinion, crucial to any substantive reform of teacher education, for the present answer is elusive at best. In this book one can find allusions to at least six role groups who are considered "teacher educators": the academic professors—both liberal arts and specific content area professors; the professors of education—including foundations, generic methods, and subject specific methods, administrators—who may coordinate teacher education without directing the teacher education faculty or the curriculum; the student teaching supervisors—who may or may not coordinate their efforts with professors; the cooperating teachers—often selected by school districts for a variety of reasons unrelated to teacher preparation; and the professional school-based teacher educators—a new role group discussed in the reform proposals. Others, not specifically mentioned, include school principals, graduate students who serve as teaching assistants or instructors, adjunct faculty members hired specifically for instructing prospective teachers, and staff members who assist students as they work through the maze of certification requirements.

Appendix E of the Holmes Group report, a working draft of goals for Holmes Group standards, presents four standards for the faculty in teacher education:

1. The faculty responsible for preparing teachers are themselves competent and committed teachers.

2. The faculty responsible for preparing teachers include both university-based and school-based faculty.

3. The academic faculty responsible for teacher education contribute regularly to better knowledge and understanding of teaching and schooling.

4. The teacher education faculty who demonstrate competence as strong teacher-scholars are recognized for this unique and important combination of abilities.

While such standards begin to address the issue of who can best educate teachers, they still diffuse the responsibility for teacher preparation among role groups whose primary definition is not that of teacher educator. The title of "teacher educator" typically has not been a phrase associated with school teaching, while university faculty have been loath to accept the title. As Lanier and Little (1986) noted in their summary of research on those who teach teachers:

> Of those responsible for teaching teachers in higher education, the most prestigious are those most removed from dealing with teacher educators' problems. The thesis emerging from the research is that variables associated with social class distinctions in the larger society are simply mirrored in universities and then again in schools and departments of education . . . . Teacher educators closest to schools and to prospective and practicing teachers often assume professional work assignments and routines that demand minimal intellectual flexibility and breadth and require, instead, conformity and limited analysis. (p. 535)

Here we have a paradox. Reform proposals are calling for teachers who are thoughtful problem solvers and who are capable of working in complex, often ambiguous situations. Yet these teachers are to be educated by a combination of professors and practitioners who are either disdainful of teacher education or disinclined toward complexity and ambiguity. If we are to consider teaching an important, high status occupation, then should we not give equal consideration to teacher educators?

As we think through the challenges presented by the bureaucracy of teacher education, the congruence between the educational process and the vision of reflective practice, and the curriculum of teacher preparation, we cannot permit ourselves to ignore those teachers who will mold other teachers. Let us review the issues related to the teachers of teachers that have been raised in this volume. Anderson is pessimistic about a working dialogue between content area professors and professors of education. Weinstein is concerned with the question of ownership when program administration is separate from program faculty. Hoy and Woolfolk are concerned that supervisors may not enhance prospective teachers' abilities to analyze and to reflect. Borko raises the same concern about cooperating teachers, even though those teachers may be expert practitioners. Richardson-Koehler and Fenstermacher ask if practicing teachers can satisfactorily balance their responsibilities to children and to adults. All of these issues are related to the conflicts that arise when vague definitions of role groups produce overlapping and confusion.

In the case of university-based teacher educators, conflicts arise when there is insufficient time or mental energy to meet the demands of both scholarship and the needs of prospective teachers. This possibility increases when one is working with a large number of prospective teachers. Time and mental energy are also important considerations in any plan for school-based teacher educators, whether they are university supervisors or practicing teachers. If teacher education is crammed into a schedule that is already overcrowded, we will not have improved teacher education, we will only have rearranged it.

Noddings (1984) discussed the concept of a school built on an ethic of caring. To care for students, she argued, is to concern oneself with providing experiences that will enable them to reach the goals they have set for themselves. Small schools, wherein teachers are allowed to interact with students and to provide learning experiences that will help students set and achieve goals, staffed by teachers who care for children better facilitate learning and an enthusiasm for learning. She argued that our current concept of schooling is based on the concept of mass production, not on the concept of individual growth and development. Education in general has failed to meet the needs of students in an attempt to meet the diverse demands of the larger society.

Noddings' argument also applies to the education of teachers. As they rush through one system in order to fill the vacancies in another, prospective teachers provide revenue for universities, subjects for research, and assistance for overworked teachers. If we are truly to develop teacher preparation that encourages knowledgeable, reflective practitioners to learn and continue learning about content, pedagogy, and the process of educating children, we must create a system that addresses the needs and the interests of prospective teachers (and practicing teachers).

I would argue that teacher education is a specialty in and of itself. Teacher educators are professionals whose primary responsibilities are to work with teachers and to study the nature of learning to teach and the relationships between knowledge, teaching, and learning in diverse educational settings. Although the prospective teacher will study with a number of university professors and will observe in a number of schools and classrooms, teacher education is not an "all university" responsibility. Rather, teacher education is the joint effort of those university and school-based educators who work as a team to implement the various facets of the teacher education curriculum.

The teacher education community is responsible for program development, instruction, laboratory teaching experiences, and clinical teaching experiences. They assume the responsibility for engaging in a dialogue with their students that will enable those students to explore alternatives in teaching practice and study the effects of those practices on the classroom environment. Such teacher educators care for their students' development and work with a sufficiently small number of students to permit the development of a caring relationship. Additionally, they model reflective practice through their own teaching *and* through studies of teaching. Finally, they are teacher educators first, and students of one or more disciplines second.

Teacher education under these conditions is possible at either the graduate or the undergraduate level. The final section of this chapter will summarize the issues that must be addressed by institutions that are considering a move toward graduate teacher preparation exclusively.

IS GRADUATE PREPARATION MORE LIKELY TO PROMOTE QUALITY IN TEACHER PREPARATION?

This chapter began with the observation that there is no consensus on the above question. The answer is clearly "no" if graduate preparation consists of a one-year "crash course" in how to teach. An affirmative answer does not come so easily, although many educators in this volume and elsewhere argue that no other answer is possible. The answer will depend, in part, on the individual nature of teacher education institutions and on the policy decisions that affect the institutional operations. The following questions, a summary of the issues raised in this volume, are intended as a stimulus for discussion among those of us who are concerned with the placement and the practice of teacher education.

1. Will teacher educators be able to develop coherent programs in the initial preparation of teachers? Or will teacher education continue as a collection of courses designed to meet certification requirements?

2. Will states, universities, and school districts allot sufficient time to the process of learning to teach? Is this likely at the graduate level, the undergraduate level, or some combination of the two?

3. Will graduate preparation enhance the status of those who are preparing to teach and of those who are preparing teachers? Will status enhancement encourage university personnel to consider teacher preparation a specialty worth pursuing and worth a major commitment of time, resources, and effort?

4. Will states and universities encourage and reward devotion to teaching and to scholarship within the field of teacher education?

5. Will graduate teacher preparation discourage certain cultural, ethnic, and economic groups from seeking careers in teaching? Will it foster an elitist attitude that may work against caring and commitment to children in urban and culturally diverse schools?

6. Will graduate preparation ultimately restrict the numbers of people who are committed to teaching and force school districts to rely on unqualified adults who will, at best, only maintain order in schools?

7. Will teacher education curricula encourage knowledge synthesis, experimentation, and thoughtful practice? Will instructors work as a cohesive team to help develop such practice? Will school-based teacher educators, field supervisors, and practicing teachers be able to coordinate their efforts with university-based experiences?

8. Will the summative evaluations of prospective teachers communicate the importance of knowledge, problem solving, and reflective practice? Should evaluation proceed in stages (as in the medical profession) independent from the educational process?

9. Will an emphasis on professional decision making and professional licensing distance the teacher professional from the students? Will teacher preparation be able to encourage the development of caring, knowledgeable professionals?

10. Will reforms ultimately further the goals and the interests of prospective teachers and their future students? Is it possible that content, not bureaucratic power, will form the basis of current reforms?

Although thoughtful people disagree about the answers to the questions posed in this chapter, they do agree that the topic is of importance and concern. In all probability there is no "one best answer" for the form and content of teacher education, that form and content must be adapted to meet changes in the knowledge base and changes in teacher education student populations. As effective graduate or undergraduate teacher educators, we must continue to raise questions and to seek answers linking program development, evaluation, and basic and applied research so that subsequent discussions of graduate teacher preparation are more focused on knowledge gained as opposed to questions not answered or not asked.

REFERENCES

BECKER, H., GEER, B., HUGHES, E., & STRAUSS, A. (1961). *Boys in white: Student culture in medical school.* Chicago: University of Chicago Press.

BERLINER, D. (1984). Making the right changes in preservice teacher education. *Phi Delta Kappan, 66*(2), 94–96.

BLOOM, A. (1987). *The closing of the American mind.* New York: Simon & Schuster.

CARNEGIE FORUM ON EDUCATION AND THE ECONOMY. (1986). *A nation prepared: Teachers for the 21st century.* Washington, DC: Carnegie Forum on Education and the Economy.

CLIFT, R., MARSHALL, F., & NICHOLS, C. (1987). *The RITE program: A close look at participants' perceptions.* Presentation to the Association of Teacher Educators. Houston, TX.

CLIFT, R., NICHOLS, C., & MARSHALL, F. (1987, April). *Turning opportunities into problems: Anger and resistance in teacher education.* Paper presented at the annual meeting of the American Educational Research Association, Washington, DC.

DOYLE, W. (1983). Academic work. *Review of Educational Research, 53*(2), 159–199.

FULLAN, M. (1982). *The meaning of educational change.* New York: Teachers College Press, Columbia University.

HABERMAN, M. (1975). Perspectives on tomorrow's teacher education. In K. Ryan (Ed.), *Teacher education* (74th yearbook of the National Society for the Study of Education, Part 2, pp. 310-320). Chicago: University of Chicago Press.

THE HOLMES GROUP. (1986). *Tomorrow's teachers.* East Lansing, MI: The Holmes Group.

JOYCE, B., & CLIFT, R. (1984). The Phoenix agenda: Essential reform in teacher education. *Educational Researcher, 13*(4), 5–18.

JUDGE, H. (1982). *American graduate schools of education: A view from abroad* (Report to the Ford Foundation). New York: Ford Foundation.

LANIER, J., & LITTLE, J. (1986). Research on teacher education. In M. C. Wittrock (Ed.), *Handbook of research on teaching* (3rd ed., pp. 527–569). New York: McMillan.

LEINHARDT, G., & GREENO, J. (1986). The cognitive skill of teaching. *Journal of Educational Psychology, 77*(3), 75–95.

MCCALEB, J. (Ed.). (1987). *How do teachers communicate? A review and critique of assessment practices* (Teacher Education Monograph No. 7). Washington, DC: ERIC Clearinghouse on Teacher Education.

MCCALEB, J. L., BORKO, H., ARENDS, R. A., GARNER, R., & MAURO, L. (1987). Innovation in teacher education: The evolution of a program. *Journal of Teacher Education, 38*(4), 57–63.

MUIR, R. (1980). A teacher implements instructional changes using the BTES framework. In Denham, C., & Lieberman, A. (Eds.), *Time to learn* (pp. 197–212). Sacramento, CA: Commission for Teacher Preparation and Licensing.

NODDINGS, N. (1984). *Caring: A feminine approach to ethics and moral education.* Berkeley: University of California Press.

POLANYI, M. (1967). *The tacit dimension.* New York: Doubleday.

ROSS, D. (1987, April). *Teaching teacher effectiveness research to students: First steps in developing a reflective approach to teaching.* Paper presented at the annual meeting of the American Educational Research Association, Washington, DC.

SCHON, D. (1983). *The reflective practitioner.* New York: Basic Books.

SCHON, D. (1987). *Educating the reflective practitioner.* San Francisco: Jossey-Bass.

SHULMAN, L., & SYKES, G. (1986). *A national board for teaching: In search of a bold standard.* Paper prepared for the Task Force on Teaching as a Profession, Carnegie Forum on Education and the Economy. Stanford, CA: Stanford University.

TOM, A. (1986). The Holmes Report: Sophisticated analysis, simplistic solutions. *Journal of Teacher Education, 37*(4), 44–46.

WILSON, S., SHULMAN, L., & RICHERT, A. (1987). "150 different ways" of knowing: Representations of knowledge in teaching. In Calderhead, J. (Ed.), *Exploring teacher thinking* (pp. 104–124). London: Cassell PLC.

ZEICHNER, K., & LISTON, D. (1987). Teaching student teachers to reflect. *Harvard Educational Review, 57*(1), 23–48.

12

PROSPECTS FOR GRADUATE PREPARATION OF TEACHERS

Louise Cherry Wilkinson

The question under consideration in this volume is: Are graduate programs for teacher preparation more likely than undergraduate programs to prepare highly qualified, competent, reflective professionals? The authors of the chapters in this volume deliver a complex, mixed, and inconclusive message. The evidence presented in this volume does not lead to or present an unequivocal answer to the question posed above. The issues are many and are presented in a variety of ways; the debate is often at a theoretical and logical level, with little or no confirming empirical evidence.

Despite the lack of answer to the question posed above, some of the authors have developed or alluded to the arguments in favor of and in opposition to programs that prepare teachers at the graduate level. The present chapter will briefly summarize those arguments. In addition, a *position will be presented that these conceptual-logical arguments may not be the most important factor in determining the kinds of programs that will be available to prepare future teachers in this country*. Other trends in our society, both within and outside of the academy, may have a major impact on future programs to prepare teachers. The cumulative impact of these trends may well be the diminution or even extinction of teacher preparation programs at four-year undergraduate liberal arts colleges. Furthermore, one consequence of this diminution may be a bifurcation in the ways in which teachers are prepared in the future: (a) no professional education for some teachers prior to entrance into the first teaching position subsequent to award of the baccalaureate degree; (b) highly professional and specialized education at the graduate level (e.g., completion of five-year and fifth-year programs) for other teachers. *The fate of teacher preparation programs may not be determined by demonstrated quality in one kind of program versus another, but by compelling societal forces that have impact on both the design and availability of programs in the future.*

ARGUMENTS IN FAVOR OF GRADUATE PREPARATION OF TEACHERS

The chapters in this volume provide an overview of the arguments in favor of and in opposition to graduate preparation. There are three basic arguments in favor of graduate programs for the preparation of teachers:

1. *More time is available for the professional education curriculum in graduate programs.* The premise that four years is simply not enough time to prepare both an educated person and a fully professional teacher underlies the argument in favor of graduate programs. There are more opportunities to focus on professional education and learning how to teach when there is a full additional year available for that purpose. The argument for time does not necessarily have any implication for the quality of the program, however, as several authors point out (Clift, Weinstein, Woolfolk, Zeichner). The adequacy and success of teacher preparation programs does not depend exclusively upon the availability of time, but rather on how that time is used. Nevertheless, proponents of graduate preparation point out that a quality program cannot occur if sufficient time is not available for that program to be implemented. In the fifth-year programs, and in the majority of five-year integrated programs, that additional year is devoted almost exclusively to professional education and development of teaching skills. These models are differentiated from four-year undergraduate programs, which typically consist of intermingling of professional education courses with general education courses and courses that are required for the major throughout the four years. However, Weinstein (see Chapter 3) noted significant variation in the structure and the content of both the teacher preparation and the general liberal arts components of the additional year.

One consequence of having a fifth year to focus on professional education is that more time is available during the four undergraduate years to master the content area that the prospective teacher will teach, that is, the academic major. Once again, there is no evidence that more time to study the academic major and the general education curriculum will necessarily result in a higher quality teacher. The assumption is that more courses in the academic major will lead to greater mastery of the content area, which will in turn result in a teacher who is better prepared compared to an individual who has not taken so many courses in the major.

2. *Graduate programs are associated with greater status and prestige.* The awarding of a graduate degree is associated with many, but not all, five-year integrated programs (e.g., University of Florida, University of Virginia) and some fifth-year programs. There are many variations of the postbaccalaureate program. In some

programs graduates receive an advanced degree (Ed.M., M.A.T.), while in others they earn graduate credits or certification as a teacher. Higher status and enhanced prestige is only associated with graduate preparation programs that lead to advanced degrees. However, if graduate preparation simply means entrance into a nondegree program that will merely result in the accumulation of graduate credits and eligibility for certification, it is not likely to be associated with the same prestige. Both Weinstein and Zeichner have noted that there is a consistent linkage between the awarding of an advanced degree and perceptions of prestige. Students at the University of Virginia saw the master's degree as a major attraction of the program, and they asserted that they would not be likely to invest the additional time in the program if the both the B.A. and master's were not awarded. Weinstein goes on to conclude that the B.A. in the liberal arts and the master's degree taken together are regarded as prestigious because they are perceived as indicators of rigor by students.

3. *Graduate programs are more likely to attract highly qualified college students.* Undergraduate four-year teacher education programs are regarded by students as "easy majors." As Sykes (1982) has noted, easily accessible undergraduate teacher education programs actually may be a disincentive for bright undergraduates to enter education, because these programs are not perceived as rigorous.

The argument that graduate programs, in comparison to four-year undergraduate programs, are more likely to attract highly qualified college students is related to the assertion that graduate programs are perceived as more prestigious by students. The status of graduate programs, particularly with the simultaneous awarding of both the graduate degree and certification upon completion of all program requirements, may be inexorably linked with the recruitment of students into these programs and into the profession. Students perceive, perhaps accurately, that the quality of the instruction available to them in graduate/professional courses is superior to that often found in undergraduate education courses. In most universities, far fewer students are needed in a graduate course to meet minimum enrollment requirements, in comparison with undergraduate courses. Graduate courses typically are smaller than undergraduate courses, thus allowing professors to individualize their instruction to a much greater degree in graduate courses. In universities, teaching graduate courses is often preferred by faculty members, who may infuse their graduate courses with greater rigor and enthusiasm. Furthermore, graduate students, particularly those returning for fifth-year graduate programs after some teaching experience, may be more mature and more able to learn the skills and refined knowledge associated with the development of "the thoughtful, reflective professional" teacher.

ARGUMENTS IN OPPOSITION TO GRADUATE PREPARATION OF TEACHERS

Two arguments in opposition to graduate preparation of teachers can be derived from chapters in this volume. The arguments that are offered in opposition to graduate preparation programs are:

1. *Increased expense and elitism associated with graduate programs may result in a more restricted applicant pool.* This argument implies that the quality, quantity, and representativeness of the pool of applicants for teacher preparation programs is diminished by a shift from undergraduate to graduate programs.

This argument is often applied to potential applicants from minority groups, who may not be able to bear the increased financial burden of graduate study. Demographic trends support the presupposition of this argument. Current data do indicate that members of minority groups (blacks and Hispanics) are more likely to have insufficient economic resources for continued graduate, postbaccalaureate study. Thus, the addition of a fifth year of study would put an extra burden on minority students. Unless financial aid is made available to relieve this burden, minorities would not have the same access to these programs as nonminorities. One highly probable outcome of the availability of only graduate programs for teacher preparation could be the diminished enrollment of minorities in these programs. Several authors point out that the already declining trend of minorities entering teacher education programs of all types would be further exacerbated by the restriction of programs to only graduate level.

However, the availability of the "alternate route" to obtaining certification to teach may have implications for this issue of the entrance of individuals into teaching. Many states have developed and implemented successful "alternate" certification programs for teachers that do not require any professional education taken at a university or college. Individuals who want to enter the teaching profession but, for whatever reason, do not want to enroll in a college-based program, may obtain teaching positions through this route. The issue then becomes the recruitment of minorities into teaching positions, not programs for the preparation of teachers. It may be that minorities and low income individuals who want to go into teaching will choose alternate routes for obvious financial reasons. Colleges will have to supply financial aid for these individuals if they want them to enter their programs. Some states are making available financial aid for continued education of teachers. For example, in New Jersey there are programs that allow students to use loans to pay for education, and these loans are forgiven if the individual teaches in New Jersey schools for a minimum period of time after graduation.

The data supplied by Weinstein's (see Chapter 3) case studies neither support nor refute the argument regarding the restriction of the applicant pool as a result of the implementation of graduate programs. Her studies do not show that, over the long run, either the quality or the quantity of applicants to teacher preparation programs was diminished by the shift to graduate programs. Weinstein notes that in some cases new standards have had a negative impact on the number of minority students entering into graduate programs; however, it is not clear that the additional financial burden is the cause of this trend. Other factors, such as the heavy reliance on quantitative indices (e.g., GRE) as criteria for admission into graduate programs, may be related to a diminished representation of minorities in the cohort of individuals who actually enroll in graduate programs, but this factor should not affect the applicant pool.

2. *There is an increased expense for the educational institution for graduate programs.* The argument is that these additional costs are unnecessary, since it has

not been proven that graduate programs are of higher quality than undergraduate programs. Shifting teacher preparation programs to the graduate level requires a substantial investment by the institution. As Judge (1982) pointed out, universities may not support increasing standards for teacher preparation programs, because this may lead to fewer students enrolling in these programs, thus resulting in a loss of revenue. Weinstein notes that data from the University of New Hampshire do not support the link between shift to graduate programs and falling enrollments. Data from the University of Kansas do reveal that more investment is required to develop and implement programs of higher quality. Thus, the issue seems to be the relationship between financial support and the quality of programs, not graduate versus undergraduate.

TRENDS AFFECTING THE STATUS OF TEACHER PREPARATION PROGRAMS

One is struck by the paucity of data confirming or refuting the arguments regarding graduate preparation presented by the authors of chapters in this volume. These arguments are logically and conceptually developed and sometimes infused with great passion; however, the arguments have not been empirically supported. As Zeichner (Chapter 2) has pointed out, the lesson to be learned from past experiments with graduate preparation programs is that we could not determine very much on the success of these programs, because they were not evaluated in a systematic way. Furthermore, the failure to study the past programs prevented us from knowing the unanticipated consequences of the implementation of graduate programs. It would be irresponsible to have the current debate about graduate programs settled by persuasive logic and strong feeling, rather than accurate and comprehensive study.

It may be some time before adequate empirical studies are completed regarding the success and failures of the implementation of present graduate programs. Nevertheless, it may be useful to examine the current political, social, and economic context within which this debate and evaluation are taking place. There are some forces already in effect that may mitigate or intensify the movement toward the extinction of undergraduate programs for the preparation of teachers, and/or the greater viability of graduate programs. Five trends are worth noting. These trends may affect the popularity and prevalence of both graduate programs and undergraduate programs.

1. *Legislative limits on preservice teacher education.* Increasingly, legislators are placing limits on the availability of preservice teacher preparation at four-year liberal arts colleges. Currently, the preparation of teachers is regulated by many governmental entities that directly or indirectly control the content, course offerings, and sequences of courses in teacher preparation programs. In Texas, the legislature put a limit on the number of credit hours that could be devoted to preservice teacher education at colleges and universities. Texas universities may require undergraduate students to take no more than 18 hours of professional coursework, 6 of which must

be in student teaching. In addition the undergraduate degree in education has been abolished (see Chapter 11).

Similar legislation placing a cap on the number and kind of professional education courses that can be taken during the undergraduate years has been adopted in several other states (e.g., New Jersey, Virginia) and may indicate a national trend. Legislators seem to be taking a greater interest in the professional education curriculum that is available to undergraduates who wish to become teachers.

Legislative limitations on the number of credits that undergraduates can devote to teacher preparation exacerbate the problem of a lack of adequate time in the undergraduate program in which to prepare teachers. An unintended consequence of this action is that it may contribute to the perception that teacher preparation at the undergraduate level is not important, of low status, and not desirable.

2. *College-based teacher preparation is no longer necessary to obtain a permanent teaching position because of the increased availability of "alternate routes" for teacher certification.* The "alternate route" for teacher certification in New Jersey has become a popular way for individuals to enter teaching positions. In its three years of existence, increasing percentages of teaching positions are being filled by "alternate route" candidates (11, 14, and 19 percent; Cooperman, personal communication). The Commissioner of Education in New Jersey frequently refers to the high quality of the applicant pool of "alternate route" candidates. These candidates are well-prepared in their content area and would not have entered teaching positions via the more traditional college-based programs, perhaps because of the perceived low status of the programs.

Thus, the "alternate route" programs can be regarded as being in direct competition with undergraduate teacher preparation programs. Graduates of the latter programs are eligible for certification as teachers with the baccalaureate. In New Jersey, the former "alternate route" programs are open to any individual with a liberal arts major who has graduated from a four-year institution. Professional education is provided by the school district employing the individual, and the first year of teaching is an induction year in which the individual is heavily supervised by experienced teachers. Recently, the Commissioner of Education in New Jersey has proposed mandating that the same supervision be supplied to *all* new teachers, regardless of how they entered teaching positions. Thus, the financial incentive for school districts to hire graduates of college-based programs has been removed, since they did not require the high investment of resources during their first year of teaching. Graduates of liberal arts colleges who take teaching positions in New Jersey are now on an "equal footing" regarding the investment that districts must make to provide intensive supervision during the first year of teaching. The implications for the popularity of undergraduate teacher preparation programs of the Commissioner's decision are not yet known. Undergraduate teacher preparation programs may now become less popular with undergraduates, since they can obtain a teaching position and professional education without any professional preparation during the undergraduate years. We see two recent trends in governmental intervention into the teaching profession: (a) the aggressive recruitment of individuals who have knowledge of disciplines into teaching positions by provision of "alternate routes" to certification; and (b) the placing of limits on the amount and kind of professional education that can be provided to undergraduates. The combined result of these trends is to provide *disincentives for students to enroll in four-year teacher preparation programs.*

3. *The reform movement of four-year liberal arts education deemphasizes preprofessional and professional education for undergraduates.* Liberal arts education is currently under intensive scrutiny from a variety of perspectives. This trend is exemplified by the popularity of Alan Bloom's arcane treatise, *The Closing of the American Mind: How Higher Education Has Failed Democracy and Impoverished the Souls of Today's Students* (1987). Bloom is among a group of contemporary critics who are deeply troubled by the dearth of the intellectual experience presently available to undergraduate students at liberal arts colleges in the United States. It is clear that the "undergraduate experience" has now been taken on as a cause celebre by those within the academy (e.g., Bloom, Ravitch, Hirsch) and outside of it (e.g., Boyer). The faculties of liberal arts colleges are now being challenged to respond to these criticisms by rethinking the meaning of a "liberal education" in our contemporary society and designing a high quality liberal preparation for undergraduates. This upheaval in undergraduate education is by no means a one-time occurrence; as Nussbaum (1987) points out in her insightful critique of Bloom's book, scrutiny of "liberal education" does tend to recur periodically.

The provision of any vocational and professional education at the undergraduate level is noticeably absent from these current discussions about how best to ensure the liberal ideal of breadth of study, competencies in literacy and numeracy, and specialized knowledge in a content area. Indeed, some critics have asserted that an emphasis on vocationalism may be in part responsible for the sad state of the present liberal arts experience in many colleges.

Thus, one consequence of the current reform movement in the liberal arts may be a deemphasis upon preprofessional, professional, and vocational courses of study during the four years of liberal arts education. For example, at Rutgers University, the arts and science faculty is presently debating reinstating foreign language requirements for graduation. In the future at Rutgers, there may be less time available to students to take elective specialized vocational and professional courses during the four undergraduate years.

The trend within the academy to increase the commitment to nonprofessional/vocational coursework during the undergraduate years will probably enhance the effects of legislative limitations on the amount of time allowed for undergraduate study of professional education. That is, these trends, coupled with the elimination of the requirement that individuals need to take college-based teacher preparation programs to obtain teaching positions and certification, may *substantially diminish the popularity of undergraduate teacher preparation programs, which are already perceived as low in status by students.*

4. *Demographic trends suggest that a teacher shortage may not be imminent.* In a recent study of national trends in the school-age population, Hughes (1987) concludes that although the overall population of the United States will not increase radi-

cally, minorities will increase their proportional representation in the population due to their higher growth rate. The highest minority representation will be most evident in the youngest age groups. These minority children will be much more likely than nonminority children to live in "nontraditional" households, with the most prevalent structure being the single female as head of the household. Already, more than half of all black children in the United States under the age of 18 live in single-parent families. America's minority schoolchildren will be coming from family environments and living arrangements that are quite different from nonminority families. There is a greater prevalence of poverty among single-parent households, particularly those headed by females. As a result of these racial demographic variations, there will be substantial concentrations of minority children who are being raised in poverty, both now and in the future.

> The nation's educational systems will not only have to accommodate an expanding clientele for the balance of the turn of the century, they will have to face a student pool diverse in socioeconomic and family/background/environment. There will be a scaled down version of the demographic boom-bust cycle of 1950-1985. There is a period of modest expansion of school enrollment at hand. . . . Elementary school enrollments are now starting to expand. By 1991 overall enrollments will be starting to expand; by 1993-4, every grade level will be expanding. But by 1996-7, total enrollment will still be 20 percent lower than post war peaks. . . . (Hughes, 1987, p. 21)

Two implications for teacher preparation programs follow from the projected demographic trends in the future student population. The first implication is that there may not be a shortage of teachers between now and the turn of the century. Young adults are not likely to spend both time and money to prepare themselves for positions that may not exist, particularly if no formal preparation is required for obtaining both a teaching position and permanent certification. However, the *perception of both prestige and quality of five-year programs, coupled with financial aid, may lure the next generation of young people into the profession of teaching.*

5. *Demographic trends suggest that the population of future students may be more difficult to teach.* A second implication from the demographic analysis is that the population of students in schools of the near future are likely to be more culturally diverse and more difficult to teach. As a group, more students of the future are going to be minority students who reside in poverty and are from single-parent households. These students may not have had the experiences in their homes prior to enrolling in school that prepare them adequately to participate in school learning. Furthermore, demographic trends also point toward increasing numbers of students who are "at risk" for underachievement, due to handicapping conditions, including physical and/or emotional disabilities.

These trends in the school-age population suggest that, in the future, teachers will need finely honed skills and expertise to be effective instructors with students. Teachers will need to be prepared to work with students who differ from each other in their readiness to learn and in the ability of their home environments to support achievement of the basic skills. Thorough knowledge of content will not be enough preparation. Teachers will be encountering students who may be "at risk" for under-achievement, who are handicapped and/or nonnative speakers of English, and whose home environments may not be able to support school learning adequately. Taken together, all of these trends seem to point to the need for more extensive preparation of teachers, not less. It is paradoxical that at the same time the work of teachers is becoming more complex and challenging, forces are in effect that seem to be thrusting individuals into teaching positions for which they are not prepared sufficiently.

One resolution to the paradox is that more extensive preparation of teachers is only possible in graduate-professional programs. The time available to prepare under-graduates as professional teachers is being severely limited, and the programs themselves are perceived to be of low status and not necessary for obtaining a teaching position. Sufficient time can be made available in a fifth year, and, if used wisely, programs of high quality can be created. In addition, legislators do not seem to be interested in intervening in graduate-professional programs, particularly when entrance into teaching positions is possible without graduation from them.

CONCLUSION

The debate between proponents and opponents of graduate teacher preparation may be stimulating to members of the teacher education community, but it may not significantly affect the availability of teacher preparation programs in the future. Societal forces are in place now that would seem to have profound influence upon future programs offered in the United States. We see the simultaneous aggressive recruitment of individuals into teaching positions and the increasing need for more highly trained, competent, thoughtful, and reflective professionals in our schools to deal with the increasing challenges presented by the student population.

What are the prospects for graduate preparation of teachers? There seems to be little doubt that there will be a variety of models of graduate teacher preparation in the present and the future. The early success of the Holmes Group will support and stimulate these efforts. In addition, we may see graduate-professional preparation as the *only* kind of university-based program available to prepare teachers in the future. The antithetical forces of regulation of college-based teacher preparation programs and professionalization may result in a bifurcation of the way that teachers are prepared for their positions: (a) no professional education for some teachers prior to taking the first position after receiving the baccalaureate degree; (b) highly professional and specialized education at the graduate level (e.g., five-year, fifth-year programs) for other teachers. If there is no shortage of teachers in the future, the "market" will decide which type of teacher school districts will choose. This trend in concert with proposed redesign of the liberal arts curricula may lead to the extinction or diminution of undergraduate teacher education at four-year liberal arts colleges.

The future design and availability of programs to prepare teachers is not clear. We do know, however, that we have entered a period of aggressive recruitment of individuals into teaching positions and strenuous professionalization in teaching. These powerful forces, which would seem to be in opposition to each other, will undoubtedly change the nature of the teaching profession and the programs that we design to prepare teachers in the future. The debate about the advantages of graduate preparation over undergraduate preparation has academic interest and may be only peripherally related to the kinds of programs we will offer in universities in the future. Present and future research promises to provide a better understanding of how best to prepare teachers and how to ensure that the result will be highly competent, thoughtful, and reflective professionals, who can meet the challenges presented by tomorrow's students.

REFERENCES

BLOOM, A. (1987). *The closing of the American mind: How higher education has failed democracy and impoverished the souls of today's students.* New York: Simon and Schuster.

CARNEGIE FORUM ON EDUCATION AND THE ECONOMY (1986). *A nation prepared: Teachers for the 21st century.* Washington, DC: Carnegie Forum on Education and the Economy.

COOPERMAN, S. (1987). Personal communication.

THE HOLMES GROUP (1986). *Tomorrow's teachers.* East Lansing, MI: The Holmes Group.

HUGHES, J. (1987). *New Jersey Demographic Report.* Trenton: State of New Jersey Department of Education, August.

JUDGE, H. (1982). *American graduate schools of education: A view from abroad. (Report to the Ford Foundation).* New York: Ford Foundation.

NUSSBAUM, M. (1987). Undemocratic vistas. *New York Review of Books,* XXXIV (17), 20–26.

SYKES, G. (1982). Contradictions, ironies, and promises unfulfilled; A contemporary account of the state of teaching. *Phi Delta Kappan, 65*(2), 87–93.

SYKES, G. (1987). Reckoning with the specter. *Educational Researcher, 16*(6), 19–21.

WEINSTEIN, C. (1987). *A Casebook of Graduate Level Teacher Education Programs.* Graduate School of Education: Rutgers, the State University of New Jersey.

ABOUT THE CONTRIBUTORS

Charles W. Anderson is an Associate Professor in the Department of Teacher Education and a senior researcher in the Institute for Research on Teaching at Michigan State University. He holds an undergraduate degree in chemistry from Rice University and master's and Ph.D. degrees in science education from the University of Texas at Austin. His research has focused on the classroom teaching of science. In that field he has investigated problems of conceptual change in students' science learning, teaching strategies for science classrooms, science curriculum development, and teachers' knowledge and teacher education.

Hilda Borko is an Associate Professor of Curriculum and Instruction at the University of Maryland. Her current research project focuses on learning to teach and on differences in the thought processes and instructional strategies of expert and novice teachers. She is former secretary/treasurer of the Division of Educational Psychology of the American Psychological Association and is currently on committees in the APA, AERA, and the National Reading Conference. Her publications include several book chapters and articles in journals such as *Elementary School Journal, Journal of Educational Psychology, Teaching and Teacher Education*, and *Reading Research Quarterly*.

Kathy Carter is an Assistant Professor in the Division of Teaching and Teacher Education in the College of Education at the University of Arizona. Prior to joining the faculty at the University of Arizona, she was a classroom teacher and worked for several years conducting research and inservice activities for state and federal educational agencies. Her publications have addressed issues in teacher education, classroom processes, and classroom management. Her present research focuses on teacher comprehension, the development of a case literature in teacher education, and expert-novice differences in information processing.

Reneé T. Clift is Assistant Professor of Curriculum and Instruction at the University of Houston where she coordinates the Reflective Inquiry Teacher Education Program. Her research interests include how students learn to teach English language arts, the development of expertise in English language arts instruction, and collaborative frameworks for teacher education.

Michelle Comeaux is a doctoral candidate in Educational Psychology at the University of Wisconsin-Madison and a research assistant in the Center for Policy Research in Education. Prior to beginning her studies at the University of Wisconsin she taught high school English and directed a study skills laboratory. Her major research interests are teacher evaluation, teacher cognitions, and staff development.

Walter Doyle is Professor in the Division of Teaching and Teacher Education in the College of Education at the University of Arizona. From 1982 to 1985 he served as a Research Scientist in the Research and Development Center for Teacher Education at the University of Texas at Austin. He was associate editor of the *Elementary School Journal* for seven years and an associate editor of the *American Educational Research Journal* for two years. From 1986 to 1988 he was vice-president for Division K (Teaching and Teacher Education) of the American Educational Research Association. He is a member of the Editorial Board for the forthcoming *Handbook of Research on Teacher Education* and has published widely in the areas of classroom management, teaching effectiveness, teacher education, and curriculum theory.

Gary D. Fenstermacher is Dean and Professor of Educational Foundations of the College of Education, University of Arizona, Tucson. His field of specialization is philosophy of education, with emphasis on the relation between theory and practice. He was formerly a member of the faculties at the University of California, Los Angeles, and Virginia Polytechnic Institute and State University. He has received numerous awards for teaching excellence and was recently awarded the Excellence in Professional Writing Award by the American Association of Colleges for Teacher Education. His work appears in many journals and anthologies in the field of education.

Wayne K. Hoy is Professor of Educational Administration in the Graduate School of Education at Rutgers University. His primary professional interests are theory and research in administration, supervision, sociology of organizations, and the social psychology of interpersonal relationships. His most recent books are *Educational Administration: Theory, Research, and Practice* (with Cecil Miskel) and *Effective Supervision: Theory Into Practice* (with Patrick Forsyth).

Penelope L. Peterson is Professor of Educational Psychology and Teacher Education at Michigan State University, Director of the Michigan State Center for Teaching and Learning, and Co-Director of the Institute for Research on Teaching. She co-edited the now classic volume, *Research on Teaching: Concepts, Findings and Implications*. She also co-edited *The Social Context of Instruction: Group Organization and Group Processes*. In 1980 she received the Palmer O. Johnson award given by the American Educational Research Association (AERA) for her article on teachers' decision making during interactive classroom teaching. In 1986 she received the Raymond B. Cattell Early Career Award from AERA for her outstanding programmatic research on effective teaching and student mediation of instruction. Currently, she is editor of the *Review of Educational Research*.

Virginia Richardson-Koehler is Associate Professor in the College of Education, University of Arizona. Her research interests include research on teaching and teacher education. She has just edited *The Educators' Handbook: A Research Perspective*, completed a research project on at-risk elementary students, and is now the principal investigator on a grant that is exploring teachers' practices in the instruction of reading comprehension. She is currently the editor of the *American Educational Research Journal*.

Carol Weinstein is Associate Professor of Elementary Education at Rutgers Graduate School of Education, where she served as Associate Dean of Teacher Education from 1984-1986. Her research has focused on the impact of classroom design on students' behavior, attitudes, and achievement. Together with Tom David, she edited *Spaces for Children: The Built Environment and Child Development* (1987). Recently, she has conducted research on teacher education students' beliefs about teaching; in particular, she is interested in preservice teachers' "unrealistic optimism"—the belief that the typical problems of first-year teachers "won't happen to me."

Louise Cherry Wilkinson is an expert in classroom communication. Her training is in educational psychology and child development, and her research and publications have focused on the development of normal children's language and communicative skills in school. She takes a sociolinguistic approach to peer communication, classroom instructional grouping, and cultural differences in children's communicative styles and the consequences for learning. She is the author of more than 50 articles/chapters and the editor/co-editor of three volumes on classrooms published by Academic Press. Dr. Wilkinson is a Fellow of the American Psychological Association and is presently Dean of the Rutgers Graduate School of Education.

Arthur E. Wise is the director of the RAND Center for the Study of the Teaching Profession in Washington, DC. He is the author of *Rich Schools, Poor Schools* which conceived the idea for school finance equalization lawsuits. *Legislated Learning* critically examined some of the effects of government regulation on the American classroom and foreshadowed the emergence of teacher professionalism. Wise served as chief consultant to the Governor's Commission on Equity and Excellence in Education in Connecticut and to the Commissioner's Task Force on the Teaching Profession in New York State. In this capacity, he helped to develop major new legislative proposals to professionalize teaching.

Anita E. Woolfolk is Professor of Educational Psychology in the Graduate School of Education at Rutgers University. Her areas of research are classroom management, student motivation, and teachers' beliefs about these topics. She has published a leading text in the field of educational psychology, now in its third edition, as well as many journal articles. She is on the editorial boards of the *Elementary School Journal* and the *Review of Educational Research* and is an associate editor of the *American Educational Research Journal*.

Kenneth Zeichner is a Professor in the Department of Curriculum and Instruction at the University of Wisconsin-Madison and a Senior Researcher with the National Center for Research on Teacher Education at Michigan State University. His major professional concern is the study of teacher education with a particular interest in how teachers learn to teach and in inquiry-oriented teacher education. His articles on these topics have been published widely in this country and abroad.

AUTHOR INDEX

SUBJECT INDEX